Tomás Prower takes us on a global journey, a que  across the world. Our stories are not confined t or religion, and this book is truly a diverse guide to understanding ou. often lost and forgotten myth and history. Certain to inspire LGBTQ+ magickal practitioners for years to come!

—**Christopher Penczak**
author of *Gay Witchcraft*

In his latest work, *Queer Magic*, Tomás Prower takes us on a journey that spans both time and continents to examine the myths, magic, and spiritual lives of those who exist outside the culturally-sanctioned heterosexual binary. Surprisingly detailed, Prower examines not only the practices of pre-modern native cultures, but also the effects of Christian colonialism and its devastating and history-robbing effects upon them. He demonstrates how those cultures' near-universal acceptance of queer sexual expression has been usurped, and he shines a light on how those traditions have found ways to survive—and even thrive—in spite of being the victims of revisionist history. With interesting bits of history and lore (I may never think of Dracula quite the same way again) combined with practical exercises to help us view sexual expression and gender outside of our common modern restrictions, this book should be considered essential reading for all LGBT+ practitioners of magic and spirituality. Highly recommended.

—**Storm Faerywolf**
author of *Betwixt and Between*

More often than not, people whose sexual identities, gender identities, social roles, affectional preferences, relationship styles, and so on are in the minority tend to be erased or misrepresented in our culture. *Queer Magic* is a journey around the world and through the centuries to uncover some of these hidden stories. This book is not only history and mythology, it also contains vignettes, experiences, and practices from modern people from diverse backgrounds. One book cannot address everyone and everything, but *Queer Magic* is a heartfelt effort that will encourage you to continue the work of discovering these treasures of the spirit.

—**Ivo Dominguez Jr.**
author of *The Keys to Perception*

QUEER
MAGIC

ABOUT THE AUTHOR

Tomás Prower is a graduate of the University of California, Santa Barbara. He holds two degrees, one in global studies and the other in Latin American and Iberian studies. A natural-born globe trekker, he sought additional education at the Universidad de Chile while working as a translator for their literature department. Due to his fluency in English, French, and Spanish, he was given the opportunity to become a cultural liaison for the French government in South America between France, the United States, and the member states of Mercosur. During this time he traveled extensively in the Amazon jungle, learning as much as he could about the region's indigenous peoples.

Upon returning to the United States, Tomás worked as a bartender at a well-known gay bar in Los Angeles before moving to Reno and becoming the external relations director for the American Red Cross in Nevada. He then moved back to his home city of Los Angeles, where he worked for a time as a mortician while writing and researching the city's LGBT+ scenes and macabre subcultures. Nowadays he resides in fabulous Las Vegas, Nevada, where he can be found hiking in the desert, interacting with tourists from all over the world, and writing new books by the glow of Sin City's neon lights.

QUEER MAGIC

LGBT+ SPIRITUALITY AND CULTURE FROM AROUND THE WORLD

TOMÁS PROWER

LLEWELLYN PUBLICATIONS

Woodbury, Minnesota

FIRST EDITION
Sixth Printing, 2022

Cover design by Shira Atakpu
Interior design by Rebecca Zins

Llewellyn Publications is a registered trademark of Llewellyn Worldwide Ltd.

Library of Congress Cataloging-in-Publication Data
Names: Prower, Tomás, author.
Title: Queer magic : LGBT+ spirituality and culture from around the world /
    Tomás Prower.
Description: First Edition. | Woodbury : Llewellyn Worldwide, Ltd., 2018. |
    Includes bibliographical references.
Identifiers: LCCN 2018002503 (print) | LCCN 2018018088 (ebook) | ISBN
    9780738755649 (ebook) | ISBN 9780738753188 (alk. paper)
Subjects: LCSH: Sexual minorities—Religious life—History.
Classification: LCC BL65.H64 (ebook) | LCC BL65.H64 P76 2018 (print) | DDC
    200.86/64—dc23
LC record available at https://lccn.loc.gov/2018002503

Llewellyn Publications
A Division of Llewellyn Worldwide Ltd.
2143 Wooddale Drive
Woodbury, MN 55125-2989

www.llewellyn.com

Printed in the United States of America

CONTENTS

CONTENTS

CONTENTS

9: Pagan Europe   109

10: Christianity   123

CONTENTS

CONTENTS

EMBARKATION

*If all the world's a stage, then
identity is nothing but a costume.*
MARC JACOBS

What makes a man a man? What makes a woman a woman? Is a man someone with facial hair who is tall, strong, aggressive, and sexually attracted to females? Could be—but then again, we all know some men who aren't. Is a woman someone who wears makeup and is petite, family-oriented, gentle, and sexually attracted to males? Sometimes, yeah—but we all know some women who aren't.

So maybe the answer has something to do with science. Our biology must be what defines and divides the genders, right? A man is a human with an X and a Y chromosome, and a woman is a human with two X chromosomes. But still, this doesn't seem to fully satisfy our question, does it? After all, what about the people with XXY chromosomes? Plus, modern medicine and surgical advances allow a male to biologically become a female and a female to biologically become a male. So, then, is being a male the definition of being a man, and being a female the definition of being a woman?

Well, what would your answer be? Go ahead and think of your response; you don't have to say it out loud. To *you*, what makes a woman a woman and a man a man? Now, let's take it a step further. If you had lived one hundred years ago, would your answer be the same? Five hundred years ago? One thousand years ago? What if you had been born into another culture? In another religion? In another country? You see, the concept of what it is to be a man and what it is to be a woman is not, has not, and never will be set in stone.

Interesting, isn't it? But perhaps you're thinking "What does defining men and women have to do with our magical tribe of LGBT+ people throughout the globe and throughout time?" A lot, really. I mean, let's take the acronym apart and look at those letters individually. Lesbians are women who are sexually attracted to women. Gays are men who are sexually attracted to men. Bisexuals are either men or women who are attracted to both men and women. Transgender individuals are people who were born as one sex and transitioned into the other. And the list goes on and on, including queer and intersex individuals and more! But if our sexual and gender identities are based upon us being men or women who are attracted to men and/or women, and we already established that what defines men and women varies from culture to culture and from era to era, then how can we, with absolute unchanging certainty, define the LGBT+ community currently or at any point in history? Or, for that matter, how can we define the sexual and gender identities of the all-powerful, omnipresent immortal gods with these limiting labels?

So far I've just thrown a bunch of questions at you and played devil's advocate a bit without giving any solid answers, but that's where this book comes in. Like you, I've had a lot of questions—not just about the world but about myself, my sexuality, my identity, and my spirituality. From an early age, I knew I was attracted to men, but did that mean I wasn't a man? Anyone who knew me never would've labeled me a woman because I was too manlike in my behavior, but still, I didn't seem to act like other men anyone knew. And nobody seemed to act like me. What was I?

I felt like I didn't belong, and I just wanted to get away—not in some nihilistic sense, but I wanted to go out and explore the world to find my tribe. I wanted to go beyond my Irish-Mexican heritage and Catholic school bubble and find the answers that I knew I couldn't find at home. Of course, being a teenager economically dependent upon my parents, I couldn't just get up, quit school, and go on a globe-trekking adventure. So, I had to use what was available.

Books, specifically nonfiction books, served as my map to finding my tribe. Within the pages of non-scholastic history books, especially religious myths from around the world, were tales of "otherness" that contained sexualities and genders of which I had never heard!

The more I learned about my queer tribe of "others" that was spread throughout the ages and the globe in so many religious traditions and spiritual beings, the more I realized how vast and diverse our tribe is. Lesbian, gay, bisexual, and transgender are just a small handful of the flavors under the umbrella of queerness that have existed in our history and religious traditions on every inch of land on the earth. And therein was the inspiration for this book.

Throughout history in every part of the globe and in every spiritual plane are members of our tribe. Had schools taught queer world history or queer religious studies, so much more of my youth would've been soothed and comforted in knowing that I wasn't alone in both community and spirit. This is the book that contains all the information I wish someone had given me when I began my quest. Because what good is knowledge if it isn't shared and acted upon? So here for you all is my collected knowledge and research about our tribe of queer humans and gods, as well as the magical ways our queer brothers and sisters interact with these queer gods.

For easy reference and flow of reading, I have mapped out our global expedition into seven parts that'll be our ports of call, each spotlighting a specific region of the world. These parts are further divided into chapters, each focusing upon a specific religious culture from the region. And because you cannot truly separate the human experience from spirituality or spirituality from the human experience, the first half of each chapter will illuminate the hidden queer history of each cultural tradition, followed by a quick takeaway summary on how to implement the tradition's queer wisdom into our own everyday queer lives and spellwork. The second half of each chapter will focus on the queer deities, legendary figures, and mythic lore of the tradition, along with their appropriate correspondences and devotional preferences when applicable.

But with that in mind, I highly discourage you from immediately and arbitrarily incorporating these cultures and deities into your personal practice just because of capricious curiosity. Eclectic spirituality and cosmopolitanism are one thing, but appropriation and lack of cultural reverence are another. Yes, many of these queer traditions and deities from around the world will call to you and speak to you on some intrinsic level, but do personal research before jumping into foreign waters.

Here's a parallel example of what I mean. Growing up Catholic, I can tell you that if someone one day read a book on Catholicism and suddenly decided to pray that the Virgin Mary be the intercessor of manifesting their prayers, not only are they not really a Catholic, but they also really don't know what they are doing or the significance and meaning behind why Catholics do that. Does that mean no one can practice Catholicism who wasn't born into it? Absolutely not. But it does mean that anyone interested in truly practicing Catholicism should go beyond that one book, do their own personal research, talk with members of the community, and find out the appropriate reasons why and how Catholics do what they do. The same is true for all other religions and faiths found in this book. This is a tour of all the queer options out there for our community; what resonates with you deserves your time for more in-depth, independent research before jumping into their magic.

To help with this, since it is a book for the community, I felt it should be a communal effort. And so in closing each chapter, I have invited a special guest from the worldwide queer community to share a little something for us all. Some will share their personal experience growing up and being queer in a particular culture or religion, and others will share queer-focused spells, prayers, meditations, and cultural exercises from their tradition.

This kind of queer communal gathering of wisdom, magic, and personal experiences is truly a blessing of our time. Throughout history, our voices had been silenced, our people ignored, and our gods and practices normalized to fit the social mores of times gone by.

But the times they are always a-changin', and humanity is always progressing to become more socially inclusive and better than we once were. For example, in this book you'll see a lot of things from the past that you may not agree with, and some of them rightly so, in particular the antiquated practice of homo- and heterosexual erotic partnering of adults and youths. Nowadays we have a higher value and empathy for children and childhood in general, and we have almost universally stopped the social acceptance of such horrid practices in this day and age. But to ignore these terrible practices of the past as if they never happened is to not learn from them. So as you read this book, know that what was once socially acceptable in a certain place at a certain time has to be acknowledged, but it doesn't have to be condoned or practiced today, especially if it is illegal.

Also, you might notice a bit of imbalanced queer representation in this book. I have tried my best, with the historical information and research available to me now in the early twenty-first century, to find as much info on our tribe's spiritual lesbians, gays, bisexuals, transgender individuals, and every other flavor of queerness. But for most of recorded history, almost everywhere, the lives of women were seen as so unimportant that they didn't merit to be mentioned in historical records. Because of this patriarchy through the ages, there exists less information available on females than there is on males. Compounding this, historians' favoritism of men, and modern queer researchers' focus on gay men in particular, have left us with a disproportionately larger amount of info on the "G" of the LGBT+ community than any of the other letters. Still, I have endeavored to give representation for everyone in this book as much as is available. There is something for everybody.

And lastly, for practical purposes, I will use the term LGBT+ to refer to the entire spectrum of queer gender/sexuality/identity. Different people spell that acronym differently: GLBT, LGBTQ, GLBTQI, and so on. But each form seems limited since there is an innumerable amount of subtle shades of gender/sexuality/identity than can and do exist. So, to keep things uniform, I will utilize the most well-known acronym of "LGBT" and add a "+" next to it to signify the seemingly infinite spectrum of queerness. In addition to saving ink and page space (thus making the book physically slimmer and therefore less expensive), this seems the most fair, practical, and inclusive way to refer to our community.

As we head out on our global expedition in search of our queer tribe, both human and divine, stay close and keep an open mind. It'll be your passport to worlds you never knew existed, populated by people and spiritual beings just like you, regardless of who you are.

All aboard! Our first port of call in the Middle East is just around the page.

PART 1

GREATER MIDDLE EAST

I, you, he, she, we.
In the garden of mystic lovers, these
are not true distinctions.
Rumi

Since our earliest days, the Middle East has been the crossroads of the world, where cultures, religions, and ideas collide. The desert sands and fertile floodplains of the region saw the birth of humankind's earliest civilizations and monotheism. Known to many cultures as the center of the world, it is the origin of three of the modern world's most widespread religions: Judaism, Christianity, and Islam.

While we're here, we'll focus more on Judaism and Islam; we'll save Christianity for when we reach Europe, wherein it truly took hold and became synonymous with European culture. Today the Middle East and North Africa are strongly Islamic. Since World War II Judaism has seen a fevered resurgence in the area, with the recent creation of the State of Israel carved from Palestinian lands. Through it all, though, in this place where the topic of religion is as hot and as changing as the sands they were built upon, LGBT+ leaders and events have had their place in every faith. But let's start at the beginning and look at the queer contributions of our first urban ancestors who established civilizations on the Tigris, Euphrates, and Nile Rivers millennia ago.

1

CRADLES OF CIVILIZATION

Cultural

MESOPOTAMIA

Around the fourth millennium BCE, the peoples in Mesopotamia and Egypt gradually stopped their nomadic ways of life as hunter-gatherers and began to settle. The floodplains of the Tigris, Euphrates, and Nile Rivers were ideal for agriculture, and with the domestication of animals and edible plants and the invention of granaries in which to store surplus foodstuffs, humans began to grow their own sustenance in a reliable manner. With food in abundance assured by dedicated farmers, it was no longer necessary for everyone to focus their lives on obtaining food for the community, which thus led to the creation of diversified talents, skills, and careers such as masonry, astrology, pottery, military, and bronze working.

The combination of everyone's unique skills contributing to the greater good of the whole of society and the peace necessary to maintain this intricate society became known as civilization.

One specialized career that held great prominence in these ancient empires of the Middle East was the priesthood. For the first time in human history, people could dedicate their entire lives to the study of the Divine and its mysteries since other people were now laboring to supply the food and drink for all. Their initial insights into the nature of the Divine included many gods and goddesses that we would nowadays label as queer.

In Mesopotamia a number of civilizations rose and fell, but their idea of the cosmos and of the Divine were quite similar to one another. While not exactly the same, these various empires often retold similar mythological stories within their own cultural context. While collectively known as Mesopotamian, these peoples are known to the world today as Sumerians, Phoenicians, Akkadians, Babylonians, and Assyrians. A commonality among many of these Mesopotamian civilizations was their belief in the spirituality of third-gender individuals.

In Akkad and Babylon, Ishtar (called Inanna among the Sumerians) was the goddess of fertility, love, sex, and war, and she was known to magically feminize her male priests, known as *kurggaru* and *assinnu,* during ritualized possession ceremonies. Some of the male priests who became vessels for the goddess were known to remain forever feminine in mind and manner, while still some others subsequently castrated themselves so as to become a physically feminized vessel to better receive Ishtar.[1]

Another example of priestly queerness comes from the Sumerian mythologies of Enki, god of mischief, creation, bodies of water, intelligence, and craftspeople. As legend goes, Enki created a special class of androgynous priests, known as the *gala,* as a gift to the goddess Inanna. Their dedicated purpose was to sing soul-soothing laments to the goddess, a position usually reserved for women. They were known as being gender

---

1   Stephen O. Murray, *Homosexualities* (Chicago: University of Chicago Press, 2002).

fluid and ranged the spectrum on sexual orientation. Some were androgynous biological females, some were biological males who adopted female names, some were homosexuals, and so on. In fact, in their native script, the word *gala* is a portmanteau of "penis" and "anus," an obvious nod to the widely acknowledged gay homosexuality of the male priests.[2]

The Sumerian creation myth shows another link between Enki and non-binary beings. According to the tale, in addition to men and women, the goddess of creation and mountains, Ninmah, created an additional gender comprised of women who were biologically barren and individuals who had neither male nor female genitalia. Enki took a liking to this other gender and bestowed upon them the sacred positions of priestesses (known as *naditu*) and servants to royalty (known as *girsequ*). In the Akkadian version of this myth, it was Enki himself who requested that this third gender of humans be specifically created and called the *gallu* (also known as the *galla*). As opposed to priestesses and royal servants, however, the Akkadian *gallu* were hellish demons who acted as psychopomps to the underworld.[3]

These third-gender *gallu* play a small yet prominent role in the legendary Descent of the Goddess myth from a Sumerian poem. In brief, the story is about how the goddess Inanna descends into the underworld to console her older sister Ereshkigal, queen of the underworld, who is mourning the death of her husband. While down there, Inanna is imprisoned by Ereshkigal. Enraged by Inanna's imprisonment, Enki sends his loyal *gallu* to rescue her, but they arrive too late as Ereshkigal had already murdered her little sister. Nevertheless, the crafty *gallu* see that Ereshkigal is in agony (some versions say due to labor pains, others due to guilt from killing her sister) and so they overtly show compassion for the panicked murderess. Soothed by their sympathy, Ereshkigal promises to give them a

---

2   Stephen O. Murray and Will Roscoe, *Islamic Homosexualities: Culture, History, and Literature* (New York: NYU Press, 1997).

3   Ernest L. Abel, *Death Gods: An Encyclopedia of Rulers, Evil Spirits, and Geographies of the Dead* (Westport, Greenwood Press, 2009).

gift of their choosing, in which the *gallu* select Inanna's corpse as the gift. The *gallu* revive Inanna, thus allowing her to escape from the underworld.[4]

Aside from the leisure that civilization provided to the pursuit of mysticism, the codification of laws was another advantage that arose with the development of urban societies in Mesopotamia. With so many people living together, there had to be set guidelines on what was and was not permissible, as well as punishment and reparation for damages done. One of the earliest code of laws in human history came be known as the Code of Hammurabi. In his code of laws, the Babylonian king Hammurabi established progressive judicial theory for the times, such as the accused's presumption of innocence, the necessity of evidence to garner a conviction, and the regulation of preset punishments that befit the crime.[5]

While fascinating from a jurisprudence standpoint, the Code of Hammurabi is worthy of note in our travels here because it makes no mention of homosexual acts. In fact, no Mesopotamian legal systems lay out standards or punishments for queerness. Since it can be safely assumed that LGBT+ individuals and activities were happening in these heavily populated urban centers of early civilization, LGBT+ actions and propensities were either a non-issue to be addressed in codes of law or simply not seen as negative or harmful to society. Modern Mesopotamian scholars now generally believe that these early civilizations saw sexuality as far too natural to write about, let alone regulate through laws.[6]

Nevertheless, in the legal codes of Middle Assyria, two ancient laws directly mention homosexuality, and though it's mentioned in a negative light, the reason for punishment is not homosexuality itself if we read between the lines. In brief, the first law dictates that flogging, fines, and castration shall be the punishment for anyone who spreads unsubstantiated rumors of a man who goes around letting other men have sex with him. In

---

4   Diane Wolkstein and Samuel Noah Kramer, *Inanna: Queen of Heaven and Earth* (New York: Harper & Row, 1983).

5   Ann Wolbert Burgess, Albert R. Roberts, and Cheryl Regehr, *Victimology: Theories and Applications* (Burlington: Jones & Bartlett Learning, 2009).

6   Jean Bottéro, *Everyday Life in Ancient Mesopotamia*, trans. Antonia Nevill (Baltimore: Johns Hopkins University Press, 2001).

this context, the criminal act is technically slander and defamation of character for essentially calling a man a slut (to use modern slang). The second law dictates that if a man forces himself upon another man, the punishment will be for the aggressor to be physically forced upon and then castrated. In this context, the criminal act and punishment is technically rape.[7]

Mesopotamian Takeaway:
DIVINE QUEERNESS

Now it's time for our first takeaway lesson/activity. Unlike the larger rituals and stories that our special guests will share, these cultural takeaways will serve as short, immediate things you can adapt and implement into your own queer daily life and magical practices right away.

It's amazing to discover how widespread and disproportionately high our queer ancestors were represented in the priestly classes of Mesopotamian society. Making this more impactful is how these are some of the earliest civilizations in human history. This shows that our earliest urban ancestors oftentimes saw queer individuals as especially able to have a connection to the Divine.

Since queerness was a preeminent quality for the clergy at a time when the clergy was intricately tied with magic and special knowledge, it shows that we, as LGBT+ people, have always been seen as magical, special beings. Our inability to perfectly fit in with those around us just might signify that it's because we are better suited as dual citizens of the physical and spiritual worlds.

So, for your first magical activity, take time in meditation to discover how your queerness gives you a unique insight and outlook within your own magical tradition. Embrace not fully fitting in, and see what kind of uniqueness you can add to your tribe thanks to your divine differentness. Like the ancient Mesopotamians, own your queerness within your own tradition, and know that since earliest history the world has seen a unique magic within us. It's time you see it within yourself.

---

7   James B. Pritchard, *Ancient Near Eastern Texts Relating to the Old Testament* (Princeton: Princeton University Press, 1969).

ANCIENT EGYPT

This is going to be a controversial leg of our global expedition. You see, when it comes to the ancient Egyptians' views on homosexuality and queer culture, there is practically no direct information about it in their writings and art.[8] There is some talk about it in their mythology, but we'll save that for later. For now, we're looking at the day-to-day culture of LGBT+ persons in ancient Egypt. Unlike a people's physiology or diet, sexuality leaves no trace behind for us to examine. Without direct written or artistic evidence, Egyptologists can only guess the ancients' attitudes based upon a mix of vague, indirect evidence and personal bias depending upon what the researcher is trying to affirm or disprove.

One of the best places to discover a society's stance toward a certain subject is in its code of laws. Nowhere in the legal system of the ancient Egyptians is non-heterosexuality either protected or criminalized. Unlike other cultures wherein the documented day-to-day lives of the people could more or less explain why a legal system has such an omission and allow us to read between the lines, the lack of LGBT+ anything in other ancient Egyptian writings prevents us from making such assumptions about them. Even if we look up writings about sex and sexual topics, whether in official documents or artistic literature and poetry, they shed no real light on queer identity and sexuality. This is because, for better or for worse, the way about which sexuality was written involved the use of forced and contrived flowery language as well as talking about the act in a roundabout way without ever mentioning the act itself. So, what we have today is a lot of descriptions that are up to interpretation, without concrete contextual clues to hint one way or the other.[9]

One of these interpretive and controversial writings about alleged queerness is the fictionalized tale of Pharaoh Neferkare (aka Pepi II) and General Sasenet. Mind you, the tale only survives in fragments, but the

8   George Haggerty and Bonnie Zimmerman, *Encyclopedia of Lesbian and Gay Histories and Cultures* (New York: Taylor & Francis, 2015).
9   Richard Parkinson, "Homosexual Desire and Middle Kingdom Literature," *The Journal of Egyptian Archaeology* 81 (1995): 57–76.

gist of it tells how the pharaoh was rumored to steal away into the night by himself to some unknown location. To verify the rumor, a man secretly followed the pharaoh when he slipped out of the palace on a night walk. The pharaoh stopped at the house of General Sasenet and signaled to someone inside, after which a ladder was lowered down from a window and the pharaoh climbed up inside. Then the narrator says that after four hours had passed, "his majesty had done that which he had wanted to do with him," at which point the pharaoh climbed back down and returned home.[10]

Now, it's easy to immediately assume that the king was off having nightly sexual liaisons with one of his generals because that would be the more scandalous and fun answer, but the reality is that he could've been doing almost anything: consulting secret war plans with the general, asking for advice on matters of court intrigue, etc. The description of "that which he wanted to do with him" is *so* vague that the only evidence of it being at all sexual is our interpretive imagination. To make matters worse, any part of the story that might have revealed the nature of these clandestine encounters has been lost to time as a part of the still-missing fragments of the tale. Those who are on the side of believing these royal rendezvous were not sexual instead believe the whole scene to be a religious reference to Ra, the sun god, visiting Osiris, god of the underworld, for hours every night, thus explaining the phenomenon of nighttime.[11]

The most prevailing evidence of LGBT+ tendencies in ancient Egypt to date was found in the tomb of Khnumhotep and Niankhkhnum in Saqqara during the 1960s. The initial clue to the sexuality of these two high officials was the fact that they shared the same tomb together, but the bigger clue was all the artwork covering the walls of the inner sanctums. Throughout the structure there are images of the two men so close together that their

---

10   André Dollinger, "King Neferkare & General Sasenet," *An Introduction to the History and Culture of Pharaonic Egypt*, Oct. 2006, http://www.reshafim.org .il/ad/egypt/texts/sasenet.htm (accessed Sept. 30, 2016).

11   Emma Brunner-Traut, *Altägyptische Märchen: Mythen und Andere Volkstümliche Erzählungen*, 10th ed. (Munich: Diederichs, 1991).

pelvises touch, and in one particular depiction their noses touch, which, in ancient Egyptian art, generally symbolized kissing.[12]

The naysayers were quick to point out that these two high officials couldn't possibly be queer because they each had wives and children. But because you and I live in the real world and don't like to delude ourselves, we know that this kind of stuff is actually *not* uncommon, and marriage doesn't necessarily mean that a person is heterosexual. Another rationale used to explain away the queerness of the two men is that they are obviously conjoined twins because of how they are always seen as so close and touching one another in the artworks. Again, though, you and I know that this is *really* reaching for an explanation and goes through too much mental gymnastics for it to be the most likely answer.

The most popular argument against their queerness, however, is that they were simply brothers and nothing more. When it comes down to it, though, let's look at it this way. If all these intimate Egyptian images were of a man and a woman instead of two men, everyone would automatically assume that the art depicted lovers because it would be the most obvious answer, and if someone started insisting that this man and woman were more likely conjoined twins, it would be a scarcely defended position. So, were these guys ancient Egyptian lovers? Probably, but as of now there's no definitive proof aside from making assumptions based on the obvious.[13]

Nevertheless, Khnumhotep and Niankhkhnum belonged to a very privileged class, and what is acceptable for the wealthy aristocracy is often not acceptable for the lower classes. Therefore, their elaborate burial chamber still isn't a good indicator of society-at-large's attitudes toward LGBT+ people. The ways in which people expressed their queerness and to what extent such expressions were accepted by the culture are the questions that still remain a mystery about ancient Egypt.

---

12   John Noble Wilford, "A Mystery, Locked in Timeless Embrace," *New York Times,* Dec. 20, 2005.

13   Alissa Lyon, "Ancient Egyptian Sexuality," *Archaeology of Ancient Egypt,* Oct. 23, 2014, http://anthropology.msu.edu/anp455-fs14/2014/10/23 /ancient-egyptian-sexuality/ (accessed Sept. 30, 2016).

But before we wrap things up here and head on over to Israel, it's interesting to mention that the Egyptians' contemporaries make specific mention to ancient Egypt's widespread acceptance of lesbianism. This outside group is the Hebrews, and the mention comes in the Talmud. Meant to be negative, the literature portrays ancient Egypt as a sexually liberal place of debauched decadence, so much so that female-female sexual acts were known to the Hebrews as "the acts of Egypt," denoting how widespread it was there. This Talmudic evidence should be taken with many, many grains of salt since the Hebrews historically were not too fond of the Egyptians, it was written many centuries after ancient Egypt fell to Greece and Rome, and the Hebrews have had their own biases against queerness. Modern scholars see these references as a way of Judaism linking female homosexuality to an evil society in the same vein as male homosexuality is linked to Sodom and Gomorrah—but more on that when we get to Israel.[14]

Ancient Egyptian Takeaway:
THE POWER OF THE LENS

The uncertain significance of those seemingly homosexual ancient Egyptian artworks we just talked about is an example of "the power of the lens." Different people have come to different conclusions as to what the artworks signify. This is because, like art, everything depends on the interpretive lens from which it is viewed. You see, everything we hear is actually an opinion, not a fact, and everything we see is a perspective, not the actual truth. All things are inherently neutral; it is our personal lens that gives them their meaning.

I'll give you a recent and funny queer example of this power of the lens. In 2014 an Australian arthouse horror film premiered called *The Babadook*. It was a critically acclaimed financial success, but it didn't rock world culture in any significant way. A few years later a couple of people on social media made a vague claim that the film's titular monster was gay. At first seen as a joke, the joke kept building, with more and more people

14   Rebecca T. Alpert, *Like Bread on the Seder Plate: Jewish Lesbians and the Transformation of Tradition* (New York: Columbia University Press, 1997).

defending the queerness of the Babadook in a very tongue-in-cheek way. The more it was talked about online, the more people began watching the film through a queer lens, trying to understand and see the queer meaning behind it. And the more people watched it through the lens of a queer horror film, the more it seemed like a queer horror film. Without any spoilers, it's about a flamboyantly dressed monster with a flair for the dramatic living in the shadows of a house. His presence and desire to be acknowledged cause chaotic tension within a family that fears him yet doesn't fully accept his identity. Sounds a lot like growing up in the closet, doesn't it?

But for years no one thought of *The Babadook* as a queer film, and it certainly wasn't intended to be one. However, once viewed through a queer lens, the Babadook monster became a queer icon all over the world. So, for your next magical activity, take a neutral magical spell and convert it into a queer spell via seeing it through a queer lens. I suggest starting with a spell you've done many times before; don't try to get all fancy. Do nothing different except change the lens and notice the different result that will manifest.

Deities & Legends

GILGAMESH & ENKIDU

Gilgamesh was a hero king of Sumer believed to have actually lived sometime around 2800–2500 BCE. Stories of his greatness passed through the generations until he eventually gained the status of a demigod and cultural legend. The story of his divine heroism is known to posterity as *The Epic of Gilgamesh*, widely agreed to be humankind's first literary epic.

Featured prominently in this epic is the special relationship between Gilgamesh and Enkidu. The two men are described as polar opposites: Gilgamesh is the brutish yet arrogant leader of civilization and Enkidu is the cunning yet irreverent wild man of the rural lands. Their relationship's story arc commences with them being at odds with one another; specifically, Enkidu is created by the mother goddess Aruru in response to prayers of the people of Uruk (Sumer's capital city) because Gilgamesh has become a tyrant who uses his strength to bully the weak and force himself on people in the city. Enkidu and Gilgamesh fight each other, but it ends in a draw, each recognizing the other as an equal and sealing their respect with a kiss.[15]

As the epic goes on, their relationship deepens, forming the stereotyped masculine-feminine roles of equality between gay male lovers: Gilgamesh as the brash alpha male, ultra-masc "top" and Enkidu as the smart, sensitive, femme "bottom." Their love for one another eventually changes them for the better. Enkidu sensitizes Gilgamesh and tames his brutish ways, and Gilgamesh makes Enkidu more assertive and gives him a sense of stability from his wandering ways.

Their story arc is a tragic one, though, as Enkidu is sentenced to death for protecting Gilgamesh and killing the Bull of Heaven. Although the beast was sent by Inanna specifically to kill Gilgamesh for spurning her sexual advances, the gods agreed that someone had to be punished for killing the sacred bull, and Enkidu took the fall. The death of Enkidu then becomes the impetus for the other story arcs of the epic wherein a distraught and mourning Gilgamesh searches for the secret of eternal life.[16]

Traditionally, Gilgamesh had been associated with shades of blue and purple and with water elements due to his tempestuous emotional nature and the necessity of rivers for Sumerian civilization. Enkidu, on the other hand, has traditionally been associated with shades of green and earth elements due to his reputation as a wild man of the woods and fields. Also, the way the Sumerians worshipped their deities is a lot like how modern Pagans worship theirs. A singular patron deity was chosen based on their magical domain, and continued contact was made between the individual and the deity. Home altars, incense burning, and daily prayers were common, especially written prayers in praise of their patron deity.

---

15   Will Roscoe, *Queer Spirits: A Gay Men's Myth Book* (Boston: Beacon Press, 1995).

16   H. N. Wolff, "Gilgamesh, Enkidu, and the Heroic Life," *Journal of the American Oriental Society* 89:2 (1969) 392–398.

HAPI

Hapi is the Egyptian god of the flooding of the Nile, which was the annual lifeblood for the civilization's agriculture. Generally depicted as an overweight, false-bearded male with female breasts, Hapi is usually regarded as an intersex deity. Even in Hapi's Gemini-esque dual-gender twins form, Hapi is regarded as neither man nor woman, yet both. The plants sacred to Hapi were aquatic in nature, such as the lotus and papyrus, and the conquering Romans even linked Hapi to the astrological sign Aquarius due to Hapi's position as bearer of life-giving water. Unsurprisingly, Hapi developed a strong following made up primarily of gay and gender-variant priests, but in the fourth century CE Emperor Constantine formally abolished Hapi's following due to a mix of his queerphobic nature and his conversion to Christianity.[17]

Natural waterways are the places most sacred when worshipping Hapi. Again, aquatic elements are preferred, and animals that can dually cohabit water and land, such as amphibians and crocodiles, are often associated as sacred, emphasizing Hapi's inner and outer duality.

SET

Set is the Egyptian god of storms, the desert, war, disorder, violence, and foreigners. Often depicted as a pansexual deity, his wife is Anat, a transgender female Amazonian warrior goddess, and together the couple's favorite expression of intimacy is anal sex. Among his worshipers, he was viewed with ambivalence in the sense that the ancient Egyptians disliked him for murdering and usurping the throne of his brother Osiris, god of the underworld, but they also loved him for being the protector of Ra, the sun god, both of which have homoerotic overtones.

Following the killing of Osiris, the mythology tells us that Osiris's son, Horus, the sky god, time and again battles his uncle Set for the throne of Egypt. Eventually the gods tire of this family squabble and demand that the two of them settle things. Set decides to prove his dominance once

---

17   Linda Alchin, "Hapi, God of Egypt," *Egyptian Gods: The Mythology of Ancient Egyptian Gods and Goddesses for Kids*, March 2015, http://www.landofpyramids .org/hapi.htm (accessed Aug. 18, 2017).

and for all by sexually "topping" Horus, but when Set ejaculates onto Horus, Horus catches the semen in his hand and throws it in the Nile. Isis (Horus's mother) then steps in and cuts off Horus's hand to make sure no trace of semen is left on him. She then takes some of Horus's own ejaculate and rubs it onto Set's sacred plant (lettuce), which Set then unknowingly eats.

When the council of the gods calls the two of them to make their final case of who should have the throne, Set boasts of how he is more dominant because he ejaculated all over Horus, but looking at Horus's body, the gods find no evidence of this and dismiss his claim. In turn, Horus lies and claims he is more dominant since not only did he ejaculate in Set's mouth, but also Set swallowed. The gods look into Set's body, see Horus's semen (which got there from Isis's lettuce trick), and uphold Horus's claim on the throne. But, of course, Set feels cheated and refuses to comply with the ruling, and the in-fighting continues anyway.

Nevertheless, the queerness of this story continues when Set's semen swallowing results in him giving birth to Horus's child. The myths vary as to who this child of homoerotic conception was. Some say that he grew up to be the moon deity Khonsu, others say that he turned out to be Thoth, and still others make no special mention of the child other than him being the son of Set and Horus.[18]

The winter solstice is Set's celebrated feast day. Being a sky god, he is associated with air correspondences and has the falcon as his sacred animal. But in terms of the queer lens, Set represents that "total top" segment of society. *Always* wanting to prove to everyone how he's "the man," he is that guy who sees "bottoming" as shameful. Ironically, though, for all his boasting, *he* is the one who gets impregnated and gives birth to a child after ingesting another male's semen. In this way, the magical image and story of Set can be utilized more as a curse of karmic retribution against those in the queer community who look down on their own kind or somehow feel that they're better than the rest because they only "top."

18   Randy P. Connor, David Hatfield Sparks, and Mariya Sparks, *Cassell's Encyclopedia of Queer Myth, Symbol, and Spirit* (London: Cassell & Co., 1997).

2
JUDAISM

Cultural

LGBT+ issues are a hot topic in modern Judaism. The veracity of the statement that "Judaism does or doesn't approve of queerness" is wholly dependent on about which branch of Judaism you are talking. Like most intact and living religious faiths that date back to ancient times, Judaism itself has fractured into multiple denominations, each with their own beliefs on what is and is not acceptable. On one side, there are anti-LGBT+ denominations such as Orthodox Judaism, and on the other side, there are pro-LGBT+ denominations such as Reconstructionist Judaism and Reform Judaism. To make a blanket statement saying that Judaism affirms either this or that in regard to queerness is impossible. Nevertheless, the history of Judaism has certainly had its fair share of queer leaders and figures.

Still, in regard to the naysayers, those within Judaism who abhorrently denounce the LGBT+ community usually point to a few specific passages in Leviticus and Deuteronomy within the Tanakh (the Hebrew Bible, aka Christianity's Old Testament). Both books of Leviticus and Deuteronomy generally list instructions on legal, moral, and ritual practices, and both Leviticus 18:22 and 20:13 specifically talk about homosexuality. These are the famous Bible passages stating "thou shalt not lie with mankind..." that are favorites of homophobic protesters to put on their picket signs. The other passages are Deuteronomy 22:5 and 23:17. The former is the one wherein men and women are forbidden from wearing the other gender's clothing. The latter is the one that prohibits the children of Israel from being temple prostitutes, implying that male prostitutes would have male clientele.[19]

Among Hebrew and biblical scholars, the aforementioned, apparently homophobic passages are generally seen as one part of a larger contextual issue that the Tanakh was trying to establish rather than four out-of-the-blue dictates against Jewish queerness. Like all ancient texts, the Tanakh has to be read through the lens of the time and culture of when it was written. During the time Leviticus and Deuteronomy were composed, the larger contextual message the writers were trying to spearhead was a sense of "differentness" in the Hebrew people.

The ancient Israelites were really trying to distinguish themselves as different from their neighboring tribes in order to emphasize their belief of being God's chosen people and therefore divinely special. Thus, among scholars of the liberal denominations of Judaism, the specific four passages against homosexuality and transvestitism were specifically written to show how different the Israelites were compared to the Mesopotamians and Canaanites, who had more of a goddess-centered belief system and celebrated queerness in the form of homosexual and transgender priests and priestesses. Judaism, in contrast, had one masculine God, and the sons of his chosen people were to act like men. The daughters of his cho-

---

19   Jewish Publication Society of America Version of the Tanakh, http://biblehub
      .com/jps/ (accessed Oct. 4, 2016).

sen people (as mentioned when we were back in ancient Egypt) were not be like the lascivious lesbians of Egypt.[20]

Interestingly, once the Hebrew people had successfully established themselves in the Promised Land by conquering its former inhabitants, their attitude toward LGBT+ people softened. No longer a vagabond tribe of people wandering the Middle East having to prove themselves as different, the Israelites were now more able to easily distinguish themselves from their neighbors because they were a recognized regional nation-state with defined territory, cultural achievements, and laws. This was the era of more lax attitudes toward sexuality, as most prominently evident in the highly erotic poetry that is the Song of Solomon.

Nothing lasts forever, though, and once the Promised Land came under Roman imperial rule, antipathy toward LGBT+ people peaked once more. Oppressed by foreign invaders and in order to emphasize a sense of nationalism and special differentness as God's chosen people, the Israelites focused upon how Rome's permissiveness toward male-male sex and religious cults of transgenderism went against those four passages in Leviticus and Deuteronomy. Homosexuality and blurring of the genders was something evil Rome did; as true people of virtue and respect for God's law, the people of the Jewish faith were certainly not homosexuals, nor did they desire to be the opposite gender. This was also the time wherein the Sodom and Gomorrah tales of the Hebrew Bible started becoming associated with homosexuality, as opposed to their original intention of showing the importance of hospitality toward others.

Even after the fall of Rome, though, the Jewish people still had no national self-sovereignty in the Promised Land, and the emphasis of "differentness" continued through the medieval era under the rule of the Byzantine and then Ottoman Empires. Outside of the Promised Land, the Jews more or less adapted to the prevailing attitudes of the region; those in Christian Europe continued their harshness toward LGBT+ people, while those in the Islamic empires shifted back to a more permissive acceptance,

20   Alpert, *Like Bread on the Seder Plate.*

perhaps best exemplified by the gay male poetry of the Hebrews living in caliphate Spain.

The exception came from the more mystical branches of Judaism that gained ground during this time, particularly that of Qabalah. Whether it grew from a branch of Jewish mystical Gnosticism or ancient Egyptian and classical Greek traditions that Jewish mystics appropriated into their own culture, one of the most underlying tenets of medieval and modern Qabalah is that of change. In a very generalized sense, practitioners of Qabalah do not see the world in terms of absolutes, but rather as gradations of change; everything can be transmuted either physically, spiritually, and/or energetically.[21]

For the most part, modern followers of Qabalah are accepting of the queer community. The underlying belief is that God doesn't make mistakes; if people are born with whatever degree of queerness in them, then it was divine destiny, not a biogenetic accident. Moreover, Qabalah's main focus is that of transforming one's self, and one's self is more than just sexuality and gender expression. To judge someone based on a single factor that Divine Providence instilled within that person since conception is to ignore the greater whole of the individual. Even the concept of male and female in this branch of Judaism has more to do with one's energy than one's biology. Therefore, to modern practitioners of Qabalah, it makes complete sense as to why a biological male with more "feminine" energy would be effeminate, why a biological female with more "masculine" energy would be butch, and why a person with an equal mix of energies could be both and yet neither simultaneously.[22]

21   Kieren Barry, *The Greek Qabalah: Alphabetic Mysticism and Numerology in the Ancient World* (Newbury: Samuel Weiser, 1999).

22   Kristóf Yosef Steiner, "Confessions of a Gay Kabbalist," *White City Boy*, Oct. 15, 2014, http://whitecityboy.com/2014/10/15/confessions-of-a-gay-kabbalist/ (accessed Oct. 6, 2016).

Jewish Takeaway:
OWNING OUR DIFFERENTNESS

For much of their history, even into today, many of Judaism's follow-ers have proudly professed their faith, even in the most dire and darkest of times. They knew who they were and refused to change just because the world around them was telling them that they were evil. And though times are changing, it is still an act of bravery in this world of negative connotations to live unapologetically as a Jew.

This is a mighty lesson. Never hide your queerness or change in order to accommodate society. It is much easier now for you to do this than it was for our ancestors, so don't go giving me excuses. Even if you cannot fully be yourself because you are young and financially dependent upon an unloving family, find your outlet of queer expression and community online. Just always, always, always remember who you are, and love that person.

So, for your next magical activity, come out of the broom closet. Depend-ing on your circumstances, that might be more difficult; if so, start with baby steps. Publicly wear your tradition's symbol as a pendant around your neck. Fashion a bracelet or some accessory that has magical significance to your tradition. As a worker of magic, do not hide who you are.

Harvey Milk's campaign for all people to come out openly as an LGBT+ person showed the world that queer people are their neighbors, relatives, friends, and coworkers. It created familiarity and, from there, dialogue, which eventually helped to reject then-California Proposition 6, which would have made mandatory the firing of all public schoolteachers who were gay or supported gay rights. Though not as dire, the same kind of positive familiarity campaign can be done with your magical tradition. But if you continue to hide it from the world, then it either doesn't exist to the world or it only exists in the way hateful people describe it to the world. Have the courage to start being more public in your queerness and your magical tradition. Own your differentness and educate the masses at the same time.

Deities & Legends

JONATHAN & KING DAVID

Like most same-sex biblical relationships, that of Jonathan and King David is somewhat controversial in that while many see it as a homoerotic love, many others refuse to see it as anything other than a passionately platonic friendship. The love between these two men can be found in the Book of Samuel: Jonathan being the royal son of King Saul of Israel, and David being the famed sling-wielding giant slayer. As the story goes, Jonathan, who had been fighting the Philistines for a while, took a liking to David after his impressive underdog victory against Goliath, the Philistine warrior. Jonathan formalizes his affection by making a "covenant" with David because he "loved him as he loved himself."[23] Granted, there could be any number of interpretations for this, but the profundity of their love eventually becomes clearer.

However, Jonathan's father, King Saul, shows little affection toward David, who is Israel's new golden boy, riding high on his popularity as the giant slayer. This unprecedented popularity among the people unnerves King Saul, who suspects David will inevitably use his clout to be the next king of Israel. As per court conspiracy protocol of the time, King Saul plots to preemptively kill David before David can usurp the throne, but Jonathan warns David of his father's plans, allowing David to flee and find refuge among, ironically, the Philistines, who in the meantime kill both Jonathan and King Saul.

Upon hearing of Jonathan's death, David grieves deeply and publicly laments losing someone very dear to him, proclaiming "Wonderful was thy love to me / Passing the love of women."[24] David later goes on to unite Israel and Judah, defeat the Philistines, and bring the Ark of the Covenant to newly conquered Jerusalem, where he establishes his new capital

---

23   1 Samuel 13:3-4. Jewish Publication Society of America Version of the Tanakh, http://biblehub.com/jps/ (accessed Oct. 8, 2016).

24   2 Samuel 1:26. Jewish Publication Society of America Version of the Tanakh, http://biblehub.com/jps/ (accessed Oct. 8, 2016).

city. Since the Middle Ages, Jonathan and David officially making their love to be a covenant (which scholars see as an early form of Jewish same-sex union)[25] and David's elegy for Jonathan that states his love surpassed that of all women are the main reasons why Jonathan and David have been seen as gay lovers.

In magical workings, the most popular and defining icon of King David is the Star of David. It's the symbol emblazoned on the center of the Israeli flag, the six-pointed star made of two stacked equilateral triangles: one right-side up and the other upside-down. Traditionally, the Star of David has been used in magic, especially by followers of the Qabalah, as a talisman for protection and an amulet for good luck.

JOSEPH & HIS COAT OF MANY COLORS

Not to be confused with the stepfather of Jesus Christ, this Joseph appears in the Book of Genesis and is most memorable for his coat of many colors. In brief, the tale of Joseph begins with him not only having the power to interpret dreams but also him being daddy's favorite and given a flashy, colorful coat to prove it. Naturally, his brothers are extremely jealous, and they steal his coat and sell him off into slavery. The wife of his new master makes sexual advances toward him, but when he refuses, she falsely accuses him of raping her, landing him in prison. Other events ensue until eventually Joseph is asked to interpret the Egyptian pharaoh's dream, which no one else can do. Joseph's interpretation is prophetically accurate and he becomes vizier of Egypt. Later, he gets revenge on his brothers, reunites with his family, and becomes a phenomenal success until dying around the age of 110.[26]

Scholarly research into Joseph's story arc in the Book of Genesis generally associates his coat of many colors to be a priestess gown or even his mother's wedding gown. His mother, Rachel, was still a follower of their

---

25   Michael Vasey, *Strangers and Friends: A New Exploration of Homosexuality and the Bible* (London: Hodder & Stoughton, 1995).

26   Book of Genesis, http://biblehub.com/jps/genesis/1.htm (accessed Oct. 8, 2016).

native Canaanite religion of goddess worship wherein gay and transgender priests and priestesses were still in full practice. The fact that their father gave Joseph the coat/gown may have been a sign of approval for him to join the gender-variant priesthood of the Canaanite religion. So, more than just being their parent's favorite, it could be interpreted that Joseph's brothers essentially saw him as a cross-dressing queer and reacted in a very homophobic way to get rid of him.

Also, Canaanite dream interpretation was generally seen as a type of womanly magic, thus further emphasizing Joseph's association with femininity. Since the story goes on to say that Joseph eventually married and had children, it is within reason to believe that he was an effeminate man, either heterosexual or bisexual, who enjoyed cross-dressing in his mother's clothes and had supportive parents but was nevertheless hated by his unaccepting homophobic siblings. Magically, Joseph emphasizes the functionality of clothing and fashion in representing our true selves and awakening the power within.

NAOMI & RUTH

Within the scriptures (both Hebrew and Christian), the relationship of Naomi and Ruth is perhaps the single most common go-to reference when advocating lesbian love. The Book of Ruth tells of a famine that devastated Israel, causing Naomi and her family to flee to nearby Moab, where her husband dies and her sons marry two Moabite women, one of which is Ruth. Years later both of Naomi's sons die, and in a gesture of sociopolitical compassion, she tells her daughters-in-law to go ahead and return to their original families and remarry so as not to be strapped with the lifelong burden of taking care of their mother-in-law without a man to support them. Remember, this was a time when women were essentially a form of property, unable to make a good living on their own. Women depended upon either their parents or their husband for economic survival, so this was a very altruistic thing for Naomi to do for her daughters-in-law since there were no men left to take care of them. Ruth, however, refuses to leave Naomi, agreeing to go wherever she goes and help shoulder the burden of living as widows in a man's world. Ruth's self-sacrificing dedication to her mother-in-law (and her sexual aggressiveness, which is a whole 'nother story) eventually caught the eye of a man named Boaz, and the two married and had children, making Ruth the great-grandmother of David the giant slayer.[27]

While not overtly lesbian, the homoerotic aspect of their relationship is often argued for in the semantic details of the Book of Ruth. By far, the most memorable part of the tale is Ruth's vehement refusal to leave Naomi and remarry. The passage claims that while her sister-in-law kissed Naomi goodbye, Ruth "cleaved unto her." In the original Hebrew, the word used is *dabaq*, which was used in the preceding Book of Genesis to mean uniting with a spouse and being romantically or sexually drawn to someone.[28] Moreover, Ruth's passionate declaration to stay by Naomi's side, come what may, is often a passage used in Jewish wedding ceremonies between heterosexual couples, causing many to point out that the love between Naomi and Ruth is indeed a love between lovers.[29]

For obvious reasons, the Book of Ruth has been held in high esteem by both feminists and queer scholars. It is the story of resourceful women sticking together and, through mutual cooperation, defiantly surviving in a man's world without men. And although Ruth does eventually remarry, it is evident that she doesn't need a man by the time he shows up in the story. In a magical sense, Ruth is an icon of female self-determination and all-female covens and communities, as well as the mutual sisterhood of support between queer women.

27 Book of Ruth, http://biblehub.com/jps/ruth/1.htm (accessed Oct. 8, 2016).

28 Thomas Marland Horner, *Jonathan Loved David: Homosexuality in Biblical Times* (Louisville: Westminster John Knox Press, 1978).

29 Claudia Card, *Lesbian Choices* (New York: Columbia University Press, 1995); Connor, Sparks, and Sparks, *Cassell's Encyclopedia of Queer Myth, Symbol, and Spirit*.

3

ISLAM

Cultural

Islam probably takes the most heat on being anti-LGBT+ in our modern world, and it's not undeserved. Casual online research consistently shows that Muslim-majority countries (by no means all, but many) have unkind and severe laws against queer persons ranging from imprisonment to public executions. And while it is true that non-Muslim countries also have similar laws, if you were to look at maps of worldwide LGBT+ rights, there is consistently a large swath of the most anti-queer countries flooding over Muslim Africa, the Middle East, and into Bangladesh. Those same countries are also the ones who frequently oppose LGBT+ rights on the international level.[30] In very loose terms, it seems that what the Christian-majority nations were to our queer ancestors in the Middle Ages, the Muslim-majority nations are to our queer brothers and sisters today.

But why is that? Truth be told, it hasn't always been this way, and it isn't that way for all denominations of Islam or all nations and people in the denominations that are. Like all religions on our globe trek, it's important to separate the faith from the cultural mores of the times. Only then can we get a better understanding of how, when, and why things are as they are today. Due to the severe negative connotations Islam has to many of us in the West, we'll start by getting a better understanding about the religion and then get into what role it has played in queer history.

Islam can be considered the third monotheistic religion that traces its roots back to Abraham of the Book of Genesis. It is the worship of the same singular masculine God as the Jews and the Christians, but where they all differ is in regard to who was the best prophet that had the final say on things. Very generally, Judaism is the faith of Moses, and they believe that the Messiah has yet to come and lead a new era for them as God's chosen people. Christianity takes it a step further and believes the prophesized Messiah did already come in the form of Jesus Christ. Islam takes it a step even further and believes that while Jesus was a holy prophet, he wasn't the Messiah. To them, Muhammad was the supreme prophet to whom God revealed his final revelations until the preordained Day of Resurrection (Judgment Day).

Officially, all teachings of Islam have to originate from one of two places in order for them to be considered authentic: either the Qur'an or the hadiths. All rules, laws, and social/spiritual conclusions are based on these sources. The Qur'an is the holy book of Islam. Unlike Judaism and Christianity, which are often internally split on whether their holy books are God's word, divinely inspired, or just a human attempt to record what they learned from the Divine, Islam believes that the Qur'an is the direct

---

30   Jessica Geen, "UN Passes Gay Rights Resolution," *Pink News*, June 17, 2011, http://www.pinknews.co.uk/2011/06/17/un-passes-gay-rights-resolution/ (accessed Oct. 10, 2016).

word of Allah (God) as given to the prophet Muhammad by the archangel Gabriel. So pure and unalterable is the Qur'an that any translation of it is considered merely commentary; only the original version in Arabic, as given to Muhammad, is the true Qur'an.[31]

The hadiths, for their part, revolve around the life of Muhammad. Specifically, a hadith is a report, narrative, or teaching directly from Muhammad himself. While the Qur'an was composed during and directly after Muhammad's lifetime, the hadiths remained oral tradition until centuries after the death of Muhammad, when they were finally collected and written down. Because of this, each denomination of Islam has a different "official" collection of hadiths by which they follow, and some even reject them altogether since they can't be unequivocally traced back to Muhammad as can the Qur'an.

The Qur'an and the hadiths are important to our discussion of Islamic queer cultural history because together they form the basis of Islamic law (also known as Sharia law), which, in turn, dictates if, how, and to what extent a person can express their queerness in everyday life. In regard to LGBT+ people, both the Qur'an and the hadiths make direct mention of them in a very negative light.

In the Qur'an, the anti-LGBT+ sentiment comes from the infamous Sodom and Gomorrah story wherein the Divine smites the cities for their wicked ways. In the sacred texts of Judaism and Christianity, this tale is generally understood as a moral allegory against being inhospitable to strangers in need. In the Qur'an, however, it specifically states that the wickedness of these cities is their acceptance of and participation in homosexuality.[32] By and large, this is the main argument against gays and lesbians in the Islamic world, solidified by the fact that the Qur'an is believed to be the direct word of Allah. So if Allah specifically dictates that something is wicked, then who are mortals to argue against it or circumvent it through logic and reasoning?

31   Geoff Teece, *Religion in Focus: Islam* (London: Franklin Watts Ltd., 2003).
32   From http://cmje.usc.edu/religious-texts/quran/verses/007-qmt.php (accessed July 10, 2017).

Thus anti-LGBT+ sentiment in Islam has been tougher to change in comparison to the other monotheistic faiths who believe the holy books to be more interpretive and not necessarily dictated by God. In fact, the name of the principle character of the Sodom and Gomorrah story, Lot, became the origin for the Arabic words *liwāṭ* and *lūṭi*, which mean homosexual behavior and homosexual, respectively.[33]

For proponents of the Qur'an as a legal document, there is no direct mention of punishment for homosexuality other than it being immoral, but that is where the hadiths come into play. Accordingly, Muhammad specified that the punishment for Lot's people (homosexuals) should be to kill both the one doing it and the one to whom it is done.[34] Additionally, another hadith tells of how Muhammad cursed effeminate men and masculine women, calling for them to be cast out of their homes.[35]

These are the famous go-to references used by Islamic extremists to rationalize the death penalty for LGBT+ persons, but because the hadiths are unreliable in origin and probably tainted by the bias of the writers, Islamic jurisprudence does not consider them to be legal justification for the death penalty. In general, there are only two crimes for which Muslim blood can be legally spilled as punishment under Sharia law: intentional murder and "spreading mischief in the land" (which is up to interpretation but generally includes sexual crimes). Those Islamic empires and countries that have and do sentence queer persons to death base their legal theory on the accepted assumption that LGBT+ acts fall under the latter category.[36]

Although it is somewhat a back-handed acceptance, a unique exception can be found in the Sharia law of modern Iran regarding transgender individuals. In the 1980s the first supreme leader of Iran, Ayatollah Khomeini,

---

33   Wayne Dynes, *Encyclopaedia of Homosexuality* (New York: Routledge, 1990).

34   From http://cmje.usc.edu/religious-texts/hadith/abudawud/038-sat
      .php#038.4447 (accessed July 10, 2017).

35   From http://cmje.usc.edu/religious-texts/hadith/bukhari/072-sbt
      .php#007.072.774 (accessed July 10, 2017).

36   From http://www.bbc.co.uk/religion/religions/islam/islamethics
      /capitalpunishment.shtml (accessed July 27, 2017).

advocated for the promotion of helping transgender people receive gender reassignment surgery to live their life as the gender they felt they truly were. This position has been supported by much of the Islamic clergy of Iran as well as the second supreme leader of Iran, Ayatollah Ali Khamenei.

Considering homosexuality and LGBT+ behavior is outlawed in Iran, the reasoning for this seemingly progressive stance on transgenderism is interesting. The way the religious leaders of Iran see it, transgender individuals are essentially homosexuals since they are sexually attracted to their own biological gender, but by allowing them to surgically change their gender, they are no longer homosexuals since they will be attracted to the opposite gender as per "normal" society. Because of this "save the sinner" approach, Iran is second only to Thailand in the number of sex change operations, and the government even subsidizes 50 percent of the cost of the surgeries and facilitates subsequent birth certificate corrections without qualm.[37]

But even prior to Ayatollah Khomeini's promotion of gender reassignment surgeries in Iran, the Islamic world has been a hotbed of LGBT+ promotion and tolerance for centuries. It goes without saying that the Arabian world had queer persons in it before the arrival of Islam. But to be official about it and point to something other than common sense to back up that claim, evidence comes from the prophet Muhammad himself in the hadiths. Assuming that the previously mentioned hadiths are true (the ones wherein he called for the killing of queer people and the casting out of queer family members), then queer identity and self-expression must have been going on. Otherwise, how could he have denounced something that no one was doing?

Immediately following Muhammad's death, Islam spread rapidly, and its two major holy cities, Mecca and Medina, became global metropolises. And much like modern times, these large multicultural urban cities became centers of social liberalism. Despite the disapproval from religious authorities during this time, the effeminate dancing men known as

37   Vanessa Barford, "Iran's Diagnosed Transsexuals," BBC, Feb. 25, 2008, http://news.bbc.co.uk/2/hi/7259057.stm (accessed Oct. 11, 2016).

mukhannathun were quite popular.[38] Tolerance of social queerness soon skyrocketed under the Abbasid Caliphate, which traced its lineage back to Muhammad's youngest uncle. Caliph al-Amid was particularly known for his non-heterosexuality. Pressure kept building on him to produce an heir, but he was noticeably disinterested in women. So, to get around this problem, he forced all of his slave women to dress and act like men in the hopes that he would then be aroused enough by them to get them impregnated.[39]

As the Middle Ages went on, the Muslim empires of the time developed a "don't ask, don't tell" type of secret permissiveness toward same-sex relations. Scholars believe this developed a sexual outlet for a cultural society that disallowed socialization between the sexes outside of the home. After all, when you're only allowed go out, socialize, and have fun with members of your own sex due to mandated segregation, it is not uncommon for passionate, romantic, and even sexual bonds to form. And though the research is scant, it is generally agreed that this resulted in female-female relationships in addition to male-male ones. But because it was shameful for a man to be penetrated like a woman, younger males became the only ones who could socially get away with "bottoming." To the medieval Muslims, queerness wasn't something that you were, but rather something that you did—it was a verb, not a noun.[40]

Fascinatingly, the biggest issue medieval Muslim society had with male-male sex was not so much being penetrated, but rather the enjoyment of being penetrated. Understood as an enjoyable act, the rationale of the times lauded against males "bottoming" so as to prevent them from acquiring a taste for it, which would become shameful as they entered adulthood and prevent them from desiring a woman, settling down, and producing children of their own. Nevertheless, the exception to the rule

38   Everett K. Rowson, "The Effeminates of Early Medina," *Journal of the American Oriental Society* 111:4 (1991): 671–693.
39   P. Bearman, et al., *The Encyclopaedia of Islam* (Leiden: Brill, 1983).
40   Arno Schmitt and Jehoeda Sofer, *Sexuality and Eroticism Among Males in Moslem Societies* (New York: Routledge, 1992).

seems to be most prevalent in poetry and literature, particularly those of Iran and Muslim Spain wherein homoerotic verse, odes, and songs maintained strong appeal both among writers and readers.[41]

And before we go on to the next section of Islamic queer deities and legends, I think it's important to mention one final thing: Sufism. Although Islam has a number of denominations and subdenominations, the faith can be generally divided into two overarching umbrella denominations of Sunni and Shia, a divide stemming from disagreement over Muhammad's successor. Sunni commands the overwhelming majority of Muslim nations, with the exception of Iraq and Iran wherein the Shia denomination is the majority. The other most well-known denomination of Islam is Sufism, and it differs from the other denominations by being more inner and mystically oriented.

Sufism, by and large, has been historically much more openly accepting of LGBT+ persons than the more mainstream branches of Islam. These mainstream branches are outwardly oriented in the sense that the Divine, Allah, is outside of ourselves, and by following his teachings via his prophet Muhammad, one can meet him in the next life. But Sufism is all about searching for a direct experience with the Divine within ourselves on an intuitive and emotional level. Part of this involves seeing the beauty of Allah in others, regardless of their gender, and so when two people physically express their love for each other, it is a dance between genderless souls, not bodies limited by gender.[42]

Unfortunately, their openness in expressing and complimenting the beauty of someone of the same gender, in addition to the men's flowing, dress-like clothing, made them targets of the less tolerant branches of Islam. A number of historic Islamic texts deride Sufis as sodomites and heretics, and the cascade of homoerotically humorous and romantic Sufi

41   Kecia Ali, "Same-Sex Sexual Activity and Lesbian and Bisexual Women," *The Feminist Sexual Ethics Project*, Dec. 10, 2002, https://www.brandeis.edu /projects/fse/muslim/same-sex.html (accessed Oct. 12, 2016).

42   Kath Browne and Sally R. Munt, *Queer Spiritual Spaces: Sexuality and Sacred Places* (New York: Routledge, 2010).

writings further fueled that fire. Nevertheless, many of the region's most profound and gloriously beautiful poetry has been the result of queer Sufi mystics, one of which we will soon discuss. [43]

Islamic Takeaway:
CRAFT LIKE NO ONE'S WATCHING

For hundreds of years, the whirling dance of Sufism has been mocked by fellow Muslims because it looks odd. Moreover, it has a queer tinge to it because it is reminiscent of that gay-boy fantasy of a man wearing a long gown and spinning in circles, watching the skirt flare out like a flower. But do the dancers care? Not at all. They don't care how they look or how it comes across to onlookers. They are right there in the ecstatic motion of the dance, communing with the Divine. It is a form of moving meditation meant to separate themselves from the ego through the use of music, movement, and concentration on the Divine.

This is bold and highly admirable. Most of us are apprehensive to dance in public, let alone allow ourselves to "act queer." Highly aware that our very movements, speech, and mannerisms often give us away as LGBT+, we try to "act straight" and fit in. We move as if we're being watched at all times, like spies undercover, awaiting and dreading being found out.

But that's no way to live. I mean, if you're always pretending to be something that you're not, then your friends are actually friends with that persona, not you—not the *real* you. Stop the masquerade and start actually living your own life. Don't worry who's watching; if they don't like what they see, they can always look away.

So, for your next magical activity, live your own magical life and craft like no one's watching. Take a mental step back and see if the tradition you're currently in/studying is truly the right one for you. Every tradition has certain rules, expectations, and ways to properly do things, but if you're just going along with all that just because you want to fit in with the tradition rather than because that is how you truly desire to practice

---

43   D. J. Moores, *The Ecstatic Poetic Tradition: A Critical Study from the Ancients Through Rumi, Wordsworth, Whitman, Dickinson, and Tagore* (Jefferson: McFarland, 2014).

magic or where your true crafting talents lie, then you're just masquerading like the "straight-acting" crowd. The fact that various, vastly different magical traditions are all effective in their magic is enough to show that there aren't really any hard and fast rules to spellworking. Don't stay in a particular tradition if the rules and regulations don't resonate with you. Live your own magical life and explore other traditions. Who knows, you might realize that you have a knack for a particular brand or style of magic that your tradition doesn't promote or focus upon. Craft like your tradition isn't watching to make sure you do everything according to their way and see where your new magic takes you.

Deities & Legends

GODDESSES OF THE SATANIC VERSES

This ultra-cool name comes from an apocryphally infamous incident called the Satanic Verses Incident wherein the prophet Muhammad was allegedly tricked by Satan, who was pretending to be the angel Gabriel, to encourage people to seek divine intercession through three female deities. Of course, these verses are widely considered to be a fabricated incident due to their inability to be directly traced back to Muhammad like traditional hadiths and due to the Islamic belief of Muhammad's infallibility, thus making him theologically immune to such trickery.

Nevertheless, these three goddesses were actually real deities once worshipped in the Middle East. They were three queer-positive female deities of pre-Islamic Arabia who were integrated into a Pagan-Muslim mythology mixture found in early cosmopolitan Islamic cities. Ultimately, their worship was denounced as idolatrous and later eradicated by Islamic zealotry. Their names are al-Lāt, al-'Uzzā, and Manāt.[44]

The goddess al-Lāt was a patron deity of the city of Mecca. She was believed to be the daughter of Allah, and in some legends she is the consort of Allah. She was the goddess of the military and love, and is notable

44   Shahab Ahmed, "Ibn Taymiyyah and the Satanic Verses," *Studia Islamica* 87 (1998): 67–124.

for having a large following of women and transgender individuals. Her worship became so popular that Muhammad, in his quest to spread Islam, specifically called for the destruction of her temples and statues, which were widely eradicated during his lifetime.[45]

The second goddess is al-'Uzzā. She is traditionally depicted with black skin and thought to be African in origin. She is the goddess of travelers, nomads, the desert, the moon, and the planet Venus. She, too, had a large following of women and transgender individuals. After the destruction of her worship in Arabia, Christians syncretized her into the Marian apparition of our Lady of Madaba in Jordan, and Jewish mystics syncretized her into the angel Metatron.[46]

The third goddess with a queer following of her own was Manāt. She was the goddess of time, fate, and destiny. People prayed to her in order to tip the scales of destiny to be in their favor. She is thought to be the most ancient of the pre-Islamic goddesses of Arabia, and throughout the Arab world pilgrims flocked to her shrine near Mecca and Medina, often shaving their heads as a sign to the world of having completed this pilgrimage for their goddess.

MEHMED THE CONQUEROR

Fatih Sultan Mehmet Han, better known as Mehmed the Conqueror, was a sultan of the Ottoman Empire. He is infamous for being the leader who brought an end to the Byzantine Empire, expanding Islam into southeastern Europe, and being a patron of both the sciences and civil engineering public works. He was also known, though much less celebrated, for his sexual attraction to men, particularly to young, pretty men. Two stories, in particular, stand out.

The first story involves a eunuch who served in his court. The eunuch's fourteen-year-old son (conceived before castration, one would assume)

[45] Muhammad ibn Jarir al-Tabari, *The History of al-Tabari, vol. 9: The Last Years of the Prophet*, trans. Ismail K. Poonwala (Albany: State University of New York Press, 1990).

[46] Connor, Sparks, and Sparks, *Cassell's Encyclopedia of Queer Myth, Symbol, and Spirit*.

was rumored to have been a particularly pretty boy, and so Mehmed ordered the man to bring his son to the palace so he may enjoy him sexually. When the eunuch refused, Mehmed unhesitatingly ordered him, his pretty son, and his son-in-law to be beheaded.[47]

The second story comes from Mehmed's conquests of Europe, specifically the Kingdom of Wallachia wherein he captured two princes as prisoners of war: the infamous Vlad the Impaler and his brother. This brother was known as Radu the Fair, named for his exceptional prettiness, and he soon caught the eye of Mehmed, who made him his personal page. The two were said to be lovers and their intimacy consensual. When Mehmed finally vassalized Wallachia, he set Radu on the throne to act as his proxy ruler of the newly conquered territory. As a side note, modern historical psychologists believe that Vlad's obsession of impaling his victims on stakes through the anus represented his own pent-up hostility for being unwillingly sodomized himself as a young man living in the Ottoman Empire.[48]

RUMI

Jalāl ad-Dīn Muhammad Rūmī, known in short as simply Rumi, was a Sufi mystic, dancer, and poet. Said to be gifted as a child, he reported having visions and being able to express knowledge beyond his years. Once established as somewhat of a famous mystic, Rumi encountered the philosopher Shams Tabrizi, who became his spiritual instructor and romantic lover. Shams Tabrizi was special in that not only was he raised exclusively by women, but also that his profound wisdom was equally matched by his rugged good looks. Rumi and Shams complemented one another seemingly perfectly, with Rumi being more of a prideful intellectual and Shams

---

47   Kinross, *Ottoman Centuries: The Rise and Fall of the Turkish Empire* (New York: Harper Perennial, 1979).

48   Jamie Adair, "Dracula: Impalement, Punishment By Proxy of His Brother's Lover?" *History Behind Game of Thrones*, March 6, 2014, http://history-behind -game-of-thrones.com/historical-periods/draculaimpale (accessed Oct. 13, 2016).

being more of an irreverent, commonsense sage, and this dynamic helped in completing each another's mystical knowledge.

As their relationship grew, Rumi brought his lover to live with him at his school and began writing some of Sufism and Islam's most beautiful and romantic queer poetry. Popular topics included how Shams's beauty allowed Rumi to see the Divine, loving the Divine through loving Shams, and sex as a sacred act. However, Rumi's disciples became increasingly jealous with their teacher's attention to this new person, and they mercilessly harassed Shams to the point where Shams felt he had no alternative but to leave. Their time apart became the impetus for Rumi's most philosophic works into the nature of love itself.

Shams eventually did return, but Rumi's followers were still hotly jealous and murdered him. Legends say that in honor of Shams, Rumi incorporated music, poetry, and dance (the appreciation of which was instilled in him by Shams) into Sufism's iconic whirling trance dance meditation.[49] Nevertheless, the queerness of Rumi remains a hotly controversial subject, with avid supporters and deniers both outside of and within Islam and Sufism.

Upon reading his works, you'll see just how magical and achingly beautiful his written expression of love is. For anyone seeking to heighten the potency of a queer love or lust spell, read some of Rumi's works while in a meditative state. Its efficacy will be undeniable.

---

49 Dhwty, "The Ancient Tradition of Whirling Dervishes of the Mevlevi Order," *Ancient Origins*, April 23, 2015, http://www.ancient-origins.net/history /ancient-tradition-whirling-dervishes-mevlevi-order-002943 (accessed Aug. 18, 2017).

4

GREATER MIDDLE EASTERN MAGICAL COMMUNITY

MESOPOTAMIAN MENTORS
IN THE MODERN AGE

Our first special guest for the Greater Middle Eastern leg of our expedition is Dr. Jacob Tupper. A veterinarian by trade, Jacob is a devotee of the deities of ancient Mesopotamia. I first met him while on a book tour at a Pagan convention in the San Francisco Bay area when he stayed around to talk with me after one of my presentations. He told me of his queerness and how that caused a rift between him and his family. Nevertheless, he found strength and support from the Mesopotamian gods, who helped him become the successful medical professional he is today. So, naturally, I brought him here on our expedition to share his story with you, showcasing how the most ancient of deities are still supporting the LGBT+ community in this day and age.

Like a lot of people, my spiritual life and my mundane one are irrevocably intertwined. I entered the services of Ishtar about seven years ago, still too young and inexperienced to know who I was and what I wanted. Like many people, I was raised in a conservative Protestant household where sexuality (especially non-heteronormative sexuality) was simply not a topic up for discussion. I was painfully shy and borderline asexual due to my upbringing, so I was thrown for a loop when this vibrant and intensely sexual goddess was like, "Imma just make myself at home here and mess around a bit. You can accept it or you can fight it. Either way, I always win in the end. 'Kay, thanks!" In working with her and her husband, Tammuz, I started to break down some serious psychological blocks and discover that I wasn't just a picky straight dude but a bisexual one attracted to strength, confidence, and (mostly) men.

Things continued for many years with me simply not discussing my romantic life with anyone in my family. However, any secret that big is liable to get out, and my parents eventually confronted me and forced me to come out. They dove into despair and anger, lashed out at me, and for months basically stopped speaking to me unless it was necessary. At that point Ereshkigal joined her sister and brother-in-law as my patron. The three of them, through daily devotion and soul-searching, supported me and encouraged me to fight for my right to live and be happy on my own terms instead of subsisting off the scraps society deigned to throw to me. This proved to be one of the most valuable lessons I could learn, and it paved the way for pruning a number of unhealthy relationships over the years. Now I'm on much better terms with my family and the world at large, and I'm learning how to give back to the powers that supported and protected me.

Ultimately, the greatest thing I can tell anyone reading this is to keep going. Keep practicing, studying, and being who you are. If you look and leave yourself open, the people you most need will find you. It was only

later that I learned of the kurgarra and the galatur, devotees of Ishtar,
that were explicitly neither male nor female. As we continue to push the
boundaries of what is considered "normal," we will need a strong founda-
tion in order to manifest the world we wish to create. For me, the ancient
gods of Mesopotamia helped me cultivate such a foundation. For you, these
or other gods (or no gods at all!) may give you the strength to grow your
roots. No matter what speaks to you, I and everyone here wish you the best
in your seeking and pray that life treats you with kindness and respect.
    Blessed be.

—DR. JACOB TUPPER

PROTECTION PRAYER TO THE BAWY

Up next is the Rev. Tamara L. Siuda. In addition to being a professional
Egyptologist and Coptologist (MA 2000, MA 2008, Ph.D. in process), she
is the founder of the Kemetic Orthodox Religion, which is a modern practice of ancient Egyptian spirituality. She is a female king (as the Kemetic
Orthodox Nisut and as a *mambo asogwe* of Haitian Vodou, which we will
explore in an upcoming chapter), and she identifies as biracial, genderqueer, and bisexual. She founded the Marriage Militia (marriagemilitia
.org) to provide advocacy and information on same-sex marriage in the
USA, and she is active in LGBT+ and other human rights movements.
So, without further ado, I'll let her take the lead and explain more about
ancient Egyptian queerness and give us a prayer of gratitude, survival, and
balance for uncertain times.

Ancient Egyptian polytheism does not make a statement on modern
LGBTQ identity. Ancient Egyptians did not discriminate against people
we understand as LGBTQ, and texts describe same-sex relationships
and gender difference in ways that neither highlight nor disparage. The
ancients did have similar conceptions around gender binary as their con-
temporaries, and some things privileged men in certain spheres and women
in others. However, they were not as patriarchal as contemporaries.
Ancient Egyptian women had more equality, as we understand it, than
any other ancient Near Eastern civilization.

However, we must acknowledge that the difference we understand in LGBTQ identity today also existed then. In some cultures this difference is considered exceptional, and such people are held up as especially powerful or magical. For the ancient Egyptians, any difference in a person, from hair color to sexuality, was notable simply because it was different. Their philosophy was based on harmony and symmetry between complementary opposites. Difference itself was a way of understanding otherness as one part of a larger whole.

In ancient Egyptian religion, two gods, Horus and Set, appear as complementary opposites. Horus, embodied as the sky whose eyes are sun and moon or as the avenging son of Osiris, represents the strength of tradition. From the eternal sky he maintains order in the form of Ma'at, the balance of justice. When something is evil or unjust, Horus restores Ma'at and provides strength and protection to those with none. Set, who is often oversimplified as evil or chaotic, does not embody constancy but the reality that, for our existence, our only constant is change. Set is also a sky god, but he manifests in storm, lightning, and desert: unpredictable, sometimes violent natural forces that keep life moving. Set is Horus's loyal opposition: the change that keeps order from becoming stale or complacent. If Horus is a protector, Set is a challenger. Set forces us to know who we are and confront our reality. He pushes us out of comfort zones and outdated beliefs and helps us grow.

Together, Horus and Set maintain creation in a balance between same and other, tradition and change. These two gods protected the two lands of Egypt: Egypt was one country made of two lands, and humans are one being made of constancy and change. Together these gods were sometimes depicted as a single being with two heads called Bawy, "twin powers." Today's LGBTQ Pagans and polytheists can call upon Bawy to help us as we struggle for survival and balance. I offer this modern prayer to the ancient Bawy in gratitude for their presence in our lives.

Bawy, you who are Horus and Set,

Black land and red land, white crown and red,

Hear me as I come before you and ask your blessing.

As Horus I seek to know you and do your work,

To be and bring justice to an unjust world.

Grant me courage. Help me be true to myself.

Help me speak for the voiceless and vulnerable.

May I walk with your hand on my right shoulder,

    proud and strong.

As Set I seek to know you and do your work,

To be and to become everything I am.

Grant me strength. Help me know myself.

Challenge me to confront change in myself and my world.

May I walk with your hand on my left shoulder,

    proud and confident.

Bawy, you who are Horus and Set,

Black land and red land, white crown and red,

May I balance myself as you balance yourselves.

May I live in Ma'at as you do,

Constant and changing, as two who are one.

—*Rev. Tamara L. Siuda*

BISEXUAL BALANCE IN JUDAISM

Here to give more insight into growing up queer and Jewish is my friend Keren Petito. I had the honor of meeting her in college; she was a coworker of mine back at my first job on campus. Since I'm Irish-Mexican, most everyone I knew growing up was Catholic, so she was one of the first Jewish people with whom I bonded. When it came time to find an LGBT+ Jewish special guest for this book, I immediately turned to her. She was kind enough to meet us here in our expedition to share a little bit about being a bisexual woman raised in a Jewish Orthodox household and how she found the appropriate balance in her life of faith and identity.

Growing up, I never thought about my sexual identity as more than what it was. It was already assumed I'd marry a nice Jewish (Israeli preferred) man. It probably wasn't until middle school where I started to feel some queer tendencies that I ignored or set aside. The religious aspects of my life started to become less important or relevant and I began to stray from the religious beliefs. When I came out, and most importantly when I felt comfortable with my sexual identity, I felt that I related to very little of my religion and mostly with my cultural upbringing that is associated with Judaism.

Recently I came out to my parents and siblings, and that, even more so, separated me from my religion because it separated me more from my family. My family was my outlet into Judaism. I celebrated holidays with my family and family friends, who are all Orthodox Jewish, straight, and for the most part conservative or Republican. Since I've come out to my family, I no longer live with them. If I were to live under their roof, I would have to live under their rules, and dating a woman or thinking about spending my life with a woman does not exactly fall in line with their rules. I now celebrate Judaism and holidays with my family and alone, but now I focus on celebrating in a more personal way—a way in which I'd realistically like to raise my children to celebrate my religion. I still visit my family for the important meals and prayer rituals, but I try to not spend the night there or go there every weekend of the month.

Now that I live on my own, I feel more inclined to practice my religion the way I want to and without any outside influences. I don't light Shabbat candles, but I do light a memorial candle for my maternal grandfather and close family friend. I say a prayer in hopes of elevating their souls and bringing them closer to God. In Judaism it is regarded as most respectful to honor the dead, more so than the living. This is just one example of how I have kept the tradition of my religion.

Since I moved out of my parents' house for college, I stopped keeping kosher. I still don't eat the same foods we were taught not to eat, but I don't follow the same rules with the food, such as mixing meat and dairy or buying specifically kosher meat. I do this out of convenience and out of lack of desire to seek out special foods. I know that, like my sexual identity, this is something my family and surrounding Jewish community would not approve of.

I find it most comforting to think about how at the end of the day, it's me and not anyone else that I should be trying to please. I think most people forget this at times.

—KEREN PETITO

ISLAMIC PRAYER FOR THE LGBT+ IN LOVE

Our last special guest before we travel down into sub-Saharan Africa is Saif Mohammed. As he'll soon tell you, growing up as a gay Muslim in India was far from easy. Nevertheless, he persisted. He never forgot who he was, and he survived it all to be the happier man he is today. So without further ado, I'll move the spotlight over to him so he can share not only how he got through the bad times, but also a special Islamic prayer for those of us who feel our queerness destines us to be forever loveless and alone.

My name is Saifuddin Mohammed, aka Saif. I am from India and identify myself as gay and Muslim. Growing up in India in a very multicultural society, I was never very much inclined toward religion. But I was very spiritual due to the influence of my mother. Struggling about my sexuality in my teens and in early adulthood, I suffered from depression and loneliness and had very few friends. One day I happened to meet one of my close friends whom I had not met in a long time; on asking him about his long absence, he told me that he now had a girlfriend and preferred to spend time with her. On knowing this, I was very much saddened, in part due to my loneliness and due to the fact that I identified myself as gay. I thought finding a soulmate would be next to impossible in a society which was inherently homophobic.

That night I cried and prayed in my heart. I prayed that I too should find someone.

Here's my supplication:

"Oh Allah! You are the most benevolent and merciful. Your kindness and compassion encompasses the worlds; you love all your creatures, and I am one of them. You love me so much, yet I am in pain. Please show some mercy upon me and guide me to someone who would love me and whom I shall love. I am incomplete without him. Let him complete me and let me complete him. Take away all my sorrow and fill me with happiness.

Rabbana atina fid-dunya hasanatan wa fil 'akhirati hasanatan waqina 'adhaban-nar.

(Our Lord, give us good in this world and in the hereafter, and protect us from the torment of the fire.)"

And my earnest prayers were answered very soon. In a fortnight I met the person whom I loved the most and who completed me.

I feel closest to Allah in my own way and not in the way in which traditional religion describes. I feel that I am very spiritual and not religious. It reminds me of what my grandma used to say: "Religion and spirituality are two totally different things; religion gets you closer to society, while spirituality gets you closer to Allah."

Every single day I feel closer to Allah and always pray,

"Rabbana atina fid-dunya hasanatan wa fil 'akhirati hasanatan waqina 'adhaban-nar."

—Saifuddin Mohammed

PART 2

SUB-SAHARAN AFRICA & LANDS OF THE AFRICAN DIASPORA

Love doesn't rely on physical features.
MOSOTHO PROVERB

Our next destinations are sub-Saharan Africa and the New World nations whose majority populations are descendants from the slave trade. Now, these are controversial regions of the world when it comes to LGBT+ history and mysticism. Right up there with many Islamic nations who do not separate church and state, many modern African and diasporic nations are openly hostile to the queer community. So brace yourself because we are about to explore regions of the world that pridefully hold themselves as societies wherein legalized discrimination up to and including the death penalty is popularly supported by the masses. The exception, of course, is South Africa, which is the only country in this next leg of our world tour to provide LGBT+ protection.

Interestingly, these regions' anti-queer sentiments are rooted in the populist idea that homosexuality and queerness are not native to Africa or the people of African descent. It is widely believed that LGBT+ people and behaviors are a product of Western colonialism wherein the European powers introduced gayness and queer culture into Africa like a disease. Therefore, the common remedy is that all things queer must be eradicated from these countries in order to not only put the death-nail in the coffin of their colonial past, but also to return to a "purer" state of African culture the way it was *before* Europeans arrived with their evil practices such as slavery and homosexuality. Unsurprisingly, this same affirmation of something being un-African and an import of Western colonialism is also often used by those in power in Africa toward many progressive ideas and movements in these regions, especially regarding women's rights to sexual liberation and bodily sovereignty.[50]

If that line of reasoning sounds reactionary and ridiculous, it's because it is. But to countless people in sub-Saharan Africa and its diasporic nations, this reasoning is ironclad. Ironically, though, to justify the evils of Western-imported ideas such as queerness, the people almost always point to the Christian Bible—the holy book of a Western-imported faith forced upon the people during colonialism. The hypocrisy here is off the charts, and a look into the history and religious practices of precolonial Africa reveals many queer leaders and spiritualities throughout the continent.[51]

While the information on precolonial queer Africa is very patchwork and not fully studied (partially due to modern Africa's denial of such a past and refusal to research it, as well as academia's own historic marginalization of both queer and African history), there do exist numerous albeit less fully fleshed-out examples of our community in these lands, so let's get exploring.

50   Sylvia Tamale, "Homosexuality Is Not Un-African," *Aljazeera America*, April 26, 2014, http://america.aljazeera.com/opinions/2014/4/homosexuality -africamuseveniugandanigeriaethiopia.html (accessed Oct. 20, 2016).

51   Wanjira Kiama, "Homosexuality Takes Root in Kenya," *Daily Nation*, June 24, 1998, http://archive.globalgayz.com/africa/kenya/gay-kenya-news-and -reports-199-2/#article1 (accessed Oct. 20, 2016).

5
SUB-SAHARAN AFRICA

Cultural

EASTERN & SOUTHERN AFRICA

Religious culture in Eastern and Southern Africa is unique in that, depending on which region of which country you are in, the people are strongly Protestant Christian or Muslim, with a bit of indigenous beliefs added to the mix. But back in precolonial Kenya, there were two tribes in particular that were historically noted for their queer inclusiveness: the Kikuyu and the Meru, who recognized special religious leaders called *mugawe*. Equivalent to a priest, these non-heterosexual males not only dressed and wore their hair like women, but they also publicly acted like women. A notable number of them were even recognized as being married to other men.[52]

Traditional Kenyan society also allowed for same-sex marriages between two women. In the Akamba tribe this practice was called *iweto*, and despite initial assumption to the contrary, its practice had nothing to do with lesbianism but rather fertility. You see, in this particular society, males literally embodied the past, present, and future of the family. Without a son, a family's future as well as all its past ancestors would be spiritually erased. This extreme emphasis on a woman to produce boys was especially problematic for women who were barren, widows who never bore a male child, and the wives of men whose Y chromosomes were consistently not making it to the finish line. Therefore, to preserve the literal spirit of the family, Akamba society allowed women to take another woman as a wife and allow her to act as a surrogate. The original wife was expected to go through all the motions of courting the other woman, paying her bride price, and (if the husband was dead) selecting with whom she should mate. Regardless of the father, the male child born of this matrimonial surrogate was considered the next torchbearer of the original husband and wife's family spirit.[53]

In the Sudan a number of tribes have been recorded as accepting transvestitism as part of the culture. The Otoro are one of these tribes, but unlike many other tribes around the world, the socially accepted cross-dressing of men in their culture is neither religious nor spiritual in nature. Otoro men dressed and even sometimes lived as women simply because it was what they personally wanted to do, and everyone was okay with it.[54] Elsewhere in the Sudan the Tira, Nyima, and Moru tribes all had

---

52   Rodney Needham, *Right and Left: Essays on Dual Symbol Classification* (Chicago: University of Chicago Press, 1973).

53   Martha Mbugguss, *Same Gender Unions: A Critical Analysis* (Nairobi: Uzima, 2004).

54   Dynes, *Encyclopaedia of Homosexuality*.

preestablished transgender bride prices that grooms were expected to pay to the bride's family if they desired a transgender female wife.[55]

Two other Sudanese tribes, the Mesakin and the Korongo, were studied back in the 1930s by British anthropologist Siegfried Frederick Nadel, who wrote copious notes regarding the males' reluctance within these tribes to leave the all-male camps and return to the women in their settled villages. According to Nadel, the males of the tribe believe that marriage and sex with women are detrimental to their physical strength as men. He goes on to describe how even the older men of the tribe will frequently leave their home at night in preference for the company of the other men who are camping outside the village.

Nadel makes it clear, though, that he doesn't want to dive too deep into the psychology of why Mesakin and Korongo men prefer to exclusively be surrounded by other men, but he does leave the subject with two observational notes. First, that this behavior is almost exclusively seen among matrilineal African societies, and second, that there is widespread open homosexuality and transvestitism among the tribes that exhibit this male-bonding preference.[56]

The area of modern-day Uganda, now infamous for its draconian witch-hunt legislation toward LGBT+ persons and allies, was once an area of Africa well-known for its queerness. Homosexual, cross-dressing priests were common among the Bunyoro tribe, and the Teso tribe recognized a third gender exclusively for men who dressed like women. The most famous of the queer tribes, however, was the Langi tribe of northern Uganda, who had a special class of people known as *mudoko dako*. In general, a Langi tribesperson would be recognized as a mudoko dako from birth due to being born impotent. Now, how could anyone know if a baby was born impotent, you ask? Good question. The general theory is that

55   Randy P. Connor and David Hatfield Sparks, *Queering Creole Spiritual Traditions: Lesbian, Gay, Bisexual, and Transgender Participation in African-Inspired Traditions in the Americas* (Binghampton: The Haworth Press, Inc., 2004).

56   Siegfried Frederick Nadel, *The Nuba: An Anthropological Study of the Hill Tribes in Kordofan* (London: Oxford University Press, 1947).

there had to be some sort of immediate physical sign, most likely some sort of irregularity with the genitalia, and it seems as if being born intersex was how one would be labeled mudoko dako. At the very least, it had little to do with one's sexual orientation and more with one's physiology.

These mudoko dako existed well before their lands became colonized by foreign powers. Legally and socially, it was acceptable for a mudoko dako to marry a man or a woman. And since they were considered a third gender that was neither man nor woman, they could take on traditionally male work and dress as men or they could take on traditionally female work and dress as women. Some of them assumed the social identity of a woman so strictly that anthropologists have observed a number of them simulating menstruation with each moon cycle, though they could not do so naturally.[57]

In Ethiopia the Maale tribe has been historically documented for their queer *ashtime* people. In general terms, ashtime are biological males who dress, behave, and act like women and even have regular sex with other biological males. What made the ashtime special in relation to other transgender persons in East Africa was that they were given special protection by the king of the Maale, arguably making them one of the world's first cultures to establish specific protections for LGBT+ persons.[58]

Elsewhere in Ethiopia the Harari tribespeople were noted for their liberal attitude toward sex in general. Mutual masturbation between two women or two men was commonly accepted, and sexual relations between or even within the genders were not limited to persons of the same age, allowing no stigma toward two people of differing generations who mutually consent to engage in lovemaking. Furthering their progressive attitude, the Harari also recognized a third gender, which they defined as a person who had the spirit of one gender and the body of the other. These

57 Jack Herbert Driberg, *The Lango: A Nilotic Tribe of Uganda* (London: T. Fisher Unwin, Ltd., 1923).

58 Donald L. Donham, *Work and Power in Maale, Ethiopia* (New York: Columbia University Press, 1994).

third-gender persons were allowed to romance and fool around with men and women, depending on their preference.[59]

In the 1990s a first-of-its-kind lesbian-led anthropological study was conducted in the small landlocked country of Lesotho, focusing on the sexuality and same-sex relationships between the women there. The lead anthropologist, K. Limakatso Kendall, initially began her research by trying to identify *Basotho* (the plural demonym for Lesotho citizens) who self-identified as lesbians like herself, but in a surprising twist, not a single woman she met would self-identify as a lesbian.

What made this an odd finding was the fact that Basotho women would, in private, often engage in passionate makeout sessions with one another that would frequently lead to touching, fondling, oral sex, and even intercourse. According to Kendall's finished research, Basotho women did not see these as erotic acts but rather as ways of expressing non-romantic love and affection with one another. To them, something could only be considered sexual if a penis was involved; therefore, in their worldview, nothing sexual was going on because no one had a penis. Furthermore, a few women whom Kendall interviewed told of how their female best friends would sometimes conduct large public commitment ceremony feasts to strengthen their special friendship with one another, and both women's husbands would be in attendance, giving their wives their blessing for these wedding-like union celebrations.[60]

59   Irving Bieber, et al., *Homosexuality: A Psychoanalytic Study of Male Homosexuals* (New York: Basic Books, 1962).

60   K. Limakatso Kendall, "Women in Lesotho and the (Western) Construction of Homophobia," in *Female Desires: Same-Sex Relations and Transgender Practices Across Cultures*, ed. Evelyn Blackwood and Saskia Wieringa (New York: Columbia University Press, 1999).

Eastern & Southern African Takeaway:
SEPARATING LUST, LOVE & FRIENDSHIP

Basotho women maintain a healthy separation of lust, love, and friend-ship. They've been known to interact with each other on a profoundly deep and intimate level because they adhere to very sharp distinctions between a lustful relationship, a romantic relationship, and a platonic friendship. For our queer community, these are often tangled together with disastrous results.

Think back to that timeless *When Harry Met Sally* question of whether men can have friendships with women that are nonsexual in nature and vice versa. In hetero society men and women form strong, special bonds with their own gender because there is no lust added to the mix to compli-cate things. If a person is attracted to their own sex or all sexes, then that same-sex platonic bonding and friendship is always complicated because there is always a hint of lust and sexual attraction, maybe even romance, that exists or could develop from either party. Plus, if a gay guy has a straight female friend or a lesbian has a straight male friend, there is still the possibility that this friend may develop feelings or desires. So what are we to do?

Well, we follow the Basotho example and teach ourselves the under-standing of what each relationship is and isn't. As queer people, we may not be able to control our romantic or sexual affinity for a particular person, but we can control how we act upon those feelings. If you start developing feelings for a friend, think to yourself two things: Is it worth complicating the friendship in order to pursue those feelings? Can you handle and continue on with a friendship wherein you will always have unreciprocated feelings for someone or in which someone will have those feelings for you?

Magically, these are important questions, too. If we do a spell to find new friends, are we *really* wanting friends or are we just wanting some-one with whom we can do social activities? If we do a spell to manifest a lover, are we *really* wanting a lover or are we looking to satisfy our need of being loved? So, for your next magical activity, go into meditation and honestly assess your current relationships. Think of all your friends and people with whom you interact on a regular basis, and ask yourself into which categories they fit.

For example, say you have a friend named Renée; in the stillness of meditation, contemplate: Am I at all sexually attracted to Renée? Do I sense that she is sexually attracted to me? Do I have romantic feelings for Renée? Do I sense that she has romantic feelings for me? If I had to hang out with Renée one-on-one as friends, could we have a great time together or are we only comfortable with each other in the presence of a larger group? Once you know where you stand in all your relationships, you can more readily decide how to move forward. With all your socio-romantic emotions untangled and organized, you can be more mentally clear and efficacious in your socio-romantic spellwork.

WESTERN & CENTRAL AFRICA

In regard to spirituality, Western and Central Africa differ from Eastern and Southern Africa in two main ways. First, Western and Central Africa were colonized mostly by Catholic nations, Catholicism being much more Pagan-based in nature than Protestant Christianity or Islam due to their pantheon of saints with magical spheres of influence and their reverence for the divine feminine embodied in the Virgin Mary. Secondly, Western and Central Africa tend to be more personally involved with deities than elsewhere on the continent. Rather than the gods being separated from humanity by their divine nature, the gods of Western and Central Africa are often invoked by people to possess them and physically interact with them.

In regard to queer culture, these regions of Africa have many recorded examples, although again, due to a number of reasons, the research is not as fleshed out and fully realized as other non-LGBT+ and non-African his-tories. Nevertheless, the colonial conquerors did make note of the queer customs of the native tribes.

For example, in the modern region of Burkina Faso (a country wherein homosexual activity has never been criminalized), the Dagaaba tribe uti-lizes the unique, inherent talents of their LGBT+ tribespeople. Specifically, they act as the tribe's intermediaries for conflict resolution. Spiritually, queer persons are seen as having the ability to intercede between the people and the spirits as a type of gatekeeper who has direct contact with the Divine. On a more mortal plane, queer persons are also the primary liaisons whenever there is a problem between the sexes. Whether it be on a smaller level as de facto marriage counselors or on a grander scale if the women and men of the tribe are fiercely divided on a specific issue, the queer tribespeople are seen as the best people to handle these problems since they possess both male and female energies within them, allowing them to see both sides of the issue and suggest the best resolution.[61]

In present-day Ghana, the Ashanti Kingdom of the eighteenth and nineteenth centuries was well-known for its homosexual permissiveness within the luxury of the upper-class aristocracy. Male concubines were a common sight. However, these concubines (aka slaves) were expected to dress and act like women in order to please the societal preference for masculine-feminine relationships despite their allowance of homosexuality. Grimly, most of these Ashanti gay sex slaves met unfortunate ends due to the custom of being executed whenever their master died. Elsewhere in Ghana, the Dahomey Kingdom utilized ritually castrated males as royal wives within the upper court. These eunuchs were regarded as more female than male, and they often held positions of great power in the court, thus having great power over the kingdom at large.[62]

Down in Gabon and Cameroon, the Pangwe and Fang tribes shocked European explorers by their use of queer sex magic. German anthropologist Günther Tessmann writes about how these people used sodomy as a means to instill spiritual "medicine" into another person. Uniquely, though, the "top" is not the one delivering the medicine into the "bottom," but it is actually the "bottom" who is passing on the medicine into

61   Carolyn Baker, "Men, Women, Collapse and Conflict," *Transition Voice*, June
      2013, http://transitionvoice.com/2013/06/men-women-collapse-and-conflict/
      (accessed Oct. 25, 2016).
62   Anthony Kwame Appiah and Henry Louis Gates Jr., *Encyclopedia of Africa*
      (Oxford: Oxford University Press, 2010).

the "top." Tessmann, in his unfortunate homophobic worldview befitting turn-of-the-century colonizers, goes on to say that in addition to the inherent shame felt by the people who engage in this immoral superstition, both parties involved inevitably end up dead or suffering from a debilitating disease. Unsurprisingly, Tessmann provides no personal evidence of witnessing such side effects and shame, and neither has any other anthropologist who has since studied the Pangwe and Fang.[63]

When it comes to the Hausa, one of the largest ethnic groups in all of Africa, it makes sense that their acceptance of queerness throughout their history has created an intricate social system and verbiage specifically for their own LGBT+ community. Located throughout much of Western Africa, though mostly in northern Nigeria and southeastern Niger, the Hausa have a term called 'dan Daudu, which contextually best equates to "men who are like women," but it is not meant pejoratively. A child recognized to be a 'dan Daudu at an early age would be given female-specific toys and encouraged to express the gender of their spirit despite their biology. In adulthood they would be expected to fulfill female chores and forms of livelihood ranging from preparing and selling food at the marketplace to pimping prostitutes. In their private lives they would live among other women until taking on a husband. If they married another 'dan Daudu, the new couple would be seen as practicing lesbianism, which they called kifi. However, a 'dan Daudu would also be allowed to marry a biological female and become a father while still maintaining their status as a woman in society.[64]

Also in Nigeria, the Yoruba are a native people who have recognized LGBT+ individuals in their society throughout their history. The Yoruba differ from the Hausa in the sense that queerness is not based on what you identify as, but rather how you act. A colloquialism for a gay man would

---

63   Roscoe, *Queer Spirits*.

64   G. G. Bolich, *Transgender History & Geography: Crossdressing in Context*, vol. 3
      (Raleigh: Psyche's Press, 2007).

be *adofuro*, which essentially means "one who has anal sex."[65] Nowadays, however, Nigeria has seen a religious revival of both extreme Christianity in the south and extreme Islam in the north, making the queer community there highly persecuted and seen as a type of Western, first-world poison that is infiltrating and weakening Nigerian strength and sovereignty.[66]

Nevertheless, queer African history isn't *all* about homosexual and effeminate men. Lesbians play out the other half of the continent's controversial history, and two major examples stand out as being well documented. The first is a powerful African lesbian warrior queen, but we'll talk about her more in the upcoming deities & legends section. For now, we'll talk about the other example of societal lesbianism.

Located in the northern regions of what is now the Democratic Republic of the Congo, British anthropologist E. E. Evans-Pritchard documented the Azande as a highly homosexual culture. He noted that the men had developed a type of pederasty similar to the ancient Greeks wherein older, more prominent males would take on younger adolescent males and instruct them on the ways of manhood in addition to engaging in both penetrative and non-penetrative sex.[67] It was among the women, however, that he found the most fascinating homosexual relationships.

Azande women were noted to engage in sexual relations with other women quite frequently, but nowhere was this more so than in the royal court, most notably among the wives of the princes. Azande women would fashion a dildo out of a root and use that to pleasure their female lovers. Azande men had a respectful fear of lesbians. This was due to the belief that women who have sex with each other effectively double their spiritual

65 Bisi Alimi, "If You Say Being Gay Is Not African, You Don't Know Your History," *The Guardian*, September 9, 2015, https://www.theguardian.com /commentisfree/2015/sep/09/being-gay-african-history-homosexuality -christianity (accessed Oct. 25, 2016).

66 Monica Mark, "Nigeria's Yan Daudu Face Persecution in Religious Revival," *The Guardian*, June 10, 2013, https://www.theguardian.com/world/2013 /jun/10/nigeria-yan-daudu-persecution (accessed Oct. 25, 2016).

67 E. E. Evans-Pritchard, "Sexual Inversion Among the Azande," *American Anthropologist* 72:6 (1970).

power, making them more powerful than men. Because of this, lesbians were rarely harassed or crossed in society.

Evans-Pritchard also noted that the Azande word for lesbian lovemaking was *adandara,* which was also their word for supernatural catlike magic beings believed to be the offspring of sex between two women. Aside from their own pleasures, lesbians in Azande society were also revered as spiritual officials for the tribe whose inherent double power from their sex with other women gave them mighty prowess in sorcery and magical favors for the community.

Due to his research, Evans-Pritchard became not only one of the first, but also one of the most outspoken people in academia to insistently argue to both the Western nations and to the modernizing nations of Africa that LGBT+ people and behaviors were not the result of foreign imports from colonialism but rather a part of the indigenous history of Africa. A glimpse into the legal history of Africa seems to corroborate these assertions, as criminalization of queer people and practices only became realized en masse during the age of colonial rule and then further revived with the modern fanaticization of Christianity and Islam of Africa.[68]

Western & Central African Takeaway:
KNOW OUR HISTORY

The modern-day Hausa, one of the largest ethnic groups in all of Africa, have become some of the world's most anti-LGBT+ tribes. In Nigeria, where they predominantly live, queerness is criminal, but only in the northern Hausa territories is the death penalty allowed for the crime of queerness. The coupled beliefs of fanatic Islam and of how queerness is not African but rather a colonial import have fueled this hateful fire. But a look into the history of the Hausa people shows that queerness used to once flourish in their own society.

---

68   Val Kalende, "Africa: Homophobia Is a Legacy of Colonialism," *The Guardian,* April 30, 2014, https://www.theguardian.com/world/2014/apr/30/africa -homophobia-legacy-colonialism (accessed Aug. 18, 2017).

Ignorance of the past is common in queer culture, too. As a community, we forget how hard it was for our ancestors from even just a decade ago. Nowadays there are drag queens being celebrated on TV, queer radio podcasts that can be broadcast into any home, federal protections of queer rights, etc. But we have had it too good, to the point where we have become lazy in our activism and take these hard-earned rights as if our people have always had them. And the price of this complacency has been the rise of anti-queer individuals into positions of power and their revocation of our rights.

So, for your next magical activity, get in touch with your deceased queer ancestors via a ritual spell, meditation, or prayer. Often meditations and magical workings to commune with our ancestors are focused on our biological family, but we are also members of a worldwide queer family. Make time to reach out to these ancestors, learn of their stories, and ask for their strength to do as they have done and create a better world for our future queer family members. To forget and lose touch with our queer predecessors is to lose everything they have gained for us. Show your thanks and get in touch with them lest they be forgotten.

Deities & Legends

ERINLE

In Yoruba mythology, Erinle is the orisha (spiritual deity) of hunting, animal husbandry, prosperity, health, and sexual diversity. He is unique in that although he is a "wild man" deity, he is also financially wealthy, with a taste for the refined; he wears only the best garments, often accessorized with animal plumage. Because of his expert knowledge of wild plants and herbalism, he has become the de facto physician of the gods.

His patronage of queer people stems from his own ability to switch genders. In his male form he is the solid hunter of the wilderness, but in his female form he is the flexible and flowing water of life-giving rivers. Depending on which form one is trying to contact, earth element and water element correspondences should be used, and they should always be of the finest quality due to his penchant for the luxurious.

He is known for having two relationships, one with a male orisha and another with a female orisha. The same-sex relationship is, unsurprisingly, more controversial. As the legends go, Erinle used to sing to himself while out in the solitude of the woods, and one day Ogún (orisha of metalworking, war, and invention) was awestruck by his singing. Ogún offered to teach Erinle how to play the drums in exchange for being taught how to sing, and the two formed a close bond over their mutual tutelage. They eventually became so close that neither would wander the woods alone anymore, preferring to always be by each other's side when out in the wild. Some say this remained a purely platonic friendship, but others have argued that it developed into something more romantic and sexual.

As for his heterosexual relationship with Oshun (orisha of fresh waters, pleasure, beauty, fertility, and love), things didn't go so well. Attracted to Erinle's ability to understand waterways and women via his gender transformations, Oshun fell in love with him, and the two married and had many children. But she could never get over his need for solitude out in the wilderness, which he did for half the year. This separation severely bothered her, and it didn't help that he had formed such a close bond with Ogún, with whom she saw as having to share Erinle's time and affection. Ultimately, Oshun petitioned Olorun (the ruler of the heavens) to absolve the marriage, denied claim to all her children with Erinle, and abandoned her family. This left Erinle to raise the kids as a single father, a position over which he is also seen as having special magical patronage.[69]

69   Simon E. Davies, "The Orisha: Gods of Yoruba Mythology," *Ancient Code*,
      https://www.ancient-code.com/orisha-gods-yoruba-mythology/ (accessed
      June 11, 2017); Udee Bassey, "Yoruba Orishas: Erinle, Orisha of Natural
      Forces," *Beudeeful*, February 5, 2015, http://beudeeful.com/orisha-erinle/
      (accessed June 11, 2017).

NZINGA MBANDE

Nzinga Mbande was the legendary physical and spiritual leader of the kingdoms of Ndongo and Matamba of the Mbundo people in what is now Angola. She was the ruler of her people during the pivotal time in African history when the slave trade was in full swing and the Portuguese were looking for new African kingdoms to conquer that the French and British hadn't already gobbled up for their own.

Born into royalty, Nzinga was her despotic father's favorite child, and he allowed her to be with him during high council meetings, effectively teaching her how to govern. Due to her intelligence and skills in diplomacy, her brother (who succeeded the throne after their father) appointed her as ambassador to Portugal wherein she successfully negotiated peace treaties, winning herself admiration among the people and the election of queen by the Mbundo aristocracy after her brother's death.

Her haters both respected and despised her for her feminist displays of dominance. When holding court, for example, rather than sit on a throne, she preferred to sit atop one of her powerful male warriors who was on his hands and knees beneath her, allowing her to demonstrate that *she* was the strongest, most dominant person around, regardless of her gender. Moreover, she was widely believed to be what we would call in modern times a transgender male. She dressed in men's clothing and kept a harem of the kingdoms' most pretty men, whom she called her "wives" and forced them to dress as women at all times. She demanded to be addressed with masculine titles and vocabulary. She also greatly advocated and advanced the rights of transgender people under her reign.

Militarily, she was a master of guerrilla warfare, often fighting alongside her troops. When the Portuguese failed to live up to her peace treaties, they went in full force to conquer her people and ship them to Brazil as slaves. Despite their initial successes, they could never deliver the final blow to Nzinga's people. Her charisma kept her people fighting even in the face of insurmountable odds, and her guerilla tactics prevented the invading armies from being able to hold on to territory. Ultimately, as a direct consequence of her leadership, the Portuguese saw the Ndongo and

Matamba Kingdoms as more trouble than they were worth and ceased expansion into their lands until her death at the age of eighty.

Nonetheless, Nzinga's status in queer history remains controversial. Many detractors claim she purposely acted like a man in order to be taken seriously in a man's world, a tactic taken by other female leaders throughout world history. But what often makes the case for her female-to-male transsexuality is largely the fact that female rulers were not unheard of among her people, but they never kept a harem of men whom they forced to dress and act like women, nor did they themselves dress as men and demand to be addressed as a man. Moreover, her advocacy of transgender rights among her people seems to have been a personal crusade for her, most likely since Nzinga identified as one of them.[70]

THE RAIN QUEEN

The Rain Queen is a hereditary position of royal and spiritual authority among the Balobedu in South Africa. Although born as a mortal, she is believed to be divine in nature and have the supernatural power to influence and control the weather. Her areas of expertise for which her people most revere her is specifically her manipulation over the clouds and especially the rain. The Rain Queen's power has been respected by African leaders for centuries, from Shaka Zulu to Nelson Mandela.

In many circles, the Rain Queen is always thought to be lesbian, or at least non-heterosexual, due to the nature of her royal court wherein she is disallowed from marrying a man and having sex with men. Instead, she is exclusively surrounded by a harem of the neighboring chieftains' most beautiful daughters, all of whom are officially recognized as her "wives." These legally recognized marriages are the longest unbroken historical line of evidence of same-sex marriage in sub-Saharan Africa implemented by

---

70   Tomás Prower, "Royal Queerness: Gay Monarchs of the World," *Dandy Dicks*, May 30, 2016, https://dandydicks.com/blog-entry/royal-queerness-gay -monarchs-of-the-world (accessed Oct. 26, 2016); Leslie Feinberg, *Transgender Warriors: Making History from Joan of Arc to RuPaul* (Boston: Beacon Press, 1996).

native Africans and recognized by international courts since their beginnings in the early 1800s.

The sexual life of each Rain Queen has always been the subject of much controversy. Some claim her "wives" are really nothing more than handmaidens, while others insist that the queen exercises her marital privileges upon them. So common is the belief in the queen's sexual fluidity that the most recent Rain Queen's counselors had to make a public statement upon her ascension to the throne that her relationship with her wives would "not be lesbian business."[71] Still, in a time of religious zealotry and increasing continental hatred toward the LGBT+ community, many believe that these statements were made as a way to appeal to the mores of modern times. And lastly, of course, because the divine power is passed down from mother to daughter, her council will approve a single male, usually a close relative, to preserve the bloodline, whose sole duty it would be to impregnate the Rain Queen, although after that he is not allowed to interact with her or the child in any way, shape, or form.[72]

---

71   Rory Carroll, "She Who Must Be Surveyed," *The Guardian*, April 14, 2003, https://www.theguardian.com/world/2003/apr/14/worlddispatch.southafrica (accessed Oct. 27, 2016).

72   "Homosexuality Once Accepted in Pre-Christian Africa—But Now Persecuted," *Metal Gaia*, January 28, 2014, https://metal-gaia.com /tag/rain-queen/ (accessed Oct. 27, 2016).

6

LANDS OF THE AFRICAN DIASPORA

Cultural

During the Atlantic slave trade, Europeans transported more than Africa's people from their native lands to the plantations of the Americas. They transported cultures, worldviews, and religious beliefs millennia old. Out of self-preservation and pressure from their un-Christian-like Christian masters, children of the African diaspora disguised their native spiritual traditions under the guise of mystic Catholicism. Over the centuries, the religions blended together to create unique new faiths that mirrored the traditional faiths of both slave and master, though with a dominant under-current of West African practices. Three in particular rose to great promi-nence and can count among them legions of openly LGBT+ worshippers: Vodou, Santería, and Candomblé.

VODOU

Between dolls with pins in their eyes, zombies, and associations with the macabre, Vodou (alternately spelled Voodoo or Vodoun) is one of the most sensationalized religions around. Most of its morbid undertones come from the fact that it is an ancestral religion because revering one's ancestors involves revering the dead. There are different types of Vodou such as Haitian Vodou, Louisiana Voodoo, and the Vodou still practiced in Africa, but in general the New World versions are the Creole offspring of West African tribal religions and French Catholicism.

In and of itself, Vodou is very welcoming to the queer community, and in some Caribbean cultures where anti-LGBT+ sentiment is societally strong, the practice of Vodou acts as a safe and welcoming space for queer people to be themselves. There are no legal protections for LGBT+ people in the Vodou capital of Haiti, and in the other Vodou Mecca of Louisiana, the protections are minimal and often not enforced outside of New Orleans. In these geographies of where Vodou is most widely practiced, being outwardly queer often comes at the risk of repercussions ranging from being fired from your job to being the victim of varying degrees of hate crimes. The Vodou community, however, is an accepting and tolerant oasis in a sea of discrimination, and oftentimes it is the only place wherein queer Haitians and Louisianans can be themselves.

Because of this, many LGBT+ people are drawn to the inclusionary, come-as-you-are nature of Vodou; consequently, Vodou has a disproportionately high number of openly queer practitioners in comparison to other religions.[73] One's sexuality and gender expression is never judged by moral standards since there is an inherent understanding that you are as the Divine made you, and the inherent perfection of the Divine means that the Divine doesn't make mistakes. Therefore, you—however you are—are not a mistake. Moreover, procreation is not a focal point of the

---

73   International Gay and Lesbian Human Rights Commission and SEROvie, *The Impact of the Earthquake, and Relief and Recovery Programs on Haitian LGBT People,* 2011, https://www.outrightinternational.org/content/impact-earthquake-and-relief-and-recovery-programs-haitian-lgbt-people (accessed Oct. 28, 2016).

religion as it is in pure Catholicism, meaning all forms of non-procreative sex are neither taboo nor seen as unnatural. On the contrary, even the Vodou divinities themselves take pleasure in homoerotic acts of sexuality, but more on that in a bit.[74]

One of the more well-known parts of Vodou involves the invocation of a spirit (known as a *lwa*) into one's own body. This is usually done during a heavily rhythmic type of freeform dance ritual, and sometimes a lwa of one gender will inhabit the body of a human of the opposite gender. At this point, the possessed dancer begins to think, behave, and act like the lwa within them. A masculine man inhabited by an effeminate lwa will begin to act effeminate, an effeminate woman inhabited by a masculine lwa will begin to act masculine, and never are the man or woman's personal sexuality and gender identity called into question because in that moment, through the ecstasy of the dance, the lwa is in control; the human's body is just a vessel. As a side note, it's important to know that Vodou doesn't label its lwa with LGBT+ labels, though humans often recognize LGBT+ traits in their character.

Not all, but a number of Vodou practitioners also believe in a form of reincarnation wherein the body is ephemeral, but the soul is eternal. To them, the soul is a genderless thing, and each person, regardless of their current sexuality and gender, has been many things from many past lives. A flamingly gay white homosexual male today may once have been a Kinsey 1 heterosexual Asian female at one point or maybe a bisexual black woman or even a gender-fluid pansexual tribesperson in the jungles of Papua New Guinea. Thus one's outward appearance, labels, and personal desires do not define the true soul of a person, making them null and void in conversations regarding right and wrong. They are just facts of life, all subject to change during the next transmigration of the soul.[75]

74   Elizabeth A. McAlister, *Rara! Vodou, Power, and Performance in Haiti and Its Diaspora* (Berkeley: University of California Press, 2002).

75   Rev. Severina K. M. Singh, "Haitian Vodou and Sexual Orientation," in *The Esoteric Codex: Haitian Vodou*, ed. Garland Ferguson (Morrisville: Lulu Press, Inc., 2002), 50–53.

Vodou Takeaway:

INVOCATION OF OPPOSITE GENDER DEITIES

The Vodou practice of spirit possession is an obvious magical takeaway activity. Now, until you learn more about Vodou traditions or already have a relationship with them, don't go invoking Vodou lwa in a Vodou way. Start with your own magical tradition. Specifically, if your faith involves a pantheon of deities of different genders, invoke a deity of the opposite gender to which you personally identify. But do so, of course, in the manner of your own tradition with which you're familiar.

It is one thing to talk, act, and empathize with other genders, but to totally lose control and allow another gender to take the reins and make you think, feel, and act like them is a whole 'nother thing. So, for your next magical activity, do an invocation ritual of a deity who is the stereotypical epitome of the gender opposite your own. Try it out, see what it's like, and rather than just get in touch with another gender, allow that other gender to get in you.

SANTERÍA

Santería is similar yet very different from Vodou in a number of ways. They are similar in the sense that they are both Caribbean in origin, created from the mix of colonial Catholicism and West African traditional religions, and believe in a pantheon of spiritual beings who are often called upon to possess a devotee during ritual dance. Their predominant differences, however, come from the specific branches of their religious roots, from which their other differences evolved naturally. Specifically, while Vodou is more of a mix of French Catholicism and African spirituality from the Dahomey tradition, Santería is more of a mix of Spanish Catholicism and African spirituality from the Yoruba tradition.

Rather than the lwa of Vodou, Santería's spirits are known as orishas. The Yoruba slaves who once lived under colonial Spanish rule in the Caribbean disguised their orishas as Catholic saints, having each orisha correspond to a specific saint. Through the years, the traits, mythologies, and sphere of spiritual domain that each orisha and saint possessed blended together to form the unique spiritual tradition known today as Santería, which is still popular in their native Spanish-speaking Caribbean countries as well as in the US and Latin American cities with large Spanish-Caribbean immigrant populations.

From the outside, Santería has all the trappings of sensationalism: divination with deceased ancestors, possession, heavy use of drumbeat dance rituals, trances, and, most notoriously of all, animal sacrifice. Added to all this is the fact that Santería also has a statistically large percentage of LGBT+ practitioners in comparison to other religious traditions. The reasoning for this is very similar to the reasoning for the same social phenomenon found in Vodou: Santería places a higher emphasis on the genderless soul of a person rather than their physical body or bodily appetites. This allows for a nonjudgmental and welcoming come-as-you-are attitude to pervade the faith. Moreover, the queer community within the larger *machista* Caribbean/Catholic cultural society of the islands finds refuge in their religious community of Santería because they can safely and openly be themselves, find others like themselves, and meet other open-minded people. Queer identity is also found in the myths and lore of their orishas.

One example of this is the Santería origin story of homosexuality itself. According to legend, it developed naturally between two male orishas in response to their mother's attempt to hide her own shame. As the story goes, Yemaya (the orisha of the moon, ocean, feminine mysteries, and the mother deity to all the orishas) was tricked into having sex with her son Shango (orisha of thunder, lightning, fire, and war) in front of his two brothers Abbatá and Inlé (the orishas of healing and the medical profession). Embarrassed and horrified over anyone finding out about this, she banished Abbatá and Inlé to live at the bottom of the sea, away from the rest of the world, and just for good measure she caused Abbatá to become deaf and she cut out Inlé's tongue. Despite their inability to communicate to one another, they were still able to understand each other empathically. And together, in their mutual loneliness and suffering, the two developed a deep bond that grew into romantic and sexual passion, thus giving birth to homosexuality in the world.[76]

Other than the obvious origin story, this myth also contains much deeper reflections of gay society. The bonds of being outcasts, rejected by their family, their inability to fully express themselves, and punishment for actions beyond their control all are common themes in the lives of the queer community as a whole. Moreover, it also hints at the natural empathy of LGBT+ persons for others who suffer. The other connection lies in Abbatá's symbol of intertwining snakes, which, while having associations with the medical caduceus, also has strong homoerotic undertones. Abbatá's spiritual role as Inlé's nurse also has a gay undercurrent to it, owing to stereotypes of male nurses being gay. Nevertheless, the specifics of these two lovers vary depending on the preference of the individual practitioner. Preferences range from people seeing Inlé as an androgynous being to people hetero-normalizing their relationship by seeing Abbatá as a full-on female.[77]

According to some Santería practitioners, one cannot be a solitary practitioner. To them, and to many, Santería is a communal religion. Due to the large percentage of queer practitioners in Santería, exposure to them allows the non-LGBT+ practitioner majority to interact with them and come to see the queer community as good, ordinary people just like them. This creates a societal snowball effect wherein more and more people become more and more accepting, and they, in turn, raise their children to be more socially liberal, leading to even greater acceptance within Santería. Furthermore, many leaders within Santería are openly queer; as leaders, they direct the course of the religion to become even more accepting and open-minded.[78]

---

76   Randy P. Conner, "Gender and Sexuality in Spiritual Traditions," in *Fragments of Bone: Neo-African Religions in a New World*, ed. Patrick Bellegarde-Smith (Champaign: University of Illinois Press, 2005).

77   From https://www.viejolazaro.com/en/ (accessed Nov. 1, 2016) and http://agolaroye.com/Inle.php (accessed Nov. 1, 2016).

78   Scott Thumma and Edward R. Gray, *Gay Religion* (Walnut Creek: Altamira Press, 2004).

Nevertheless, like most religions, Santería is a far from utopian ideal of perfect acceptance. Despite around 30–50 percent of practitioners being LGBT+ individuals and the majority of all practitioners being women, the hierarchical structure of Santería prevents queer people and women (in most lines) from rising to the highest leadership roles of being a *Babalawo* (the highest-ranking level in the priesthood). Also, gay men are restricted from playing the sacred drums known as the *batá*. Lastly, the religion maintains a strict division of labor between the sexes, and when one's sexual orientation, expression, and identity don't line up with conventional gender roles, one's hierarchical place within the religion can become complicated and subject to the discretion of regional leadership. But despite these limitations, the LGBT+ community is generally greatly accepted within Santería and experiences much more freedom than in many other religions in our modern world.[79]

Santería Takeaway:
SACREDNESS OF COMMUNITY

Santería is a very communal faith, and the togetherness aspect is highly revered. More than just helping each other and always being there for each other, the Santería community holds sacred their communal interactions with one another. So, for your next magical activity, get out there and help your community. Magical intentions, words, and correspondences are all great, but what do they amount to if we don't act upon them? Volunteer, get involved in activism, help out a literal neighbor. The more we interact with society in a positive and beneficial way, the more society sees us as positive and beneficial. After all, a helping hand is often the most powerful spellwork one can do for the greater good.

---

79   Salvador Vidal-Ortiz, "Sexual Discussions in Santería: A Case Study of
      Religion and Sexuality Negotiation," *Journal of Sexuality Research & Social Policy*
      3:3 (2006), http://www.academia.edu/1953070/Sexuality_discussions_
      in_Santer%C3%ADa_A_case_study_of_religion_and_sexuality_negotiation
      (accessed Nov. 1, 2016).

CANDOMBLÉ

To round out our tour of African diasporic religions, we'll sail out of the Caribbean and dock at the South American nation of Brazil, which has the dubious double dishonor of not only being the number one destination for most of the African slaves taken to the New World (about 40 percent of the slave trade total), but it also was the very last nation in the Western Hemisphere to abolish slavery altogether. The sheer number of slaves combined with the extended timeline of legalized slavery created a unique and lasting spiritual and cultural fusion among the Brazilian people. Nowadays, Brazil is a country with one of the largest populations of people of African descent, second only to Nigeria.[80]

Of all the eclectic spiritual traditions to emerge from this unique history, Candomblé is one of the largest and most well-known. It shares similar characteristics with its northern cousins Vodou and Santería, but Candomblé is more a result of West African traditions melding with Portuguese Catholicism and the various native religions found in Aboriginal Brazil. Like Vodou and Santería, though, Candomblé also places high emphasis on a spiritual pantheon of *orixás* (their spelling of orishas), as well as ritualistic drumming, freeform dance, and spirit possession. It also has a very strong queer following.

It is important to note that Candomblé was not always accepting of the queer community. Originally, its strict rules and hierarchies placed severe, prejudiced limitations on anyone LGBT+. But in the early 1900s a separate branch of the religion known as *caboclo* developed and rapidly gained in popularity due to its preference for bawdier, more irreverent orixás and lack of restrictions toward its LGBT+ members. Consequently, the rise in popularity of caboclo forced more mainstream Candomblé to become less strict and more open to its queer adherents. Still, though, the caboclo branch of the religion, due to its history, is known as the "queer" version

---

80   Nicolas Bourcier, "Brazil Comes to Terms with Its Slave Trading Past," *The Guardian*, Oct. 23, 2012, https://www.theguardian.com/world/2012/oct/23/brazil-struggle-ethnic-racial-identity (accessed Nov. 2, 2016).

of Candomblé and the title itself carries with it an understood nuance of queerness.[81]

Candomblé's modern popularity among the queer community is very similar to the community's affinity for Vodou and Santería. It is a welcoming and tolerant place to express one's true self in an otherwise intolerant and discriminatory cultural society, their sexual identity and gender expression is reflected in both mythology and spiritual deities, and there is no perceived morality over sexual orientation or identity.

In Candomblé there does not exist the common duality of good and evil. Rather, each person is embedded with their own personal destiny to fulfill, and the destiny of one person might require a different moral code than the destiny of another. Of course, this is tempered by the additional cosmic reciprocity belief that what you do to others will eventually come back to you, so this is by no means a spiritual tradition that condones a "to hell with the consequences" type of mentality. But all in all, there is an atmosphere of nonjudgment among the faithful, stressing the importance of letting people express themselves in the ways most correct for them, which include sexuality and gender identity. Granted, not all members are tolerant, but as a whole Candomblé is much less intolerant than many of the modern world's major religions.[82]

Queer Candomblé practitioners are often members of a "house." These houses are similar to drag queen houses wherein everyone comes together and forms a close family-like bond, often under the leadership of a more experienced "mother" or "father." In Brazilian society these Candomblé houses have been at the forefront of LGBT+ rights movements in both advocacy and mobilization. They have even been known to go out of their way to implement HIV/AIDS prevention campaigns and assist those already infected by providing references and treatment information. Because of their efforts, Brazil nowadays has some of the most progressive

81 Roscoe, *Queer Spirits*.

82 "Candomblé at a Glance," British Broadcasting Corporation, Sept. 15, 2009, http://www.bbc.co.uk/religion/religions/candomble/ataglance/glance.shtml (accessed Nov. 2, 2016).

legal protections for the queer community in the world, although culturally there still exists a tremendous amount of discrimination and intolerance.[83]

Besides houses, Candomblé excels in another highly evolved gay mainstay: reading, as in reading a fellow queen to filth. In fact, in the 1980s, gay anthropologist Jim Wafer studied the gay culture of the followers of Candomblé, and he was particularly fascinated with their own form of stylized and playful verbal abuse among one another that they call *baixa*. According to his studies, gay Candomblé practitioners have two distinct forms of baixa; one form is used in secular public settings and the other is used only in private rituals during festivals. The main difference is in the vocabulary and types of reads one does. The secular version is akin to common reading as we know it in contemporary gay culture, but the religious version purposely makes use of orixás, ritual inside jokes, and mentions of house politics. While similar, each type of baixa developed its own rhythmic flow and spoken artform that are distinct from one another. Wafer makes a final note about baixa, stating that it is very much a gay-centric thing since it is mutually understood between gay Brazilian men and those familiar with the community.[84]

Candomblé Takeaway:
SACREDNESS OF QUEER COMMUNITY

Now, I know what you're saying: "But Tomás, this was the activity from a few pages ago." And yes, it is, but with a different focus: this is the sacredness of our own queer community. You see, Santería has made great strides in Spanish-Caribbean society of bringing the queer and non-queer communities together, breaking down barriers, and showing how we can all get along. But what our Candomblé brothers and sisters do really well is take action to support their own sacred queer community.

---

83   Andrea Stevenson Allen, *Violence and Desire in Brazilian Lesbian Relationships* (New York: Palgrave Macmillan, 2015).

84   Jim Wafer, *The Taste of Blood: Spirit Possession in Brazilian Candomblé* (Philadephia: University of Pennsylvania Press, 1991).

Through their establishment of taking in runaways to form houses, HIV/AIDS activism, and developing their own forms of verbal communication, they are bringing the queer Brazilian community closer together and looking out for one another.

As LGBT+ people, we often throw around the word "community" as if we meant it, but taking a look around, fragmentation and in-fighting is everywhere. It's nice to say that we are a community and then all show up together at a Pride event, but how are we paying tribute to our sacred queer community the other fifty-one weeks of the year? Don't just say it, show it.

So, for your next magical activity, help out your queer tribe. Volunteer at your local LGBT+ center, start a queer support group on Facebook, blog about your experience as a queer spellworker; the options are endless. Regardless of how you do it, show your magical devotion to the community through action because if all you're doing is lighting a candle and sending good intentions for your queer tribe, how are you different from those who, in response to a call for aid, say things like "my thoughts and prayers are with you"? Remember, direct action gets satisfaction; as a global minority group, we need to help each other out with actions, not just words. Helping hands are holier than lips that pray.

Deities & Legends

BABALÚ-AYÉ

Known as Babalú-Ayé in Santería and as Obaluaiê in Candomblé, he is the orisha of disease and healing. In addition to being both greatly feared and greatly respected, he is one of the most popular orishas due to myriad accounts of his miraculous healing intercessions. While not necessarily considered a queer entity in and of himself, since the birth of the HIV/AIDS epidemic he has been adopted by the LGBT+ community. To many in the community, Babalú-Ayé is seen as the preeminent orisha for people suffering from HIV/AIDS, and queer-specific petitions to him for his healing powers are numerous. And although he is an orisha, he, too, suffers from physical lameness and a diseased body. This suffering grants an understanding of solidarity between him and mortals since, unlike other deities, he can directly empathize with their sickness and pain.

Beyond the HIV/AIDS connection, the LGBT+ community holds him especially sacred for his kindness to the outcasts of the world. Legends tell of how he is the orisha who goes to help those isolated by contagious and communicable diseases when no one else would for fear of being infected themselves. His sacred color is also purple, which has internationally understood connections within the queer community.[85]

The most common offering to him are grains, and he has strong earth element correspondences. When using a vessel to present or hold offerings, though, it is traditional for the lid of the vessel to have holes in it, symbolizing the impossibility of forever shielding yourself from sickness. Additionally, his vessels are never left stationary. They are traditionally kept moving to various locations in accordance with Babalú-Ayé's mythological stories wherein movement and staying active are taught to be the best forms of healing because they prevent stagnation and keep the body healthy, preventing the body from getting sick in the first place. In spellwork, devotees pray to him to both cure loved ones of diseases and punish their enemies with diseases.[86]

BARON SAMEDI

Baron Samedi is arguably one of the best-known of the Vodou lwa in pop culture thanks to his eccentric personality and caricaturized depiction in popular movies such as Dr. Facilier in Disney's *The Princess and the Frog* and as the aptly named Baron Samedi in the James Bond classic *Live and Let Die*. As the patron lwa of death, graves, cemeteries, healing, smoking, drinking, and obscenities, he is one of the most transgressive deities of any religion.

85   "Babalu Aye," *Association of Independent Readers & Rootworkers,* June 20, 2017, http://readersandrootworkers.org/wiki/Babalu_Aye (accessed Aug. 18, 2017).

86   David H. Brown, *Santería Enthroned: Art, Ritual, and Innovation in an Afro-Cuban Religion* (Chicago: University of Chicago Press, 2003).

Appearance-wise, he is often depicted as having a skeletal-thin frame, with a glass of rum or a cigar in his gloved hand and wearing a dapper purple frock coat and top hat. He sometimes complements this by adding into the mix some feminine essentials such as a skirt and pumps. Particularly, he is known for his disregard of tact and decorum as well as for his lascivious debauchery, but he does it all with an urbane air of suaveness.

Sometimes he is seen as a transgender lwa but always with an unabashed preference for anal sex. His fluid ability to go beyond the binary of man/woman, straight/gay, masculine/feminine, earth/underworld, living/dead makes him a popular lwa to the queer community and those who feel the need to transgress boundaries without shame or who feel they don't fit into a singular category of labels.[87]

In devotion, cemeteries are places sacred to him, and he often asks that his devotees wear the colors black, white, or purple. For offerings, he has a preference for heavy smoky things such as black coffee, grilled nuts, cigars, and dark rum. He is mostly petitioned for hexes and harmful magic but is also petitioned for the prevention of death during life-threatening illnesses, during dangerous moments, and in response to being fatally hexed. According to tradition, it is said that one can only die if Baron Samedi digs your grave. Because he is a capricious, spur-of-the-moment kind of personality, he may choose not to dig your grave, thus letting you live through whatever is going on with you, if petitioned to do so, or if he just doesn't feel like digging your grave for any reason whatsoever.[88]

ERZULIE FRÉDA & ERZULIE DANTOR

Erzulie is a family of Vodou lwa, of which two members are sometimes directly associated with the queer community: Erzulie Fréda and Erzulie Dantor. Erzulie Fréda can be most likened to the Greek goddess Aphrodite and is the lwa of love, beauty, jewelry, dancing, luxury, flowers, and male

87   Tomás Prower, *La Santa Muerte: Unearthing the Magic & Mysticism of Death* (Woodbury: Llewellyn, 2015).

88   "Baron Samedi—A Loa of the Dead," *Kreol Magazine*, http://www .kreolmagazine.com/arts-culture/history-and-culture/baron-samedi -a-loa-of-the-dead/ (accessed June 12, 2017).

homosexuals. Gay men are said to be under her divine protection, and it is not uncommon for men to claim that their sexual orientation was directly the result of having invoked Erzulie Fréda to possess them during ritualistic dance. She is also known to be very flirtatious toward all genders, and someone of whom she is in possession often will be seen flirting with others regardless of their regular sexual orientation. Befitting a love deity, her sacred symbol is that of a heart, her sacred color is pink, and she prefers romantic offerings such as perfume, desserts, jewelry, and sweet-flavored spirits.[89]

Erzulie Dantor, in comparison, is the lwa of women, children, and lesbians. She is often depicted as a black-skinned Virgin Mary with scars on her face and a well-endowed bosom, holding a black-skinned Jesuslike child. Her sacred colors are usually blue and gold, while her preferred offerings are Florida water, pork, rum, and especially chocolate liqueur.[90]

[89] *Des hommes et des dieux*, directed by Anne Lescot and Laurence Magloire (2002, Port-au-Prince: Digital LM, 2003), DVD.

[90] From http://ezilidantor.tripod.com (accessed Oct. 28, 2016).

7

SUB-SAHARAN AFRICAN & DIASPORIC MAGICAL COMMUNITY

QUEER YORUBAN MOTHERHOOD

To help give us a modern queer person's perspective on African spirituality, I turned to another friend from college, Sandra Zuri. A queer woman of color with mixed African and Italian heritage, she started learning about traditional Pagan religions in her early twenties. Now a mother, she has been exploring the spiritual and religious traditions of her African roots, specifically those of the Yoruba. So, in true Yoruba tradition, gather 'round and hear her story of how the ancient orishas inspire and influence her in her sacred duty as a queer mother of color to her young son.

Yoruban spirituality is a religion that comes from Western Africa. All orishas are emissaries, or messengers, of Olorun, the supreme god who created the universe. The supreme god in this religion has no gender, but is rather known as a genderless being that reflects all creation of life. I pay my high respects to the orishas called Yemoja and Obatala. Yemoja is the mother of all orishas and the goddess of the waters and oceans. Obatala is the father of all orishas and is the sky father who created land on earth and created the human form.

The reason Yemoja and Obatala call to me is because they deal with creation and are given parental titles. As a queer woman, a spiritual person, and recent mother, I find these orishas help guide me to providing my son with spiritual tools to benefit his identity, his creativity, and his spiritual self. I am teaching him that everything is a creation of our universe, including gender. Although we use male pronouns, we also use many neutral terms inspired by this spirituality, such as identifying a person with their character traits, as we identity deities or the orishas.

Yemoja rules the seas and oceans and created them as well. She is the patron of mothering qualities, pregnant women, and the protector of children. She is often shown as a mermaid and called "the mother whose children are like fish." Her noble qualities include being protective, comforting, nurturing, washing away sorrow, and aiding fertility.

Obatala governs the land and was given permission to create humankind. Obatala is a deity with both male and female aspects and usually is shown as a man or older woman wearing white. This deity created the human form and controls all heads of living beings.

Obatala is also noted for being very protective of children, given that he is held responsible for children born with disabilities due to his drinking during the creation time. He then vowed to never drink again and became the deity of purification, compassion, and wisdom once making his amends with Olorun, the ruler of the heavens.

As a queer mother, this spirituality encourages me to inspire great qualities to my son that build spirit and character. Yemoja is typically shown as a mermaid, which deviates from the typical form I've seen associated with motherhood. I admire the freedom and fluidity of her form, as well as the gendered ambiguity (although she isn't noted as being other than *female). As a mother, I find myself constantly busy and metaphorically swimming around my son, protecting, nurturing, comforting. Obatala's protective qualities with children stem from him messing up in the beginning, so to speak, and redeeming himself through his actions, not by just saying sorry. Both orishas envoke action, creation, comfort, nurture, fluid gender, and compassion, in my perspective—all things that matter most to me as a queer mother raising a healthy spiritual being. In the bigger picture, raising him this way will hopefully encourage him to be mindful of life as sacred, regardless of gender, class, and other labels, and also that life is greater than material gain—that being rich in spirit gives life more purpose.*

—*Sandra Zuri*

LGBT+ AND THE LWA

With us here is Mambo Chita Tann ("Mambo T.") to talk more in-depth about LGBT+ persons and the lwa of Haitian Vodou. You might remember her from back in our exploration of the greater Middle East as the special guest Rev. Tamara L. Siuda, who taught us that protection prayer to the Bawy. She is back with us again because, in addition to being a professional Egyptologist and Coptologist as well as founder of the Kemetic Orthodox religion, she was initiated as a mambo of Haitian Vodou in 2001 and 2006 in Haiti. She is also the head of La Sosyete Fòs Fè Yo Wè, a Vodou house in Portland, Oregon, that is part of the lineage of La Société Belle Fleur Guinea of Haiti and New Orleans. As a reminder, she identifies as biracial, genderqueer, and bisexual; founded the Marriage Militia (marriagemilitia .org) to provide advocacy and information on same-sex marriage in the USA; and is active in LGBTQ and other human rights movements. And now she joins us again on our global trek to give us more info on the lwa and the LGBT+ experience.

There's a lot of talk on the internet about Haitian Vodou, and particularly around certain lwa (Vodou spirits) as being "lwa for gay people" or being LGBTQ themselves. Some websites will tell you Ezili Danto (Erzuli Dantor) is the lwa of lesbians or that gay men are favored by Danto's sister, Ezili Freda (Erzuli Fréda), or that the phrase de manye, "two hands," in the name of Ogou de Manye means he is bisexual. There's a European-based, Vodou-flavored esoteric book that includes stories about a Gede lwa that is allegedly the spirit of a dead gay wrestler. Other lwa are described with homosexual tropes (e.g., as effeminate or in drag), and still others embody LGBTQ mysteries in ways other religions or traditions don't. News articles and academic studies talk about Haitian Vodou as a refuge for Haiti's oppressed and threatened LGBTQ population or describe it as a "gay religion." How do we unpack these stories? What does it mean to say a lwa, a non-human spirit, is "gay" (or "straight," for that matter)?

As it turns out, most talk of "gay lwa" in Haitian Vodou doesn't come from Haitians or Haiti. In Haiti, while we do talk about lwa we can invoke around LGBTQ issues, we don't generally define the lwa as LGBTQ themselves. The lwa Vodouisants talk to about LGBTQ issues do include Danto and Freda, Ogou de Manye and some of the dead humans in the Gede nation (though the wrestling lwa mentioned above doesn't exist and was invented for that book). We don't invoke the lwa because they are LGBTQ; we don't need our spirits to be like us to have a relationship. We invoke them for help because they care about our existence and our struggle to survive as marginalized people.

Our lwa came into being out of the Haitian experience, grounded in African and Caribbean slavery and the spirits of revolution that overthrew slavery in 1801 and continue to fight for equality and justice against continuing racism every day. A gay man might favor Ezili Freda because he wants to understand and appreciate the concepts of femininity, beauty, power, and desire that she represents. Freda might take interest in him simply because she loves to be loved or because she can help him know himself. Ezili Danto might be a role model or protector for a Haitian lesbian, as the lwa who protects society's most marginalized, characterized as a single woman making her way. However, Danto is also a mother and wife, and she protects other people too. Ogou de Manye is a strong model of the many facets of identity and possibility, and while he can be invoked by bisexuals *or genderqueer or asexual people around those ideas, he does not have to be bisexual or genderqueer or asexual himself for that to be useful.*

Correlation does not require causation with the lwa. LGBTQ people are not generally discriminated against in Haitian Vodou. This is powerful enough on its own without needing to embody ourselves in the lwa. The ability for our lwa to be important for LGBTQ people as well as others reminds us of the harmony between the natural and human worlds, and that LGBTQ people stand as one equal group in a large, diverse family coming from Ginen (ancestral Africa). Everyone is welcome before the creator of all things (Bondye) and Bondye's angels, the lwa. If Haitian Vodou provides an explicitly LGBTQ experience, it is as a safe space within an unsafe culture, proof that spiritual experiences can be inclusive and welcoming to all.

—MAMBO CHITA TANN

PART 3

EUROPE

That you're a woman far away
is no hindrance to my love.
For the soul, as you well know,
distance and sex don't count.
SOR JUANA INÉS DE LA CRUZ

As we dock here along the shores of Europe, many of you are probably already familiar with the magic of this continent, but the queerness that exists in European religious traditions may be something less familiar. Our travels here will focus on the ancient queerness of the Greco-Roman era, the Pagan traditions of European natives outside of the Greco-Roman world, and, finally, Christianity. So stay close because we have a lot of ground to cover and a lot of preconceived notions to raze as we blaze a trail into the hidden queer traditions of the European peoples.

8
ANCIENT GREECE & ROME

Cultural

Whenever someone mentions historic homosexuality or other forms of queerness, ancient Greece and Rome pop to the forefront of people's minds. Some look back on these ancients with nostalgic romanticism as a golden age of queer acceptance. Others look back and see a culture whose only egregious shame was the unacceptably wanton pursuit of base appetites. But, like most of history, the truth lies somewhere in between. While nonheterosexual desires were more tolerated in this time than during many other periods in European history, they were by no means accepted with open arms. Still, they were practiced and recognized enough for these classical cultures to ascribe LGBT+ tendencies to many of their gods and epic heroes.

ANCIENT GREECE

The ancient Greeks could be thought of as spiritual revolutionaries for their time since they were one of the first people to believe that the gods looked exactly like them. Adding to the similarities, they also believed that the gods acted like them, too, being equally capable of kindness and valor as they could cruelty and pettiness. Essentially, the gods were pretty much just like humans except they could live forever and possessed supernatural powers. Whether humans were made in the image of the gods or humans' own hubris fashioned the gods in their own image is debatable, but, in either case, the gods were just as queer as the mortals who worshipped them.

And if we talk specifics, Greece was by far much more tolerant than Rome. However, they did not view queerness in the same way that we traditionally view it today. The Greeks didn't have labels based on gender and sexuality like "gay," "lesbian," or "bisexual." Having sexual desires for and intimate liaisons with a same-sex lover carried with it no effect upon your social identity; rather, it was the role you took during the sexual act itself that labeled who you were. For men, if you were the active partner (the penetrator/"top"), then, according to society, you were associated with the labels of masculinity, maturity, and being higher up on the social ladder. If you were the passive partner (the penetrated/"bottom"), then you were associated with the labels of femininity, immaturity/youth, and being lower on the social ladder. [91]

In truth, ancient Greece was a strongly patriarchal society with a strict class structure. For men, masculinity was seen as a virtue worthy of the utmost respect and for which all males should strive. Being the "top" during sex was the defining masculine act and asserted one's masculinity in society. Being the "bottom" during sex, however, was seen as engaging in a womanly act and had an emasculating effect upon whomever assumed that role. Obviously, though, not everyone can be the "top" during a round of gay sex; someone had to be the "bottom" and suffer the stigma.

91   *Oxford Classical Dictionary*, 3rd rev. ed., s.v. "Homosexuality."

The solution for this impasse, for which the ancient Greeks are now notorious, was pederasty: the sexual relationship between a young male and an older man. It was the perfect way to bypass the issue of who was going to be the "top" and who was going to be the "bottom."[92] Think about it: if two men of equal rank engaged in a night of sex, one would have to lose status and give up his "man points," and no one wanted to do that. But men of different generations were already seen as different social ranks, so they could have relations without any detrimental social effects.

The younger man (*eromenos*) was the "bottom," and the older man (*erastes*) was the "top." This setup not only preserved the social order of ancient Greek male-male relations, but it also doubled as a pedagogical mentor system for young men. Besides sex, the older men imparted knowledge and wisdom to the younger ones, helping to guide them into adulthood. In some respects, it served as a prolonged rite of passage that readied an adolescent for manhood.

But pederasty was never seen as gay in the same way that we would label it today. It was just a part of growing up. In fact, around age eighteen (or whenever he could grow a full beard), it was expected that the younger man stop being the eromenos and eventually assume his own masculinity by marrying a woman and sponsoring his own male lover as the erastes. This situation of being sexually intimate with both one's wife and a younger eromenos was never seen as bisexual; it just was what it was and had no label other than the way of the world.

The biggest exception to the rule, however, was in the military. While soldiers who fought together were not expected to be sexually involved with one another, those armies comprised of male-male lovers were seen as more powerful. The line of reasoning was that by developing a romantic and sexual bond between brothers-in-arms, they would fight harder and protect one another more fiercely in combat.[93] Most famously, the Sacred

92   John Pollini, "The Warren Cup: Homoerotic Love and Symposial Rhetoric in Silver," *Art Bulletin* 81.1 (1999): 21–52.

93   Victor Davis Hanson, *The Western Way of War: Infantry Battle in Classical Greece* (Oakland: University of California Press, 1994).

Band of Thebes, a specialized military unit comprised only of male-male lovers, remained a regional powerhouse until their defeat by Alexander the Great's father, Philip II of Macedon. Alexander himself had his own male lovers while also being married a number of times to a number of women. Above all his lovers, though, his boyhood friend Hephaestion was his most beloved, upon whose death in Babylon Alexander mourned depressively for days on end.[94]

In the literature of ancient Greece, the most prime example of both pederastic and militaristic love can be found in Homer's *Iliad* between Achilles and Patroclus. One of the principal Greek heroes of the Trojan War, Achilles—who already had a history of cross-dressing due to him disguising himself as a maiden in order to dodge being drafted into the war—took on the role as the younger "bottom." Despite this, however, his legendary strength and status as the embodiment of hypermasculinity remained intact. Conversely, Patroclus took on the role as the older "top" while still engaging in his main duties of cooking, cleaning, taking care of the animals, and other "feminine" chores. So, obviously, there were always exceptions to the rule.[95]

As for the ladies of ancient Greece, not too much is written about their sexuality. This isn't to say that they weren't sexual, but rather they were viewed as property, only worth their weight in dowry and babies. For this reason, there is scarce information on female-female relations since the male historians of the time saw no merit in recording the private lives of women. Additionally, Greek men and women did not socialize with one another outside the home, thus making the private lives of women all that more a mystery to these male historians.

The exception, however, is the women of Sparta. According to Plutarch, Spartan women developed a similar erastes/eromenos relationship between an older, wiser woman and a younger, ingenuous maiden. Beyond direct lesbianism, though, Spartan women also blurred the gender lines of

94   Robin Lane Fox, *The Search for Alexander* (Boston: Little Brown & Co., 1980).

95   Statius, *Silvae*, trans. D. R. Shackleton Bailey (Cambridge: Harvard University Press, 2003).

the times by having a lot more autonomy than women in most other Greek city-states. Granted, they were still primarily seen as breeding machines to produce future soldiers, but it was not looked down upon or even second-guessed for Spartan women to display masculine characteristics. They were given a relatively good education, could inherit property and do with it what they pleased, held public influence on societal and governmental decision-making, their daughters received inheritances equal to sons, their clothing was more in the masculine style so as to allow greater range of movement, they were commonly respected as athletes, and they generally married in their late teens (other Greek women married in their preteens).[96]

But when it comes to ancient Greek female queer sexuality, no one is better known than the poetess Sappho. So notorious was her lyric poetry celebrating sex between women that the island in which she was born, Lesbos, became synonymous with female-female love and is the origin of the word "lesbian."[97] More accurately, though, Sappho would be labeled in modern times as bisexual due to her surviving first-person point of view poetry describing ecstatic love with both women and men. Even more revolutionary was how she defied the societally rigid "top"/"bottom" dichotomy in her works by expounding upon the virtues of being on both the giving and receiving end of same-sex love making.[98]

Ancient Greek Takeaway:
INTERGENERATIONAL MENTORSHIP

The obvious and immediate takeaway from the ancient Greeks is the pedagogical mentorship between the generations for both women and men. No, not the pederastic relationship of sex, as that is both illegal and

96   James C. Thompson, "Women in Sparta," *Women in the Ancient World,* http://www.womenintheancientworld.com/ (accessed Jan. 30, 2017).

97   Glenn W. Most, "Reflecting Sappho," *Bulletin of the Institute of Classical Studies* 40.1 (1995): 15–38.

98   K. J. Dover, *Greek Homosexuality* (Cambridge: Harvard University Press, 1978), 177; Claude Calame, *Les Chœurs de jeunes filles en Grèce archaïque* (Rome: L'Ateneo & Bizzarri, 1977).

not in any way acceptable in our modern society. But the pedagogical relationship of student and teacher is a powerful thing we have lost.

Youth culture has taken the world by storm, especially in the queer community where being young and beautiful is seen as our only value and social currency. While it's not wrong to be young and beautiful, the expectation of everyone to be young and beautiful certainly is, and it makes our older queer community members seem as if they have little to no value to offer younger generations.

Remember, not all magic is written down in books; much of it lives in the experience and in the minds of the people, especially older generations who created their own magic and learned their craft before books on magic had their own shelves in commercial bookstores. So, for your next magical activity, seek out these queer spellworking ancestors and learn their wisdom. Not only will it give you unique insight into magic, but it will also help a generation of people who have lost support networks of close friends during the AIDS crisis and lived in a time when both witchcraft and queerness were either illegal or highly persecuted. It's a win-win for all involved, so help our living ancestors and preserve their magical wisdom.

ANCIENT ROME

After Greece, Rome became the dominant power in the Mediterranean, soon expanding its sphere of influence to much of Europe. And while the Romans appropriated much of their culture and religious ideas from their conquered Greek subjects, some alterations were made. In regard to LGBT+ issues, same-sex love and gender expression were still quite commonplace, but there was a slightly more sinister tinge to them.

Like the Greeks before them, the Romans had no vocabulary to define and differentiate between homo- and heterosexual.[99] And also like the Greeks, sexuality was defined by the position one took during the act itself; you were either the active "top" and were associated with all the

99   Craig Williams, *Roman Homosexuality* (Oxford: Oxford University Press, 1999), 304.

positive traits of masculinity, or you were the passive "bottom" and were associated with all the negative traits of femininity, as befitting a patriarchal empire that heavily valued masculinity. So, in regard to men, it was seen as perfectly logical to have sex with other men and still be seen as a masculine individual so long you were the "top." This created the similar Greek problem of two men wanting to have sex with each other, yet neither wanting to give up their social status by taking on the effeminate role as the "bottom."

The solution to this problem is where the ancient Greeks and Romans differed. The Romans were unable to mimic the eromenos/erastes intergenerational approach that the Greeks favored. This was because freeborn male youths were absolutely off-limits with whom to engage in sex. Instead, the Romans utilized people who had no legal social standing as citizens: slaves, prostitutes, and entertainers. Since these people technically had no status in society, they couldn't lose their social standing by being the passive partner of a sexual act. And of course if they were a slave, as Roman men often preferred, then they were property and had no say in the matter whatsoever.[100]

Roman social life, however, was less divided by gender. Where in Greek society it was unseemly for men and women to socialize together outside the home and only men could educate the youth, Roman society was perfectly okay with men and women socializing, and women were often permitted to educate their children and advise their husbands and sons on political matters. This prevented Roman men from developing the all-boys'-club level of social male bonding and romance that the Greeks had simply because the Romans were not forced to be educated solely by men and hang out exclusively with other men for their entire life. Thus, male-male relationships, although commonplace, were never held in as high esteem or respect as they were with the Greeks.[101]

---

100   Elizabeth Manwell, "Gender and Masculinity," in *A Companion to Catullus*, ed. Marilyn B. Skinner (Hoboken: Blackwell Publishing, 2011), 118.

101   Marilyn B. Skinner, introduction to *Bisexuality in the Ancient World*, 2nd ed. by Eva Cantarella, trans. Cormac Ó Cuilleanáin (New Haven: Yale University Press, 2002), xi–xii.

In their infamous sexual orgies it was a frequent sight to see threesomes among two men and one woman. Artworks of the time depict a man penetrating a woman while simultaneously being penetrated by another man. And in foursomes there were usually two men and two women, sometimes involved in male-female partnerings and sometimes in male-male, female-female partnerings. Nevertheless, the male "bottoms" of these orgies were still open to ridicule and social stigma. Jokes, snide remarks, and public accusations about men being "bottoms" were both socially popular and wildly inappropriate to make, not because it was insulting to all men in the passive role, but because it was considered one of the worst things you could call a Roman man.[102] Evidence of this still exists in literature and in the preserved graffiti of excavated ruins such as in Pompeii.[103]

Still, there are always exceptions to the rule, especially when that exception is above the rules, as was the case for emperors. But perhaps none was so tender as the relationship between Emperor Hadrian and his youthful lover Antinous, who out of all his lovers became his personal favorite.

Beyond sexual attraction, Hadrian respected Antinous as intelligent and wise, and they shared mutual hobbies. Historians of the time deemed their love to be pure, and never was there mention of Antinous attempting to gain or exert political power via his relationship with the emperor. Together, they traveled the empire and had many adventures, until one fateful excursion on the Nile when Antinous fell in the river and died. To this day the exact circumstances of his death remain a mystery, but at the time, just as nowadays, everyone seemed to have their own opinion on the matter, and the lines between truth and gossip became impenetrably blurred. The grieving Hadrian, without approval of the Senate, had his lover deified, and the local Egyptian priesthood identified him as being akin to Osiris. This association grew, and ultimately the deified Antinous

---

102   John R. Clarke, *Looking at Lovemaking: Constructions of Sexuality in Roman Art 100 B.C.–A.D. 250* (Berkeley: University of California Press, 2001), 234.

103   Preston Grant, *Gay, Explained: History, Science, Culture, and Spirit* (San Francisco: Guide Media, 2016).

became accepted as a benevolent deity often associated with death and resurrection. Worship of him still exists to this day in particular circles.[104]

When it comes to female-female love in ancient Rome, though, there aren't too many positive examples. Lesbianism was simultaneously seen as a wild perversion and as a grand mystery to the male-dominated historians of Roman culture's cult of masculinity. They knew that sexual desire between women was a real thing that happened all over the empire, but they couldn't understand why. Remember, the Roman view of sexuality was only understood through the lens of the "top"/"bottom" dichotomy, and it was generally assumed that only the penetrator could receive physical pleasure during the act. It was a great confusion as to why women would want to have sex with one another if no one could be the penetrator and thus enjoy it. Of course, dildos were well in use in the Roman world, but therein lied the perversion; to men, it seemed unnatural for a woman to get physical pleasure from inserting objects into another woman.

But as evidence of the times, official writings on female same-sex attraction were scant. Most of the surviving information we have about it from the Republic Era does nothing more than vilify and condemn the practice, but from the Imperial Era there exists a bit more surviving information on it, mostly in unofficial writings such as dream interpretations, medical cases, astrology texts, love spells, and even graffiti.[105]

Perhaps most ironically in both the ancient Greek and Roman worlds, bisexuality was more socially acknowledged and accepted than elsewhere in our modern world. Granted, the Greeks and Romans did not differentiate sexuality in terms of to whom one was attracted but rather the position one took during intercourse, but if we apply our modern labels of sexuality to the habits of the times, bisexuality was seen as the most natural thing in the world. It was understood that everyone was bisexual by nature, as evidenced by the Greek expectation for men to participate

104 Royston Lambert, *Beloved and God: The Story of Hadrian and Antinous* (London: George Weidenfeld & Nicolson, 1984).
105 Bernadette J. Brooten, *Love Between Women: Early Christian Responses to Female Homoeroticism* (Chicago: University of Chicago Press, 1996), 1.

in erastes/eromenos relationships while still fathering children with their wives and by the Roman admiration for men who exerted their masculine virility through penetrating another man, again while still fathering children with their wives. To be exclusively hetero- or homosexual was seen as unnatural both biologically and socially since it went against the way society was set up and its expectations of a model citizen.[106]

But the ways in which humans could behave and the ways in which the gods could behave were often very different. Double standards on morality and sexuality abounded in the religions of ancient Greece and Rome, especially when it came to sexual orientation and identity. Granted, there are numerous examples of Greek and Roman queer deities, but soon I'll show you a few that give a good example of the range of queerness they possessed.

Ancient Roman Takeaway:
APPETITE FOR WAR

Queer Roman emperors, just as much as non-queer emperors, infused the culture with a sense of constant struggle for expansion. Of course I'm not advocating for literal war, but there is something to be said for never resting on our laurels and becoming content with the progress we've made.

In a queer sense, this is important for our civil rights movement. We have a tendency to fight hard for something, and then once we achieve it, we back off and relax in our victory. This is especially so when we achieve a victory that directly benefits us personally and then stop fighting for civil rights victories that don't directly pertain to us. All colors and letters of the LGBT+ acronym must achieve full equality. As a minority group, we have to fight for the rights of every member of the group in order to stay strong, and we can never rest in our war against those who try to oppress any one of us. No matter how much we have accomplished, there is always more to do, and only when the war is won should we relax.

106 From http://www.gaystarnews.com/ (accessed Aug. 30, 2016).

Magically this is important, too. We do spells to win our own personal battles, but once we have manifested what we personally want for ourselves, we don't continue the fight against the greater war for what will not personally benefit us yet will benefit others. As a magical community, especially a queer magical community, we have to help each other out. Never stop fighting just because you have no more to personally gain. Our brothers and sisters need our support with spellwork. Until we are all equal, there is always more do to.

So, for your next magical activity, create a spell for the promotion of queer civil rights, especially rights that do not directly benefit yourself. Don't fall back on something someone else has written. Let it come from the heart, and formulate a personal spellworking for others to support the most vulnerable of our queer tribe in the war against intolerance and hate.

Deities & Legends

APOLLO

Apollo, the god of (among other things) music, light, prophecy, and poetry, is perhaps one of the best-known LGBT+ deities of the classical world due to his tragic romance with the youthful Hyacinth (Hyakinthos). As the story goes, both Apollo and the West Wind, Zephyr (Zephyros), were competing for the love of a particularly beautiful young mortal named Hyacinth, but Hyacinth much preferred the pretty Apollo. One day while the two lovers were impressing one another with their discus-throwing techniques, Zephyr, in a case of if-I-can't-have-him-no-one-can, caused the wind to blow Apollo's discus off-course and strike Hyacinth's head, killing him. Apollo was devastated and refused to allow Hades to claim his lover's corpse. Instead, Apollo transformed Hyacinth into the eponymous flower whose blossoms resemble the tightly curled locks of the youth's hair. Possibly stemming from this myth, the hyacinth flower, with its famous purple color, became an ingredient in male-male love magic for millennia afterwards.[107]

107   From http://www.theoi.com.

In worship, Apollo's correspondences are the sun, bay leaves, oranges, the colors gold and white, and the practices of divination as well as partaking in the arts.

ATHENA/MINERVA

Athena, renamed Minerva by the Romans, is the goddess of (among other things) wisdom, strategy, law, and justice. She is an interesting queer deity because she can be viewed as a sort of asexual or gender-neutral character. Well-known for her celibacy, Athena is never described as being sexually interested in anyone, woman or man. And despite her biologically female body, she is often depicted as wearing masculine accessories, having a masculine mentality, and fitting in better with the male Olympians. In myths she also usually takes the side of the double-standard male patriarchy when it comes to male-female relations and how women should behave. Nevertheless, despite being generally accepted as "one of the guys," she is still shown to be subject to stereotypical female vanities, most infamously in her vindictiveness over losing a beauty contest to the ultra-feminine Aphrodite in the legendary Judgement of Paris that became the impetus of the Trojan War. In certain respects, she can also be viewed as a gender-fluid deity who sometimes identifies herself more as a man and other times more a woman, regardless of her physiology. [108]

In worship, her correspondences are olive trees, the colors blue and white, owls (for wisdom), doves (for victory), and partaking in textile arts such as weaving, knitting, and crocheting, as well as playing strategy games.

BAUBO & IAMBE

Baubo and Iambe are Greek goddesses, Baubo of belly laughter and Iambe of obscene speech and the iambic pentameter. Baubo is a particularly unique goddess because she is usually described as being a headless, armless torso with legs, whose breasts act as her eyes and overgrown genitals as a bearded mouth. Their most queer myth was preserved in

---

108   From http://www.theoi.com.

the Eleusinian Mysteries, which primarily deal with Demeter (goddess of agriculture) and her sullen search for her daughter Persephone, who was abducted by Hades (god of the underworld).

According to legend, both Baubo and Iambe take it upon themselves to cheer up the obviously grief-stricken Demeter by using their natural off-color talents: Iambe by reciting lewd poetry while riding upon Baubo, and Baudo by lifting up her clothes to reveal her unusual nether-region smile. The bawdy entertainment causes Demeter to laugh, effectively stirring her out of her depression. Certain interpretations of this myth suggest that Demeter's laughter was a side effect of being shyly aroused at hearing Iambe's sexual poetry and seeing Baudo's genitalia.

This queer interpretation seems to have merit considering that the Eleusinian Mysteries attracted a number of gender-variant priests, many of whom would often reenact this saucy scene. During the processional crossings over the River Cephisus known as the *Gephyrismos*, biological males and eunuchs dressed in women's clothes would suddenly lift their skirts and make fun of all the prudish onlookers who were visibly uncomfortable by the irreverence. These were also the same mysteries of which Emperor Hadrian and his deified lover Antinous were once a part.[109]

IPHIS

In Ovid's *Metamorphoses*, Iphis is the daughter of a man who desperately wanted a son. Her parents were extremely poor, her mother was pregnant, and they knew that if they had a daughter, they could never afford the dowry necessary to one day marry her off. Being the head of the household, her father proclaimed that if the baby was a girl, he would simply kill it; problem solved. However, Iphis's mother, while still pregnant, had a dream wherein the Egyptian goddess Isis appeared to her, insisting that the baby be accepted regardless of its gender. After giving birth to a little girl, Iphis's mother quickly disguised her in boys' clothes and agreed to give the child a gender-neutral name. Falling for his wife's salvational ruse, Iphis's father raises her as his son.

---

109   Randy P. Conner, *Blossom of Bone* (San Francisco: HarperCollins, 1993).

All is well and good until Iphis's father decides it's time to arrange a marriage for his "son" and receive a poverty-lifting dowry from some other family. He chooses the beautiful Ianthe to be his new daughter in-law, to which Ianthe is very pleased since she's smitten by Iphis. Iphis, in turn, also has eyes for Ianthe and falls equally in love with her, but she knows that their marriage would be forbidden if anyone ever found out the truth about her biological gender. So she goes to her mom for advice; seeing her daughter so distraught, her mother takes her to a temple of Isis, where they pray for a solution. Their prayers are answered by Isis ultimately transforming Iphis into a biological male, thereby allowing her to marry Ianthe and live happily ever after. And despite the hasty heteronormative-twist ending, the myth of Iphis is a rare Greek tale of both lesbian and female-to-male transgender love.[110]

THE ORIGIN OF LOVE

In his *Symposium*, the Greek philosopher Plato propounded upon many explanatory theories about human life. One in particular was about the mythological origins of love and companionship. He tells how humans once came in three different genders, each joined at the back in pairs with two heads, four arms, and four legs. The male gender was made of two men, the female gender of two women, and the androgynous gender of one man and one woman. These early humans had strength to rival the gods, who in turn formed a council on what to do about these too-powerful creatures they had made. At first, the plan was to just destroy them all, but they decided against this plan since without any humans, there would be no one to worship and give sacrifice to the gods anymore.

Eventually, it was decided that Zeus would use his thunderbolts to split the creatures in two, thus weakening them so they could no longer be a threat. After the violent halving of all humans, the gods fixed us up to look as we do today, with one head, two arms, and two legs. Ever since then, we wander the earth feeling incomplete, longing for our other half; upon finding each other, we hug and kiss and try our best to physically reunite

110   From http://www.theoi.com.

our bodies back together through making love. The divided male gender is what we call gay men today; the divided female gender is modern lesbians; and the androgynous gender is modern heterosexuals.[111]

111   From http://sacred-texts.com (accessed Aug. 30, 2016).

9

PAGAN EUROPE

Cultural

Gender and sexuality In Pagan Europe is often seen today with mixed emotions. Quite a bit of evidence exists on the LGBT+ tendencies of the original tribes and people of the continent, but a lot of that evidence comes from outside sources and third-party observers. Usually these foreign historians were the Greeks and Romans, who related the queerness of "barbarous" Europe in terms of their own rigid "top"/"bottom" dichotomy, or they were the imperial Christians, who maligned any form of nonprocreative sex that they witnessed these heathens doing.

Still, there is little mention of the LGBT+ tendencies from the indigenous people themselves. Does this mean sexuality and gender were not a big deal and they were living in a queer utopia? Does it mean anything queer was such an awful taboo that no one dared record its existence at length? Well, no one really knows with 100 percent certainty. But like most tainted history written by rivals and conquerors, the truth most likely lies somewhere in between. What is preserved, however, is the undeniable queerness in the religions of various Pagan tribes, especially those of the Celts and of the Vikings. So, let us again take some grains of salt along with us and begin by looking at the Celts.

CELTS

The various groups of native pre-Christian Europeans outside of classical Greece and Rome are commonly grouped together and known as the Celts (pronounced "kelts"). In this sense of the word, the Celts were the tribes of Europe who spoke neither Greek nor Latin and worshipped non-Greco-Roman deities. At their greatest extent, the Celtic people comprised many cultures and lived on a large swath of land that arched from modern-day Portugal and Spain through France, the British Isles, Germany, Scandinavia, the Eastern European borders of the Black Sea, and even pockets in Turkey. Rather than a single unified people, the Celts were comprised of numerous tribes who all shared certain degrees of cultural similarity, and one major similarity was the predominant use of oral tradition to pass down legends, teachings, and ways of life. Nowadays, though, the Celts are mostly associated with the people of Ireland, Scotland, Wales, and the French province of Brittany, wherein their cultures most vibrantly survive.

As mentioned earlier, much of the surviving socio- and anthropological writings we have of the Celts come from other people who encountered them. And in the classical world, Greek and Roman military leaders were the primary people to have such multiple, sustained encounters. This could definitely be the reason as to why the Celts of antiquity were always described as warlike, since it was through war that these cultures kept meeting, but the way of the warrior also appears quite a lot in their own mythology. In Irish mythology in particular, legendary male figures often had a special male brother-in-arms alongside whom they fought and with whom they tenderly loved.

The Celtic cultures, like human societies throughout time, had a stratified class system of the aristocratic elite and subdivisions of pretty much everyone else. The upper classes of male Celtic society, according to the Greeks and Romans who encountered them, were known to have sexual relations with other men, but since the Greeks and Romans didn't want to come across as being similar to these "barbarians," the writers of the time emphasized that the Celtic aristocracy *preferred* other men over women and even engaged in all-male three-ways.[112] Aristotle even made special mention to point out how this preferred homosexuality also had a bias for men within the same social class—a severe no-no in Greek society.[113] Again, though, the truth lies somewhere in between.

Another in-between truth is their societal disdain for homosexual men "bottoming." The modern assumption for this comes from how prevalent machismo culture dominated Celtic society. To be weak was bad, and thus for a man to act like the weaker sex was bad. In fact, being a homosexual "bottom" was one of the worst things of which you could accuse a Celtic male. Ironically, the frequency of this accusation (especially in Northern Europe) gives proof that homosexuality was a thing in Pagan Europe since such an insult could only be understood if it was practiced commonly enough to where everyday people were able to recognize the accusation.

Similar backhanded evidence of the commonality of Celtic homosexuality was written into the Irish Celts' seventh-century Brehon Laws as a legal reason for which a woman may divorce her husband. The law doesn't mention homosexuality per se, but rather it grants a legal divorce to women whose husbands prefer to have sex with other men rather than with her. Modern scholars believe this not to be a legal punishment for gay men insomuch as it is a legal safeguard for women to have the right to bear children, as evidenced by the law continuing to list a number of other legal grounds for divorce, all of which revolve around a man's inability

112 From https://historicromance.wordpress.com/2011/01/28/warrior-lovers-in -ancient-ireland/ (accessed Sept. 9, 2016).
113 Philip Freeman, *War, Women, and Druids: Eyewitness Reports and Early Accounts of the Ancient Celts* (Austin: University of Texas Press, 2008).

to impregnate his wife, such as being too obese to have sex and outright male infertility. Still, a man preferring the bed of another man must have occurred often enough for the Irish Celts to have included it in their code of laws at all. [114]

As for the women themselves, there isn't much evidence on romantic lesbianism between Celtic ladies. The same goes for transgender individuals and bisexuals. The reason for this is, again, the Romans. Most of the surviving history of the Celts that we modern-day people have to go on are the writings from the Roman military, who, by and large, mostly had contact with Celtic warrior men. And in addition to not interacting much with Celtic women, the Roman generals and historians wouldn't have paid particular interest in the private affairs of these "barbarian" women as evidenced by how little esteem they had for their own "civilized" women.

There is, of course, an exception, albeit a controversial one: Boudica, the legendary red-headed warrior queen of the British Celts who led a successful revolt against invading Roman armies. The controversy lies in the fact that we know so little about her. What we do know is that Boudica was married to the king of a Celtic tribe allied with Rome. Upon her husband's death, the Roman army pillaged her lands, raped her daughters, and flogged her mercilessly. Now an avowed enemy of Rome, she was elected leader of a united Celtic resistance against the invaders. Under her leadership, British Celts won military success after military success against the war machine of Imperial Rome until the Roman army won a decisive victory at a strategic location on Watling Street (Rome's main highway in Britain). After this unrecoverable defeat, accounts differ as to the Celtic queen's fate. Some writings say she became sick on the campaign trail and died, and others say she committed suicide via self-ingested poisoning so as not to be captured and become a Roman slave. [115]

---

114   Fergus Kelly, *A Guide to Early Irish Law* (Dublin: Dublin Institute for Advanced Studies, 2005).

115   Tacitus, *The Annals*, trans. Alfred John Church and William Jackson Brodribb, Internet Classics Archive, http://classics.mit.edu/Tacitus/annals.html (accessed Sept. 13, 2016).

Aside from the obvious and stereotypical associations of lesbianism possessed by Boudica such as being a martial leader, an aggressive and merciless warrior, and dominating men both by direct command and conquest, modern historians believe it's quite logical that, after her husband's death, Boudica would've had sexual relations with other women, although they stop short of saying that she actually did so. The reasoning is that as the *de jure* leader of her tribe, the British Celtic custom of her people dictated that she bed with women.[116] Granted, this custom was most likely established with the assumption that all their leaders would be men, so was it possible that the custom was overlooked due to her gender? Yes, it's a possibility. But was it also possible that Boudica followed that custom so as to keep up appearances as leader of her people? Yes, that's also a possibility. The truth may never be fully known.

The only other account of female-female sexuality, other than Boudica's supposed bisexuality, comes in a very brief passage of the old Irish tale of "Niall Frossach" as written in the twelfth century Book of Leinster. In the tale there is direct mention of two women having sex with one another, and it is described as "playful mating." Nothing is said of it being something abhorrent or even odd and unusual, and the characters within the tale don't react to it in any particular way other than a matter-of-fact/it-is-what-it-is kind of attitude.[117]

Celtic Takeaway:
IN-PERSON COMMUNICATION

The queer history of the various Celtic people is scarce due to their predominant use of oral tradition, but therein also lies the takeaway: actually communicating with people directly. We are shy a lot of times in magic and in queer life. We don't know how someone may react if we tell them that we practice magic or that we are queer. Plus, both magical practitioners

---

116   Carolyn D. Williams, *Boudica and Her Stories: Narrative Transformations of a Warrior Queen* (Newark: University of Delaware Press, 2009).

117   Richard Irvine Best, *The Book of Leinster: Formerly Lebar na Núachongbála* (Dublin: Dublin Institute for Advanced Studies, 1954).

and queer people are minorities, so there are less of us with whom to talk. This leads to a lot of solitary magic practice and learning about queer life via various media. Now don't get me wrong, these are both great things, but there is nothing like being able to talk about things with actual people right there in the flesh.

The Celtic people had a high regard for direct oral communication, but nowadays we see it as a sort of last resort. Why deal with other people and their flaws when we can get all the world's information from the comfort of our own room? Well, the reason is because human interaction is a magical part of life. Aside from us being social animals, there is a certain magical sensation and "knowing" in talking with people directly. Commonly it's called a "vibe"—that subtle, unexplainable feeling you get about a person that can only be received in person. You can also think back to any date you've had. Chatting online via text, photos, or videos, they all can't tell you as much about a person as being there in the room with them in conversation. That is where our magical senses kick in and allow us to truly know a person.

So, for your next magical activity, go out and test how well you can magically read a person's vibes. Pick a random person you see and make a quick assessment of their personality based on the vibes you pick up. Then engage in conversation with them face-to-face. A safe choice is to do this at a store and approach an employee with the pretense of having a few questions. Approaching random people can put them in a defensive or dismissive mood, but an employee expects it and will technically have to respond to you. The more you do this, the better you'll become at instinctively and accurately picking up on people's energies. Consequently, being able to read these energies will help you in spellworkings for other people as well as give you a heads-up in daily life on who to trust and who's just running game.

VIKINGS

During the eighth to eleventh centuries, the Scandinavian societies of pagan Europe were a bellicose people. Infamous for their raids, ferocity in battle, and extreme aggression, these northern warriors valued testosterone-fueled masculinity and the physical power that went along with it. So, unsurprisingly, they didn't look too favorably on queerness. Much like the Celts to their south, the Vikings were very much a machismo society that valued male toughness and despised effeminacy. In a sense, it was not queerness itself that the Norsemen hated, but rather the feminizing of their men, which they equated with weakness.

Nevertheless, we do know that male homosexuality was practiced by the Vikings. Besides the obvious fact that LGBT+ people have existed throughout time in all societies, the common derision of homosexual men by the Vikings proves that they were aware of it and that it was common enough to be an understood insult. In fact, two words in particular were used as such an insult: *ergi* and *argr*. Roughly translated, they mean "unmanliness" and "unmanly," respectively. In such a macho culture, one's manliness carried with it societal power and influence, so to be called these names was an extreme insult that could permanently destroy a man's reputation. So severe were these accusations that being called such was grounds for a duel known as *hólmganga*. If the accused won, then he was obviously not "unmanly" and was entitled to compensation, but if he lost, then it was supposedly his unmanliness that had lost him the duel.[118]

Of course, though, there was exception to the rule. If you were the penetrating "top" during a round of male-male intercourse, then you were not considered womanly. And in the aftermath of a battle, it was expected of a Norseman to sexually penetrate their defeated foes. In Viking conquests, rape was a weapon of war. It asserted dominance over the loser and effectively feminized him in addition to psychologically breaking his spirit. Outside of war, it was also seen as okay for macho Viking men to have sex with their male slaves/serfs since it asserted their masculine dominance,

118 Marlene Ciklamini, "The Old Icelandic Duel," *Scandinavian Studies* 35:3 (1963): 175–194.

so long as they were the "top." Thus it was not homosexuality that the Vikings abhorred, but rather the lack of masculinity associated with taking on the female role during sex and being dominated by another man.

And let's not forget about the ladies. Much like the other cultures we've discussed previously, not much is known about the private sexual lives of Viking women because women were not seen as important enough to document their lives in such depth. But there is roundabout evidence that suggest Viking women did engage in same-sex female love frequently enough to have men enact laws against the masculinization of women. Sociologists say this was due to the scarcity value of women; the ratio of females to males was drastically uneven, with far fewer females and an overabundance of males—a major side effect of a society that heavily valued sons over daughters.

Similar to the notoriety once caused by modern China's one child policy, Viking families who bore girls often left them out in the wilderness to die of exposure as a way to erase the "mistake" and try again for a boy.[119] This left child-bearing women in short supply, and if a number of these scarce women had an aversion to heterosexual lovemaking, that left even fewer potential mothers for the men to marry and impregnate. Thus laws were enacted that discouraged women from taking on male characteristics such as cutting their hair short, wearing men's clothing, taking up weapons, etc. Basically, women needed to act like the weaker sex in order to attract a mate and bear him children, since no macho Viking man would want a woman who was more masculine and dominant than he was. On the flip side, this meant women held a lot of authority in the marriage since if they divorced their husband, the scarcity of available women made finding another wife difficult, a power over men reflected in numerous Viking sagas.[120]

119   Jenny Jochens, *Women in Old Norse Society* (Ithaca: Cornell University Press, 1995).
120   Carol J. Clover, "The Politics of Scarcity: Notes on the Sex Ratios in Early Scandinavia," *Scandinavian Studies* 60 (1988): 147–188.

But, again, from a logical sexual politics point of view, if a Viking woman truly was a lesbian or even bisexual, there really wasn't anything her husband could do about it. After all, it would be unwise to divorce her due to the scarcity of marriageable women out there. And if he complained about it, then she could threaten him with divorce, effectively shutting him up. Realistically, so long as a woman did her duty of bearing her husband's children, whatever other liaisons she had with women were her prerogative.[121]

As for bisexual and transgender individuals in Viking society, hardly anything is known. The Viking notion of queerness is not the same as ours today. To them, sexuality was a matter of sexual positioning and psychological dominance, not the inner yearnings and identity of an individual. Yet it's safe to presume that, despite the rampant effemiphobia exhibited in Norse culture, everyone was probably a little bisexual. If you consider that macho Viking warriors were societally expected to father children and sexually dominate their battle foes, as well as the widespread permissiveness of sexually "topping" male slaves/serfs, then bisexuality was the norm for Viking men at least. Still, the exploits and adventures of the Norse gods reveal a fair amount of transsexualism and all-around queerness, as we will witness in a bit.

Viking Takeaway:
SACREDNESS OF THE DIVINE MASCULINE

Now, before you jump up and start screaming that I'm an agent of the patriarchy, it's important to understand that anything taken to its extreme is bad, but that doesn't mean the thing itself is bad. The cult of masculinity revered by the Vikings is still with us in our modern culture, and femininity is still seen as weak. Although this is unfortunate and not a good thing for society, we have to keep in mind that being masculine or liking masculine people and things aren't bad. Like we talked about with youth

---

121   From http://www.vikinganswerlady.com/gayvik.shtml (accessed Sept. 14, 2016).

and beauty, the possession of and attraction to masculinity isn't bad, but the expectation to be masculine certainly is.

On a day-to-day level, we have to be okay with people's personal affinity for masculinity, either in their identity or in what attracts them. Nowadays, as a reactionary movement to the patriarchy, queer men shame other queer men who have a sexual preference for masculine men. It is wrongly assumed that liking something automatically means disliking its opposite. After all, a gay man can have a strong preference to men with beards, but that doesn't mean he hates or isn't attracted to clean-shaven guys. And a lesbian can have a preference for women with long hair, but that doesn't mean she hates or isn't attracted to short-haired women.

If a straight man sexually prefers masculine women, that doesn't mean he has disdain for effeminate women. If a straight woman prefers effeminate men, that doesn't mean she has disdain for masculine men. If a lesbian sexually prefers masculine women, that doesn't mean she has disdain for effeminate women. If a bisexual person has a slight sexual preference for men, even though there is still a sexual attraction to women, that doesn't mean there is disdain for women. If a female-to-male transsexual sexually prefers men, that doesn't mean there is disdain for women. If a gay man sexually prefers masculine men, that doesn't mean he has disdain for effeminate men. You see where I'm going with this?

Everyone is into something, and shaming our own queer family for liking what they like only tears us down as a whole. And just because someone is attracted to masculinity doesn't mean they hate effeminacy; the two are not hand-in-hand. So long as it's not hurting anyone, let people like what they like. And magically, don't be adverse to the divine masculine just because the dominant monotheistic religions show disdain for the divine feminine.

So, for your next magical activity, do a ritual with your tradition that honors and worships the most stereotypically masculine deity in your pantheon. Paganism itself attracts many people because its worship of the divine feminine is a breath of fresh air in a world that worships the cult of toxic masculinity, but the divine masculine is just as important and should not be ignored or seen with aversion. Every deity, even the ultra-masculine ones, can teach us something if we are open to learning.

Deities & Legends

CÚ CHULAINN

Cú Chulainn is arguably the most homoerotic of the Irish Celtic deities in modern consciousness despite technically never being officially described as such in surviving lore. What makes him a member of the international pantheon of queer deities is his relationship with best friend and foster brother, Ferdiad. They grew up together, trained together, experienced physical love together, and were said to have been equal in all things except that Cú Chulainn was more naturally suited to "offense" in battle due to his talent with a spear, while Ferdiad was more naturally "defensive" due to his armor-tough hard skin.

Through a series of events, they're eventually forced to fight against each other in a battle to the death. The battle drags on for days until one day Cú Chulainn delivers the killing blow by thrusting his "mysterious weapon" up into the anus of Ferdiad, a part of his body where Cú Chulainn conveniently somehow knew Ferdiad's impenetrable skin didn't cover. After pulling out his weapon, Cú Chulainn greatly mourns over the corpse of his beloved friend, a scene immortalized in countless works of art.[122]

In worship, dogs are sacred to Cú Chulainn, as well as the spear and aspects of the divine masculine.

LOKI

Of all the Norse gods, Loki is perhaps the one most recognized for possessing queer traits. In the legends he is often described as a mercurial and shape-shifting trickster deity and an agent of chaos. The first telling thing about him is his full name, Loki Laufeyjarson, which is unique since

---

122   Nora Chadwick, *The Celts* (London: Folio Society, 2001).

it shows that he was named after his mother, as opposed to the macho Viking tradition of children being named after their fathers.

His appearance is described as very beautiful, but he is often found metamorphosing himself into various animals and, on three occasions, a woman. One specific story tells of how Loki turned himself into a mare and allowed himself to become impregnated by the stallion Svaðilfari, eventually giving birth to Odin's horse Sleipnir. He is also said to have gotten pregnant via eating the half-cooked heart of a woman and given birth to the demons that plague mankind.

In many other tales, Loki goes beyond showing his usual indifference for gender roles and reveals his disregard for his own gender identity. One of the more popular examples of this tells of how, in an effort to make the giantess Skadi laugh, Loki tied his genitals to a goat's beard and proceeded to castrate himself. In machismo Viking culture where a man's penis was his symbol of power, Loki's attempt to physically emasculate himself for a laugh perfectly sums up his attitude toward sex and gender.[123]

In worship, Loki's correspondences are snakes, elder and beech trees, lead, jet, peppery incense, the color black, and partaking in practical and transgressive jokes.

ODIN

One of the more popular Scandinavian deities, Odin is primarily a shamanic god of battle, death, and spiritual wisdom who is blind in one eye and is the master of the paradisiac warrior afterlife of Valhalla. His associations with queerness are primarily twofold. First, he is often regarded as a patron of outcasts by being ideologically at odds with other gods due to his support of frenzied amorality, whether on the battlefield as a berserker through the ingestion of psychotropic plants or even as an outlaw. Secondly, he practices the magic arts of women. In one famous tale, Odin derides Loki's effeminacy by calling him the forbidden insult *argr*, but Loki then counters by pointing out that Odin, too, is unmanly because he is a practitioner of *seiðr* (a type of women's magic), effectively putting

123   Roscoe, *Queer Spirits*.

Odin in his place because it was true. Although the legends don't go into detail about Odin's active involvement in *seiðr*, the real thrust of Loki's ballsy counter was a tongue-in-cheek implication that Odin had not only embraced his inner femininity but also "bottomed" during sex.[124]

In worship, his correspondences are wolves, ravens, the colors black, orange, and red, dragon's blood incense, ferns, mandrakes, yew trees, carnelian, onyx, and partaking in the healing arts as well as acts of altruism.

SAMODIVI

The Samodivi are female Eastern European Celtic deities that can best be described as a cross between a nymph, a siren, and a harpy. Visually, they are tall, attractive, blond, and wear long, flowing, ethereal gowns akin to those of *Rumours*-era Stevie Nicks, except studded with feathers. They go by differing names depending on where you are: Samodivi in Bulgaria, Iele in Romania, Vila in Poland, and Veelas in the Balkans. They are known to be very beautiful and are often depicted as bisexuals who overtly flirt with each other in order to attract men to their doom.

The folk legends vary, but they generally tell of how their beauty and never-ending seductive dancing enchant men to become their lustful servants. They are also known to purposely attract women with their Sapphic, suggestive body language, but unlike their male victims, female victims become so jealous (either of never possessing such beauty or of someone with such beauty) that they kill themselves. Those familiar with the Harry Potter series will see that it is from the Samodivi that J. K. Rowling got her inspiration for the Veela characters.[125]

124 Snorri Sturluson, *The Poetic Edda*, trans. Lee M. Hollander (Austin: University of Texas Press, 1986).

125 Ronesa Aveela, "Samodivi—Witches of Darkness or Thracian Goddesses?" *Mystical Emona*, June 22, 2015, http://mysticalemona.com/2015/06/22/samodivi-witches-of-darkness-or-thracian-goddesses/ (accessed Sept. 16, 2016).

10
CHRISTIANITY

Cultural

There's a lot of LGBT+ mysticism in the Christian faith. It's important, though, to be very specific when we talk about the dominant faith of the Western world since Roman times. When someone says "Christianity," what do they mean? Christianity itself is highly fragmented into numerous denominations that run the gamut from highly conservative Southern Baptists to highly liberal Unitarians. Roughly, however, the three main branches that make up the vast majority of the world's Christians are (in descending order of number of adherents) Catholic, Protestant, and Eastern Orthodox. Technically, Catholicism and Eastern Orthodoxy are pretty similar to each other except for a very small number of irreconcilable differences, and Protestantism is just a generic name that encompasses almost every other subdivision of the faith that is not directly Catholic or Eastern Orthodox.

As we'll explore later, there are quite a number of queer saints, mystics, theologians, and spiritual leaders who transcended traditional gender roles and heteronormativity. But for the queer culture of Christianity, the best place in history to look is in the early church era when there were no schisms or various denominations, back when all Christians were united as one.

The political climate of the time played a large part on why the early Christians were so tolerant. You see, they were still a small, obscure religion that had the stigmatization of looking like cannibals (due to the Eucharist ceremonies) in the eyes of the pagan majority, and they were also being actively persecuted, partly for political scapegoating reasons and partly because they were rebellious upstarts challenging the majority's status quo. So the early Christians needed all the help they could get, and they didn't ask too much about new converts since they needed the numbers and support. As long as newcomers accepted the teachings of Jesus Christ, all was well.

Of these regional early church groups, the Gnostics were particularly accepting of queer ideology. Labeled a "heretical" group by the Jews and most Christians of the time, Gnosticism was a radically anti-authority group that wasn't keen on the idea of God being an authoritarian who demanded unquestioning obedience and worship from humans. They would be akin to the people you see nowadays with "Question Everything" bumper stickers on their cars. They believed that God was more like a divine teacher and that salvation was ultimately dependent upon the individual to awaken to his or her inner divinity. In fact, they got their name from the Greek word *gnosis*, meaning "knowledge," and in particular that scene in the Garden of Eden when the snake hands the Apple of Knowledge to Eve, making her aware of her own self and her own potential. To the Gnostics, the snake was the good guy hero of the story; knowledge is power, and blind faith is voluntary slavery.

When it came to sex, they were all for it, *especially* nonprocreative sex. In a roundabout way, oral, anal, and homosexual acts, along with masturbation and hand jobs, were seen as morally superior by the Gnostics, specifically the Cathars and Bogomils Gnostics, because procreative sex just ended up making another human in this world for the authoritative establishment to rule over. It is from the Bulgarian Bogomils that the British slang word *bugger*, meaning sodomy, originated.[126] Furthermore, as Gnostic salvation was internal, even if you had kids, you couldn't teach them salvation. It'd be up to them to save themselves in such hard times.[127]

As for Jesus himself, well, he never mentioned anything about homosexuality or gender-based sins. Where the New Testament of the Bible turns horribly homophobic is in the Acts of the Apostles (a sort of "Where Are They Now?" sequel to the Gospels). This was because of the game-changing character now known as St. Paul. While not technically a homophobe by today's standards, St. Paul was just terribly prudish and ultra-zealous. Converting to Christianity later in his life, St. Paul felt he had to make up for lost time and made it his business to save the world's souls by spreading the Good News. He was unique among early Christians in that he was a legal Roman citizen, a former Jew, and highly educated, all of which made him the perfect missionary to bridge cultural gaps and freely travel the Roman Empire. His condemnations of everything sexual, especially the promiscuity that Greek and Roman men had with other men outside of marriage, were very influential and became the bedrock from where the Church would build its anti-queer foundations.[128]

Nevertheless, St. Paul was just one, albeit influential, man, and the early Church was still not an organized religion and still on shaky ground,

---

126 From http://www.etymonline.com/index.php?allowed_in
_frame=0&search=bugger (accessed Sept. 18, 2016).

127 Donna Minkowitz, "Religiously Queer," *The Huffington Post*, June 29, 2013, http://www.huffingtonpost.com/donna-minkowitz/religiously
-queer_b_3520142.html (accessed Sept. 18, 2016).

128 Joe Paprocki, "What Does St. Paul Say about Homosexuality?" *Busted Halo*, Aug. 27, 2010, http://bustedhalo.com/questionbox/what-does-st-paul-say
-about-homosexuality (accessed Sept. 19, 2016).

and thus fairly tolerant. The most commonly pointed-to example of this are the same-sex weddings being granted to lesbians and gays during that era, most famously starting with the relationship between St. Sergius and St. Bacchus. According to history, these two were officials in the Roman army and obviously very close. They served under the reign of Emperor Maximian, who was extremely anti-Christian, and when it was discovered that they were Christians, they were arrested, publicly humiliated, sent to trial, and tortured. St. Sergius survived the torture, but St. Bacchus was beaten so severely that he died of his injuries. As legend goes, his ghost appeared to his lover, encouraging him to stay strong for they would be reunited again in heaven. These words were prophecy as St. Sergius was soon sentenced to be beheaded.[129]

For years following their martyrdom, these two saints were recognized by Church leaders and writers as having a romantic relationship; getting into specifics, St. Sergius was known as the sweet and gentle "bottom" while St. Bacchus was the more rough and aggressive "top." Their relationship was officially documented in the oldest text of Church martyrology. Following their lead, Christian groups all over the Roman Empire began granting wedding unions to same-sex couples, both men and women, ranging from the eighth to eighteenth centuries, records of which have been found in places such as Vatican City, Paris, St. Petersburg, Istanbul, Ireland, and the Sinai Peninsula. Of course, both the Catholic and Eastern Orthodox Churches deny this, claiming that these records, including that of St. Sergius and St. Bacchus, were not of weddings but just a form of recognition for two same-sex people who were very close friends known as "Brother-Making Ceremonies," which is like the modern-day explanatory equivalent of when your parents tell you that the two middle-aged men across the street who've been living together for years on end are just "friends."[130]

The fall of the Western Roman Empire marked the definitive turning point in Christian–LGBT+ relations. The Eastern Roman Empire (Byzan-

---

129   John Boswell, *Same-Sex Unions in Pre-Modern Europe* (New York: Vintage, 1995).
130   Ibid.

tine Empire) became a severe theocracy and clamped down on queerness, while the remnants of the rest of the empire began dissolving into the Dark Ages, marked by superstition, isolating feudalism, and fear toward all those who were different. During this time all minorities were targeted as scapegoats, in particular gays, lesbians, and non-Christians. It was also when St. Thomas Aquinas popularized homosexuality as evil, sinful, and against the natural law of things since it couldn't result in procreation, the only Church-sanctioned reason for sexual activity.[131] It eventually came to the point where sodomy was a crime punishable by death, most infamously in the trials of the Knights Templar.[132]

For Christianity's lesbians, things were a bit different. Christianity had a strange time categorizing female-female love. Naturally, in accordance with St. Thomas Aquinus's "natural law" classifications of sexual acts, hanky-panky between two women was unnatural since it couldn't result in the blessings of pregnancy. As the Christian-dominated Middle Ages marched onward, though, the legal descriptions of sex began to all revolve around the penetrative power of a man's penis. This meant homosexuality was legally punishable between two men but not between two women. According to the general consensus of the times, erotic acts between two women were not truly sexual unless a dildo or some other penis substitute was used, and therefore it was technically not illegal since, in the eyes of the law, they weren't having sex. By around the thirteenth century, however, the powers that-be eventually categorized female-female eroticism as equal to sodomy, punishable by mutilation and death.[133]

Nevertheless, there did exist a safe haven for many Christian lesbians: the nunnery. By becoming a nun and moving into an all-female convent,

---

131   Louis Crompton, *Homosexuality and Civilization* (Cambridge: Harvard University Press, 2003).

132   Malcolm Barber, *The Trial of the Templars*, 2nd ed. (Cambridge: Harvard University Press, 2002); Anne Gilmour-Bryson, "Sodomy and the Knights Templar," *Journal of the History of Sexuality* 7:2 (1996).

133   Jacqueline Murray, "Twice Marginal and Twice Invisible: Lesbians in the Middle Ages," in *Handbook of Medieval Sexuality*, ed. Vern L. Bullough and James A. Brundage (New York: Garland Publishing Inc., 1996).

homosexual women were given a solid alibi by which to avoid marriage and sex with men altogether, and whatever happened behind cloister walls was their own business. While a number of lesbian nuns have been identified, arguably none were as influential and poetically open about their sexuality as Sor Juana Inés de la Cruz, but more on her in the upcoming deities and legends section.

Beyond same-sex female attraction, though, the Church was passing judgment as to what they regarded as an anomaly in God's creation: intersex individuals. Officially, St. Augustine addressed the problem of people with both male and female parts in his damning chef d'oeuvre *City of God* by letting Christians know that these people were monstrosities. Unofficially, however, average medieval Christians' day-to-day dealings with intersex people was much less hateful. The problem was not so much the physiology of an intersex individual but the moral choices that individual made. In theory, these people—then known as "hermaphrodites"—were allowed to choose their own preferred gender; however, if they chose male, then they were barred from having sex with men, and if they chose female, then they were barred from having a penetrative relationship with other women.[134]

Still, things were a bit more complex than that in Catholic cultures since it was usually the intersex individual's godparents who chose the child's sex at baptism, thus dictating all future expected gender roles and sexual preferences. Technically, once the intersex child came of age, they were permitted to choose their own gender, but having been already labeled as a "boy" or "girl" in the local village, it was highly frowned upon for them to choose to be the alternate gender. All in all, although official Christian theology has condemned intersex individuals as monstrosities, so long as they chose a side and stayed within the moral confines of their choice, they were in better shape than homosexual women and in much better shape than homosexual men of the time.

134   Sandra Alvarez, "Intersex in the Middle Ages," *Medievalists*, Jan. 9, 2015, http://www.medievalists.net/2015/01/09/intersex-middle-ages/ (accessed Sept. 19, 2016).

Christian Takeaway:
SELF-SALVATION

The Gnostic Christians emphasized being fully responsible for your own salvation. In magic, this is an ultimate truth because no matter what spell you are doing, at the end of the day it's between you and your connection to either the natural forces of the universe or the Divine. You can read books and you can pay to have other people do spells for you, but no long-lasting significant manifestation of change will occur if you do not take ownership of your own power. Thinking we can always rely on others to do our magic for us is lazy and naïve.

Similarly, it is up to our own queer selves to make life better. While comforting and uplifting, the "It Gets Better" campaign isn't universally true: *it* doesn't get better; *you* get better. With age usually comes self-confidence and self-knowledge, which in turn leads to things getting better because we stop caring what other people think of us and start living our own truth. But if we never take ownership of ourselves, never acknowledge our own truths, and expect everyone else to suddenly become more accepting in order for our lives to get better, it's never going to get better. Just like the queer-positive Gnostics understood, it is up to us to save ourselves. It's naïve to expect society and others to change for us. Really, once we as a whole take our happiness into our own hands, society usually follows suit, but it all starts within each of us first.

So, for your next magical activity, do a unique spell all on your own. Don't copy anything from your own tradition, don't use what you learned in books, and don't rely on outside information. Do a spell based solely on your divine intuition. Pick a general objective for the spell, then go out in the world and collect materials based on your intuition and what calls you. Once you have what you feel you need, assemble them how you feel they should be assembled and do whatever you feel is right for the ritual. You can, if need be, seek divine advice in meditation or prayer, but don't rely on outside information for every step along the way. Books and information are meant to be guides, not crutches. Show yourself that you have all the magic and knowledge of the universe inherent within you.

Deities & Legends

POPE JOAN

Pope Joan was pontiff of the Catholic Church for about ten years in the late ninth century. Her officially adopted papal name, however, was John VIII. These were the times when women were barred from getting a good education, so to circumvent this, Joan disguised herself as a boy under the pseudonym John and went to a German monastery where higher education was part and parcel of being a monk. As the years went by, the lie became the truth; Joan preferred to self-identify as a male and fell in love with another monk. The monk's sudden death caused their romance to be short-lived, and the grieving Joan transferred to Rome for a change of scenery.

Once in Rome, Joan's advanced intellectualism garnered admiration from prominent cardinals, ultimately leading to Joan's election as Pope John VIII since no one knew that Joan was not biologically male. Pope John VIII eventually became pregnant by one of the papal attendants. After a few months, Vatican staff members realized their new pope was a biological female, but rather than admit that God and the leaders of the Church had made a mistake in electing a transgender person to the papacy, all attempts were made to conceal the truth. Nevertheless, John VIII soon died during childbirth while on a procession in Rome. Needless to say, the Catholic Church officially denies Pope John VIII ever being female, but due to the lack of official records from this time and the conflicting extant informal records, a number of historians assert the validity of Pope Joan and the conspiracy of the Catholic Church's erasure of her despite the controversy.[135]

135   "Pope Joan," *New World Encyclopedia*, May 22, 2015, http://www
        .newworldencyclopedia.org/entry/Pope_Joan (accessed Aug. 18, 2017).

SOR JUANA INÉS DE LA CRUZ

Sor Juana Inés de la Cruz was a nun in colonial Mexico right at the end of Catholic Spain's golden age in the seventeenth century ("Sor" being Spanish for a religious "Sister"). In her youth she exhibited great distaste for gender norms, going so far as to even claim in one of her poems, "I am not a woman… / I know only that my body / Is neither one gender nor the other."

Extremely smart and unwilling to be denied higher education due to her biological sex, gender-fluid Juana schemed to pull a Yentl-like ruse on the patriarchy by applying to and attending a religious university disguised as a man. Her mother, however, would have none of that, and so Juana pursued another alternative: being a lady-in-waiting in the court of Antonio Sebastián de Toledo, the Viceroy of New Spain, where informal intellectualism would be readily available to her.[136]

It didn't take too long for everyone to realize that this new lady-in-waiting was a savant. In particular, her academic aptitude and physical beauty caught the eye of the Viceroy's wife, the Vicereine, Leonor Carreto. Far from jealous, the Viceroy held a great admiration for Juana's talents, so much so that he became her financial patron and approved of the growing intimate bond developing between her and his wife. Despite her love for the Vicereine, though, Juana's first love was always education, and the only place for women to receive the highest education in New Spain at the time was in the nunneries. And so, forsaking love for education, Juana left courtly life and became a nun.[137]

From her convent in Mexico City, Sor Juana became a prolific writer of poetry, books, academic literature, philosophical theses, and letters advocating the rights of women, indigenous people, and African slaves. Unfortunately, her outspokenness got her in trouble with the Catholic establishment. The Archbishop of Mexico condemned her liberalism and

---

136 Stuart Murray, *The Library: An Illustrated History* (Chicago: Skyhorse Publishing, 2009).

137 Sergio Téllez-Pon, *Un Amar Ardiente: Poemas a la Virreina* (Madrid: Flores Raras, 2017).

gave her the ultimatum of ceasing her advocacy against the status quo or having all of her work censored from human view. Consequently, the Church confiscated all of her works, her library of books, and her scientific equipment. Left with nothing but her mind, this gender-fluid pansexual Catholic nun continued with her religious vows until she died of sickness due to administering care to those stricken with the plague. Despite the Church's continued censorship of Sor Juana's liberal writings and erotic letters, much of her work was saved (and available to us nowadays) thanks to her longtime lover, the Vicereine of New Spain.[138]

ST. BERNARD OF CLAIRVAUX

St. Bernard of Clairvaux is the patron saint of candlemakers, beekeepers, and the Knights Templar. He was a twelfth-century French abbot of the Cistercian order who was known for being very passionate about Catholicism. He was terribly zealous, as evidenced by his prominent role in convincing the Christians of Europe and the Middle East to embark on the First Crusade, the advocacy for which the Knights Templar made him their official patron.

He also had a penchant for writing poetry about his love for Jesus Christ that verged heavily on the romantically erotic, often with him metamorphosing into a woman in order to fully be able to accept Jesus's special love for him. In many ways his writings were very much like the infamous *Faith +1* album of the eponymous band fronted by Eric Cartman, except Bernard's poetry was truly sincere. In fact, the gay subtext of these writings were so well-known even back then that "passing under the rainbow of St. Bernard" became a French euphemism for undergoing a gender change. Unsurprisingly, though, the Church asserts his writings are neither sexual nor queer, just a profoundly affectionate love for our Lord and Savior.[139] In Catholic veneration, his feast day is August 20.

138   Octavio Paz, *Sor Juana Inés de la Cruz o las Trampas de la Fe* (Ciudad de México: Fondo de Cultura Económica, 1982).

139   Connor, Sparks, and Sparks, *Cassell's Encyclopedia of Queer Myth, Symbol, and Spirit*.

ST. HILDEGARD VON BINGEN

St. Hildegard von Bingen is the patron saint of the environment, medicine, writing, and the religious life. She was a twelfth-century German abbess of the Benedictine Order who exhibited genius levels of savvy in everything she did. She wrote plays, invented her own language, and was an accomplished scientist, a respected poetess, a noted artist, and a philosopher of mysticism. She was also sexually interested in other women. With the exception of some of her devotional writings about the Virgin Mary and her medical writings on how a woman's sexual pleasure was not dependent on men, Hildegard's lesbianism was fairly under wraps—that is, until fate intervened and forced her to fight for the woman she loved. The woman in question was her personal assistant, Richardis von Stade, and the fateful agent was Richardis's brother, who happened to be an archbishop.

The crux of the problem was that Richardis's brother secured her to be the abbess of her own convent far away, and Hildegard was not having it. Perhaps more than was appropriate for someone in her position, she pleaded for her assistant to stay, but Hildegard was evidently more involved in the relationship than Richardis because Richardis was all in favor of her nepotistic promotion. So, desperate to force her lover to not abandon her, Hildegard infamously petitioned the pope himself to step in and prevent Richardis's transfer, which of course he didn't, and Richardis moved away. In a twist of fate, Richardis unexpectedly died later that year, allegedly with her last words being how she missed Hildegard and wanted to return to her lover. When Hildegard found all this out, she mourned profusely, channeling her sorrow into artistic achievements such as the world's first morality play, *Ordo Virtutum* (Order of the Virtues).[140] In Catholic veneration, her feast day is September 17.

---

140 From http://queering-the-church.blogspot.com/2010/09/hildegard-of-bingen
.html (accessed Sept. 21, 2016); Haggerty and Zimmerman, *Encyclopedia of Lesbian and Gay Histories and Cultures.*

ST. SEBASTIAN

St. Sebastian is the patron saint of archers, plague victims, soldiers, and a holy Christian death. Unofficially, he is known as the patron saint of gay male love and those suffering from HIV/AIDS. He was a martyr of the early Church era and is known as the West's first gay icon, largely due to the artwork of him following his death. In life he was noted for his youthful beauty, and in legend he was the desired of the Christian-hating Roman emperor Diocletian. Feelings changed, however, when Sebastian, a closet Christian, publicly protected two Christians from being tortured, resulting in the emperor ordering his death. His unique martyrdom has been forever immortalized in art as depictions of an athletic, loincloth-garbed young man bondaged to a phallic-shaped tree/pillar and writhing in painful ecstasy, with arrows penetrating his supple body.

This image has captured the interest of queer artists since the Renaissance due to its transgressive mix of spirituality and overt sensuality. The Church-approved imagery was so homoerotic that it became a form of safe pornography wherein Christians on the down-low could ogle at it lustfully without their intentions being obvious. Even nowadays, St. Sebastian is often used as a subject of queer art, depicting him as the archetypal tortured closet case. In the 1990s, due to his formal patronage of plague victims and informal patronage of gay love, Sebastian was adopted by liberal Catholics as patron saint of the AIDS movement.[141] In Catholic veneration, his feast day is January 20.

141 Jason Goldman, "Subjects of the Visual Arts: St. Sebastian," *GLBTQ Archive*, 2002, http://www.glbtqarchive.com/arts/subjects_st_sebastian_A.pdf (accessed Sept. 21, 2016); "Our Name," St. Sebastian Church, July 19, 2008, http://saintsebastiancatholic.com/wp/about/our-name/ (accessed Aug. 19, 2017).

11

EUROPEAN MAGICAL COMMUNITY

INVOKING DEITIES IN HOMOEROTIC LOVE SPELLS

Note: As taught to me by our next special guest, I will use special Old Spivak gender-neutral pronouns to appropriately address a metagender individual.

Our first special guest for the European leg of our travels is a metagender individual named P. Sufenas Virius Lupus, here to talk about working with the deities of the ancient world for LGBT+ spells. A polytheist, Antinoan, *fili* and *gentlidecht* practitioner, e has been practicing polytheism for more than twenty-four years, and is an author, poet, and professor with a PhD in Celtic civilizations. E has written eight books and has essays, fiction, and poetry in many periodicals and collections, and e also appeared on five episodes of *The New Thinking Allowed* with Dr. Jeffrey Mishlove. For us here, e is going to lend eir expertise by talking about homoerotic love spells in the classical world.

Love spells have been common in many cultures throughout time. While interesting in themselves for a number of reasons, one of the most signifi-cant in the present context is that they offer a unique opportunity—even if they are done by set formulae that were traditional and even prescribed by professional magicians—to read the names of actual individuals who wished to engage in homoerotic relationships (whether purely sexual or otherwise). One question to ask oneself is what deities people called upon to assist them in attempting to gain the attentions of their potential lovers in these homoerotic relationships. Sometimes no deities are invoked at all, but other times they are. Much of what is discussed in the following can be found in Hans Dieter Betz's The Greek Magical Papyri, *John C. Gager's* Curse Tablets and Binding Spells of the Ancient World, *and Bernadette Brooten's* Love Between Women.*

Greek and Graeco-Egyptian deities are the most common. Hermes is called upon in one spell, along with Anubis; Anubis and Serapis (and/or Osiris) are called in another, and the Erinyes—The Furies—are called in the same spell. Remember: these love spells were not celebrations with hearts and flowers; they were binding curses that were intended to torment one's target into succumbing to one's advances—something that does not easily recommend itself in the modern period!

Two other matters are noteworthy, however. One might ask whether or not deities who have attested homoerotic relationships were called upon in these circumstances. Hermes is certainly one such deity, but what of others? Antinous is invoked in one love spell—along with Hermes, Anu-bis, Thoth, Pluto, Adonis, and Kore-Persephone-Ereshkigal (!)—but very interestingly, despite Antinous's fame as the deified lover of the Roman emperor Hadrian, his name is invoked in this love spell to bind a woman named Ptolemaïs to a man named Sarapammon. Deities involved in love, it seems, did not discriminate based on sexual orientation.

The final example of a deity may surprise many. Abraxas is given as an epithet in one spell which primarily invokes the Hebrew God under the names Adonai and Sabaos to bring about love between two men. In another spell, a series of male-and-female "rightful" pairings of animals is given in a love spell of a man trying to attract a woman, but in the string of such animal pairings, Iao Sabaoth (the common Greco-Roman-Egyptian rendering of the Hebrew God's name) is given in the female position, and Moses is given in the male position. Thus, not only is the Hebrew God invoked to bring about love and sex between two men, but the Hebrew God himself is said to have had such an attraction for Moses. This is something one will never hear in a church or a synagogue when gay marriage is debated, needless to say!

When crafting spells that invoke deities to assist one in gaining relationships, or in sustaining and blessing them, or even in creating rituals for same-sex marriages, remember that there is no reason that any deity might not be brought into the effort. While the deities themselves will have the final say, certainly, there is no reason that Zeus and Ganymede would be more appropriate for a gay marriage than Zeus and Hera, or that Artemis and Persephone might not equally be suited to blessing a lesbian marriage.

—P. Sufenas Virius Lupus

WISDOM OF A WELSH DRUID DRAG QUEEN

Up next, all the way from the Isle of Anglesey off the coast of North Wales, is my friend Kristoffer Hughes. What makes him marvelously unique is that in addition to being a gay/trans member of our global community, he is also Chief of the Anglesey Druid Order (a polytheistic Welsh Celtic Pagan community), a coroner, a drag queen, and an award-winning author. Taking time away from his uniquely diverse activities as well as from his husband of twenty-five years and his cat, Kristoffer is here to tell us a little story about how Paganism, magic, and drag turned his life around for the better.

My teenage years were difficult. I was tall, clumsy looking, and shy, and whilst I did not want to stand out, I did, and mostly for all the wrong reasons—or so I was led to believe. To top it all off, like icing on a gigantic 6 foot 3-inch fairy cake, I was gay. However, being gay was only half the issue; the other was that I felt different. I saw the world through different eyes to my peers; the lofty green mountains and its deep forests called to me—they would sing to my soul and warm my heart, whereas the church left me feeling cold, ostracized, and unacceptable. I struggled to balance who I wanted to be and who other people wanted me to be. North Wales barely had anything resembling a gay scene, and even when I found it further afield, I did not feel a part of it. I never could see myself as a beautiful person. I have struggled with my weight all my life, and I have a food addiction that still binds me. My weight and body type caused me to distance myself from the body-perfect perception I had of the gay community. I hurt. Did I fit in anywhere?

It was Paganism, magic, and drag that turned my life around, from an insecure, shy, scared teenager into a confident man and drag queen. I met archetypes and deities whose gender identities were fluid, not set in stone; their tales inspired me to look closely at my own gender issues from another angle. I discovered a freedom of expression within Paganism that differed greatly from the oppression I felt in mainstream religious traditions. However, I also felt different to other people in the local gay community. I loved shoes, makeup, hair, colour, and so I worked to my strengths, a powerful magical ability—to make people laugh and forget the tribulations of life for a while. Through drag I learnt that what other people thought of me was actually none of my business. I could be who I wanted to be: this is my life, I am responsible for writing its pages, this is the magic of empowerment. Under the colour and glamour of drag I could be beautiful—was and am beautiful. Becoming a drag queen gave me the power to transform my life, to find an unapologetic expression. The art of drag became a fundamental part of my life and of my spirituality; not only did it take courage and brevity to perform, it also brought pleasure to others and, of course, to me. It also offset some of the anxiety I felt for having been so different to my peers. I have grown older and perhaps wiser but have lost none of the wonder that my life as a gay man and a fierce drag queen has brought to this living. I cannot cure the world of its sorrows, but I can choose to live with joy.

—KRISTOFFER HUGHES

BEING A BLATINA BISEXUAL
IN THE CATHOLIC CHURCH

To round out our tour of Europe, I have here with us someone I've known pretty much all my life: my cousin Leah Gonzales. Not unique among our family, we are both biracial children. While we differ in that I'm white/Mexican and she's black/Mexican, we both are queer individuals and grew up heavily influenced by our Latina mothers' side in the Catholic Church. As we grew into adulthood, though, I slowly became less and less Catholic, but she remained ever committed to our natal religion. Juggling the dualities of being a woman who is both black and Latina is hard enough, let alone being attracted to both men and women and being a devout Catholic. So I'll join you in the audience now since, truth be told, I've never heard this story either, but I have always been curious as to how a bisexual woman of two colors has kept the faith for so long.

> *As early as elementary, I knew that I was attracted to both males and females. However, growing up in a traditional Latino Catholic home, I never thought about acting upon these feelings, nor did I allow it to affect my views as a Catholic. I never missed church growing up and attended both Sunday school and weekly catechism classes. It was not until I was in high school where I was at a crossroads between who I was religiously and who I chose to love. I was taught that you get your sacraments to ultimately get married in the church and then have a family with someone of the opposite sex. A part of me thought that if I date only men I would not have to worry about it conflicting with the beliefs of my family and church.*
>
> *My main questions were: Is it wrong to have these feelings and would I be allowed or welcomed in the church if I ever were to come out as a bisexual?*

I always feared that by truly revealing myself to my family, my faith and the values they taught me would be questioned. However, this never changed me going to church because I felt that who I choose to love should not affect my spirituality. After years of being in the closet, I finally had the courage to come out to my family.

Though I was nervous, they showed me that regardless of who I love, my love of God should never change. Sometime after I came out and was asked to be a part of this project, a Gospel during Mass really hit home for me. It was Matthew 5:14–16, which says: "You are the light of the world. A town built on a hill cannot be hidden. Neither do people light a lamp and put it under a bowl. Instead they put it on its stand, and it gives light to everyone in the house. In the same way, let your light shine before others, that they may see your good deeds and glorify your Father in heaven."

Then the priest said the words that basically sum up the reason why I continue to be Catholic: "Light comes in many different forms, but its primary purpose is to enhance other objects in the room; we are here to enhance our diversity and share our commonality in loving God and embracing his love."

In that moment I knew that after all these years seeing so many different people in my church regardless of race, sexuality, or income, they were all there for the same reason. I am a bisexual Catholic woman of color because though some people may judge me for who I am and who I choose to love, God will love me unconditionally and I will do the same.

—LEAH GONZALES

PART 4

THE INDIAN SUBCONTINENT

Citizens with this kind of homosexual inclination,
who renounce women and can do without them
willingly because they love one another, get married
together, bound by a deep and trusting friendship.
KAMA SUTRA

Our global trek now takes us eastward into India. In addition to being its own unique subcontinent, it is the homeland of two of the world's most ancient religions that are still actively practiced on a grand scale: Hinduism and Buddhism. The latter is generally more associated in our modern world with East Asia, where it has taken strong root and flourished, but its origin and foundations came from India and out of the even more ancient practice of Hinduism. Hinduism, for its part, is the dominant religion in the region today, so it's fitting that we explore that one first.

12
HINDUISM

Cultural

The queer cultural history within Hinduism is one of ambivalence. On the one hand, its homoerotic practices and mysticisms are extremely evident, but on the other hand, any association of queerness has been vehemently denied throughout much of India's history. Even in modern democratic India, LGBT+ rights are a hot-button issue whose liberalization and criminalization ebb and flow like the tide.

One of the main reasons for this appears to be the issue of labeling. Since ancient times, queerness has played an outward role in Hindu tradition. Even in the *Kama Sutra*, the legendary how-to book on mate attraction and lovemaking, its second-century author details male-male and female-female intimate acts and describes effeminate and masculine third-gender individuals as well as lesbians who were referred to as a *svair-ini* (independent woman).[142] Nevertheless, all forms of queerness are neither seen nor acknowledged under our modern labels of LGBT+, and so when modern Indian society discusses the issue of LGBT+ rights, it becomes contentious and confusing because who and/or what does Hindu culture consider LGBT+?

The most internationally famous example of LGBT+ Hindus are the *hijra*. In the simplest of explanations, a hijra is what we'd recognize as a transgender woman. In India and Pakistan they are legally recognized as a unique gender separate from male and female, and their presence in the region has existed since antiquity, even being documented in the *Kama Sutra,* where they are shown taking both the active and passive roles in sexual intercourse. Although ostracized by most of society, they tend to live in all-hijra communities and work as prostitutes for survival. While some hijras eventually get married to heterosexual men, most simply have noncommitted sexual relations with men, and these men, so long as they act as the "tops," socially maintain their heterosexuality and masculinity in the eyes of Hindu society. Most of these men tend to be married to biological females and carry out their extramarital affairs with hijra mistresses in secret.[143]

What makes hijras a prime example of labeling confusion is the fact that they do not consider themselves as homo- *or* heterosexual. Biologically, they are what Westeners consider males (and sometimes intersex), and sexually, their desire for other biological males would make them homosexuals in Western eyes. But since they are culturally seen as neither males nor females, their sexual desires cannot be labeled as gay or straight. In fact, the self-defining characteristic of being a hijra is being born as a biological male yet not sexually desiring women. To be gay would mean being

142   Parin Shah, "Homosexuality and the Hindu Society," *Random Rants*, Feb. 6, 2016, https://parinvshah.wordpress.com/2016/02/06/homosexuality-and -the-hindu-society/ (accessed Feb. 12, 2017).
143   Serena Nanda, "Hijra and Sadhin," in *Constructing Sexualities*, ed. S. LaFont (Upper Saddle River: Pearson Education, 2002).

born a male and sexually desiring another male—and therein lies all the difference. The Western world doesn't make a distinction between men not being sexually attracted to women and men being sexually attracted to other men; they are simply assumed to go hand in hand. But in Hindu culture, they are distinctly different classifications of sexuality and sexual identity.[144]

Because of Hindu society's historical lack of acknowledging homosexuality as opposed to the more nebulous "non-heterosexuality," legal recognition and protections are largely absent in the subcontinent. Consequently, India has experienced a growing movement of men who identify as "gay" in the Western sense of the word who aim to make the vocabulary and concept more mainstream so that they can obtain much-needed government recognition and protection. The success of their movement has been both widely beneficial and widely detrimental to gay Hindu society.

It has been beneficial in the sense that homosexuality and gayness are now widely understood and recognized as an actual sexual preference, thus making advocacy for gay rights much easier and more organized. However, it has been detrimental in the sense that it's also responsible for the growing trend of shame and disapproval associated with being gay in Hindu society. The reasoning for this might seem odd at first, but it's similar to the viewpoint of non-native homosexuality shared by many African nationalist movements. Since the modern notions and labels of gayness and homosexuality were historically never recognized as a distinct sexual orientation in precolonial India, it is seen as a Western import from the era of British colonial rule.[145]

Nevertheless, if we look into Hindu cultural mythology, we find numerous examples of queerness, transgenderism, and homoeroticism between the gods. At times the gods condone acts of gayness among each other, and at other times they vehemently disapprove, thus making the theologically

144   Roscoe, *Queer Spirits*.

145   Sheena Asthana and Robert Oostvogels, "The Social Construction of Male 'Homosexuality' in India: Implications for HIV Transmission and Prevention," *Social Sciences & Medicine* 52:5 (2001).

sanctioned attitude toward queerness in Hindu society one of moral ambiguity. Still, sexuality is never considered a static thing. Just like the gods, mortals, too, can change their sex, and through the belief of reincarnation, it is generally accepted that one has been male and female and third gender many times over in the wheel of samsara.

In fact, within the pantheon of the many deities that are in Hinduism, there exists a god who represents the infinity that lies beyond the duality of male and female. This special divinity is Ardhanarishvara, whose name best translates to "the lord who is half woman." This deity is considered to be simultaneously man and woman and is seen as the fusion of Shiva (god of creation and destruction) and his lover Parvati (mother goddess of fertility, love, and devotion). Hindus look to Ardhanarishvara as an intercessor that bridges the gaps between seemingly opposite things such as between men and women and between mortals and gods.[146]

Despite the myriad of sexually fluid gods and innumerable gender transformations of mortals and gods in Hindu mythology and texts, which we will explore in a second, modern Hindu culture is quite hostile toward the queer community. The major cultural shift of Hindus condemning queerness as a social evil largely came about in the 1920s, 30s, and 40s spearheaded by, of all people, Mohandas Gandhi. For all his virtues, Gandhi had many faults, and one of them was his vociferous homophobia, which historians generally believe he developed from his years of being educated in Britain, where homosexuality was a known thing and ingrained into him as utterly deplorable.

As the leader of India's independence movement from Great Britain, Gandhi advocated for a return to traditional Hindu values and ways of life and against all things seen as a negative British import, homosexuality being one of them. To help disassociate homosexuality with Hinduism and emphasize its association with colonial rule, he ordered his followers to go through Hindu temples and destroy all artwork and literature that represented homoerotic acts or positive references to transgender-

---

146 Krish Jeyakumar, "Ardhanarishvara," *Beyond the Binary*, Sept. 12, 2016,
     http://beyondthebinary.co.uk/ardhanarishvara/ (accessed Aug. 19, 2017).

ism and homosexuality as understood in Western terms. Thanks to the intervention of philosopher and writer Sir Rabindranath Tagore, many of these sacred sites were saved from such queerphobic vandalism, but in the psyche of Hindu society the damage was already done. Blind idolatry of Gandhi made his teachings nearly infallible, and thus his position on homosexuality as a Western-imported plague upon Indian society became unofficial cultural doctrine that still survives today in the subcontinent.[147]

Hindu Takeaway:
SACREDNESS OF THE DIVINE FEMININE

We haven't really talked about this in Hinduism yet, but it's a major recurring theme in the upcoming deities and legends section. Forgive me for jumping the gun a bit, but it's an important lesson. As you'll see, many of the Hindu male gods honor the sacredness of their own femininity.

This is similar yet opposite to the divine masculine takeaway we learned from the Vikings. This time we have to learn to accept the divine feminine in the form of our own inner effeminacy and attraction toward effeminacy. For gay men in particular, this is often difficult. The cult of masculinity places a high value on masculine men: being tall, muscular, with facial hair, the more like a "straight man" the better. Many gay men don't want to be seen as effeminate because they associate effeminacy with weakness. But, in fact, being an effeminate man is highly courageous and transgressive. In a society of toxic masculinity, it is an act of rebellion to be a male that embraces his own inner feminine, a very punk-rock statement to society. Many Hindu male deities exemplify this in spades; on the mortal plane, revolutionary artists Prince and David Bowie perfectly embodied how a man's embracing of his inner effeminacy exuded an even more powerful sexual masculinity.

---

147 Amara Das Wilhelm, "India's Slow Descent into Homophobia," *GALVA-108: Gay & Lesbian Vaishnava Association*, 2014, http://www.galva108.org/single -post/2014/05/09/Indias-Slow-Descent-Into-Homophobia (accessed Aug. 19, 2017).

Women are not exempt from this, either. In a time where women are still having to fight for their equality, those women who embrace feminine stereotypes are seen as traitors. Beauty pageant contestants, girls obsessed with the color pink, cheerleaders, and more are all seen as empty, vapid, and shallow in the eyes of many progressive women. There is nothing wrong with women openly embracing stereotypically effeminate things. People like what they like, and as long as they aren't actively trying to turn back the clock on women's rights, let them enjoy what makes them happy. The divine feminine comes in many forms.

And this all goes for magic, too. Think of the well-known goddesses Aphrodite and Artemis. They're two very different aspects of the divine feminine, but is any one form better than the other? When we do spell-work, especially queer spellwork, we have to be open to the dynamic range in which feminine energy can present itself. It can just as easily manifest in a warrior woman as it can in a beauty queen or even in a male who honors and unleashes his inner divine feminine, as many of the Hindu deities do.

So, for your next magical activity, do a ritual in your tradition that honors the most stereotypically effeminate deity in your pantheon. The "dark" goddesses and more transgressive female deities are usually the most popular, but the pretty-in-pink ultra-femme ones are just as divine. Again, all deities can teach us something, so get in touch with the most effeminate one you know and see what there is to learn.

Deities & Legends

AGNI

Agni is the god of fire, wealth, and creativity. He is an interesting queer Hindu deity because he engages in homoerotic acts not for reasons of sensual pleasure but for reasons of magic. Appearance-wise, he is depicted as somewhat of a wanderer with a long beard and riding atop a ram, but he also has flaming red skin, multiple arms, several tongues, and sometimes two faces. While he is technically the husband of the goddess Svaha, he is often shown having a side relationship with Soma, god of the moon, where he delights in swallowing Soma's semen.

Agni's thirst for semen doesn't end there, though. Another major myth involves him volunteering to accept the semen of Shiva (god of creation and destruction) after Shiva is forbidden to ejaculate into Parvati (mother goddess) due to the other gods' fear that if they conceive, their child would be too powerful. So, Shiva gets around this prohibition by using the pull-out method and having Agni eagerly catch his divine semen and lap it up. Modern mythographers believe Agni's obsession with semen represents sacrifices to the gods, usually done by tossing the sacrifice into a fire.[148]

In worship, Agni's correspondences are staffs, rams, and fire. He is particularly celebrated in rituals involving fire, especially rite-of-passage ceremonies and cremations.

GANESHA

As the god of wisdom, beginnings, removing obstacles, and prosperity, Ganesha is one of Hinduism's most popular deities. To non-Hindus he is easily recognizable as being the chubby deity with four arms and an elephant head. Generally, he is thought to be androgynous more than anything since his head is that of a female elephant, yet his body is of a human male. And because he is overweight, his chest has the appearance of "man boobs" that are sometimes believed to lactate, further adding to his androgyny. And while his trunk is often seen as a phallic symbol, it is always depicted as flaccid and never erect, as are most Hindu phallic symbols.

Ganesha is also deity of the root chakra, which is located at the perineum, between the genitals and anus. Because of this, he is said to preside over ritualistic anal sex among certain cults in an effort to release Kundalini energy. And because of his notoriety for having the power to

148 Amara Das Wilhelm, "Hindu Deities and the Third Sex (2)," *GALVA-108: Gay & Lesbian Vaishnava Association*, 2014, http://www.galva108.org/single-post/2014/05/04/Hindu-Deities-and-the-Third-Sex-2 (accessed Aug. 19, 2017).

both bless and curse as well as crossing the boundary between masculinity and femininity, he is associated with eunuchs, who, in Indian society, are also believed to have those same magical abilities.[149]

In worship, his correspondences are elephants, mice, axes, nooses, hibiscus, and the colors red and yellow. His devotees are known to leave offerings of modak dumplings and chant the sacred sound "om/aum."

KRISHNA

Like Ganesha, Krishna is another popular Hindu deity who is also well-known to Westerners thanks to the popularity of the Hare Krishna movement in the West since the 1960s. He is the god of love, beauty, knowledge, and divinity. He is portrayed as blue-skinned and forever young. Involved in countless myths, he is commonly known to change his gender and be sexually fluid, seducing anyone and everyone regardless of gender, as befitting a deity of love. In one myth he even seduces himself and makes love to his own reflection in a lake.

Many of Krishna's devotees see him as the symbol of feminine masculinity, the supreme representation of a man embracing the divine feminine within him. It is further believed that all men are like this underneath their self-imposed macho exterior, and to strive for this balance of gentle femininity and sexualized masculinity is a goal for his male worshippers.[150]

In worship, his correspondences are butter, flutes, rubies, basil, bees, and cows. His circular, sharp-edged throwing weapon, the chakram, is well-known to the LGBT+ community as the signature weapon of the 1990s lesbian pop culture icon Xena, warrior princess.

149 Christopher Penczak, *Gay Witchcraft: Empowering the Tribe* (San Francisco: Red Wheel/Weiser, 2003).

150 Devdutt Pattanaik, *The Man Who Was a Woman and Other Queer Tales from Hindu Lore* (New York: Routledge, 2012).

SHIKHANDI

In the *Mahabharata* Shikhandi is a female-to-male transgender hero. According to the texts, Shikhandi, in a past life, was once a woman who obsessed over avenging her honor after the great warrior Bhishma publicly rejected her and deemed her unmarriageable. Being but a mere woman (because remember, this all took place in ancient India), she had no way of enacting her revenge over the mighty Bhishma and ended up killing herself after Krishna promised that her reincarnation would be able to carry out the vendetta.

But in a plot twist for the ages, Shikhandi is reincarnated as a biological female again, rather than as a male, as she was led to believe. She was adopted by King Drupada who, desiring an heir, raised her as he would a son, fooling everyone into believing that Shikhandi was actually a boy. Eventually he married her off to a princess who finds out about Shikhandi's true gender and complains to her own father that they've been duped. Fearing her father-in-law's wrath, Shikhandi runs off to the forest, where a sympathetic nature spirit agrees to swap sexes with her. Now a biological male, Shikhandi finds himself in the epic battle of Mahabharat, wherein he plays a pivotal role in bringing about the demise of Bhishma, just as Krishna had foretold.[151]

151   Krishna Dharma, *Mahabharata: The Greatest Spiritual Epic of All Time* (Imperial Beach: Torchlight Publishing, 1999).

13
BUDDHISM

Cultural

What makes Buddhism different from any other religion we've explored thus far is the fact that it's much more philosophical and based on logic. Aside from reincarnation and the attainment of nirvana, Buddhism isn't really too preoccupied with the hereafter. Its focus is on the here and now, seeing the world as it is and adjusting one's thinking and mental outlook to get through this thing called life as smoothly as possible.

At first glance, the four noble truths that dictate the non-sugarcoated reality of the world may seem ultra pessimistic. They essentially point out that (1) life is suffering; (2) suffering is caused by our desires; (3) if we want to rid ourselves of suffering, we have to rid ourselves of desire; and

(4) the noble eightfold path (Buddha's personal recommendations of ways to stop desiring stuff) is the best way to go about doing it.

Without the threat of afterlife punishment to keep us in line, the LGBT+ community is free to be themselves in the Buddhist faith. Everyone's path to nirvana is different because we all have our own unique upbringings, circumstances, demons, and past karma to overcome. Thus, there is no set road that any divinity mandates you follow. Rather, Buddha simply suggested that if you follow the middle way (an avoidance of extremes), there will be less suffering in your life and it'll be easier to attain enlightenment. But if you don't, then no worries—you'll reincarnate into this world over and over under various different circumstances until you eventually do get it right.

The man himself, Siddhartha Gautama (aka the Buddha), was personally very open to LGBT+ people, but there were times when he placed practicality over total equality. As pro-queer, he accepted anyone as a disciple as long as they were committed to striving for enlightenment. Even one's sexual orientation didn't matter since never in his teachings did he distinguish homosexual sex as different from heterosexual sex. Really, he was against labels of all kinds, as evident in his disapproval of India's caste system, slavery, racism, and nationalism.[152]

Another pro-queer attribute of the Buddha was his own appearance. From multiple sources of his contemporaries, they all say the same thing: Siddhartha Gautama was sexy as hell. Now, if you're thinking of that big-bellied image of Buddha, that isn't him; that's a bodhisattva called Budai, akin to a saint in the Catholic sense, but more on bodhisattvas when we reach East Asia.

The real Buddha was documented to be very tall, with great skin complexion, an athletic build from outdoor activity, and a mesmerizingly masculine sense of calm assertiveness. Men and women alike would all make particular mention of how attractive he was, and of course the Buddha had to be aware of it. In fact, Buddhist historians generally agree that he

152 Donald Lopez, *Buddhist Scriptures* (New York: Penguin Classics, 2004).

knew his sex appeal attracted people's attention, so he purposely used his good looks to get attention from women and men—whatever worked to get people to listen to him and his teachings. In a sense, one could argue that he directly marketed himself to the gay community in order to spread his message. And although it would make sense to reason that, as the leader of a religion, people would exaggerate their flattery of the Buddha's appearance, all descriptions of him weren't flattering, as evidenced by contemporaries' later descriptions of him in old age as withered and unattractive, like he had been when he was in his prime.[153]

Still, on the anti-queer side, he was very exclusionary with his monastic orders. Remember, in Hindu India there was already a social recognition of alternate genders beyond male and female, and it was these alternate genders that the Buddha didn't allow to join the monastic life known as the sangha. He specifically forbade anyone who did not identify as what we would call a cisgender person from entering the sangha. Nevertheless, for a long time this exclusion has been seen as a pragmatic practicality of the times. The sanghas were just being started, and because of their nature, they relied heavily on financial assistance from the lay community. Buddhist scholars believe that although the Buddha very obviously approved of all people of alternate genders, it was too controversial to have them be a part of the ordained community. Accepting women was revolutionary enough already, but the unpopularity of alternate genders would prevent laypeople from supporting the sanghas during their most critical years of infancy.[154]

Outside of India, the spread of Buddhism eastward into various cultures resulted in three very distinct forms: Vajrayana, Theravada, and Mahayana. Vajrayana Buddhism is the type found in Tibet. Although it has the smallest number of followers, internationally it is the best-known type

153 S. Dhammika, *The Buddha and His Disciples* (Singapore: Buddha Dhama Mandala Society, 2005), http://www.buddhanet.net/pdf_file/bud-disciples.pdf (accessed Nov. 11, 2016).

154 Peter Harvey, *An Introduction to Buddhist Ethics* (New York: Cambridge University Press, 2000).

of Buddhism thanks to its charismatic leader, the Dalai Lama. Theravada is the type found in Southeast Asian countries such as Thailand, Laos, and Cambodia, and it is the most visually iconic of all Buddhist traditions in pop culture due to its famous use of shaved heads and orange togas. Mahayana Buddhism is the type of Buddhism found in East Asian countries such as China, Korea, and Japan. It constitutes the majority of modern Buddhists, but more on that one when we get to East Asia.

Vajrayana Buddhism has a wobbly love-hate relationship with LGBT+ people. As the most hierarchical denomination of Buddhism, the Dalai Lama is the ultimate authority on Vajrayana ethics and morality. In general terms, the ultimate goal of a follower of Vajrayana is to obtain Buddhahood, but unlike more popular traditions where one must strive to obtain Buddhahood via enlightenment, the Vajrayana school of thought is that we are all born into this world enlightened, and obtaining Buddhahood is just a matter of realizing one's own inherent Buddha nature.[155]

To help awaken to one's Buddha nature, reading Buddhist texts is heavily emphasized in Vajrayana. Unfortunately, these Vajrayana texts were written long ago in a less tolerant time, and they tend to fill in the Buddha's silence about LGBT+ people with their own distorted cultural prejudices of the time. Because of this, the current Dalai Lama (Tenzin Gyatso) has a history of playing both sides of the fence on the topic of queerness. In his personal point of view, there is nothing evil or bad about LGBT+ people, and, with his bully pulpit of constantly being in the international limelight, he has advocated for the full equality on all levels for LGBT+ people. However, because Vajrayana Buddhism is heavily reliant on its own sacred texts that don't see queerness in the most positive of lights, he also admits that nonheterosexual intercourse is technically a sin. To smooth out any anti-LGBT+ sentiments that might be perceived of him and Buddhism in general, he has made an effort to point out, through his iconic use of spotlighting irony, that almost all Buddhists sin in one way or another, and in comparison to all the things one could do that Vajrayana

155 Tenzin Palmo, *Reflections on a Mountain Lake: Teachings on Practical Buddhism* (Ithaca: Snow Lion Publications, 2002).

Buddhism disapproves of, loving a person of the same sex is pretty low on the totem pole of egregiousness.[156]

Down in Southeast Asia, the Theravada branch of Buddhism has been historically less jovial and ambivalent toward the queer community. Speaking in generalities, Theravada Buddhism differs from other denominations of Buddhism in three main philosophical ways. First, their sacred texts are seen as containing the ultimate and entire truth to enlightenment and are therefore taken much more literally than the other Buddhist branches. Second, because the texts are perfect and all-encompassing, there is little to no emphasis on the musings of ascended masters. Lastly, rather than the gradual attainment of enlightenment, Theravada Buddhism emphasizes enlightenment as an all-or-nothing understanding that comes at a singular instant. You either get it or you don't; there is no in-between.

Their attitude toward LGBT+ people is equally different and severe. At best, being queer is seen as a karmic consequence of having been a wicked person in one's previous life, and while queer sexual desire and self-expression is to be abhorred, LGBT+ people are more to be pitied than scorned. At worst, being queer is seen as a disgusting and voluntary preference for perversion that is the result of few morals and an inability to control unnatural desire.[157]

Buddhist Takeaway:
THE POWER QUESTION

From its inception, Buddha framed his teachings as logical solutions to mitigate and remedy the sufferings of life. His approach is much akin to a

---

156 Dennis Conkin, "Dalai Lama Urges 'Respect, Compassion, and Full Human Rights for All,' Including Gays," *Bay Area Reporter*, June 19, 1997, http://quietmountain.org/links/teachings/gayrites.htm (accessed Nov. 14, 2016); David Shankbone, "Dalai Lama's Representative Talks About China, Tibet, Shugden and the Next Dalai Lama," *Wikinews*, Nov. 14, 2007, https://en.wikinews.org/wiki/Dalai_Lama%27s_representative_talks_about_China,_Tibet,_Shugden_and_the_next_Dalai_Lama (accessed Nov. 14, 2016).

157 Peter Jackson, "Thai Buddhist Accounts of Male Homosexuality and AIDS in the 1980s," *The Australian Journal of Anthropology* 6:3 (1995), http://ccbs.ntu.edu.tw/FULLTEXT/JR-EPT/anth.htm (accessed Nov. 14, 2016).

doctor treating an illness. If you feel sick, there is a singular cause at the root of your suffering. There are numerous symptoms and ways to treat the sickness, but if you look at things logically, by exploring your past (where you've been and what you've done), you can pinpoint the problematic root and treat it directly. So, to solve a problem that is causing us pain, Buddhists ask themselves the power question: "What is so?"

This is the reverse of the Power of the Lens takeaway we learned in ancient Egypt. By adopting different lenses, we can see a thing in different ways, but the power question is the removal of all lenses to see a thing as it actually is, without bias, without it being obscured by emotion, without any assumption of meaning whatsoever.

On a daily queer level, we have to ask ourselves "What is so?" in order to prevent victimizing assumptions. I'll give you a quick example from my own life. When my queerness became more apparent to my family, I was hurt that my parents weren't more supportive and that it was an uncomfortable topic for them. With my ego and emotions, I assumed this was because they disapproved and were unhappy with me. As I grew older, I found out that this was not so. The real root cause for their lack of enthusiasm was their fear for me. They knew that their little boy would have a more difficult time at life than most people. I would have to fight harder, suffer from grand prejudices, and be the target of hate. Because they loved me, they worried for me and didn't want me to have the additional discriminatory burden of being queer when life in general is tough enough already. Therefore, the extra hardship I would inevitably experience because of my queerness was the cause of what made them unenthusiastic. If I had asked myself "What is so?" and not allowed my emotions to assume the root cause of the problem, it would've saved me many angry years. Remember to ask yourself this power question and not be the victim of everything you think.

So, for your next magical activity, practice the habit of asking yourself "What is so?" before doing any and all spellwork. Remove your ego and emotions, which often blind you to what's really going on. Since magic is often utilized to solve a problem, being able to look at a problem as it is, without emotional bias, allows us to pinpoint what exactly is going on and thus be more direct and efficacious with our magic. Otherwise, if we let our ego and emotions dictate the entirety of spellworking, we may be exerting energy and effort to problems that don't actually exist or we may be manifesting solutions to the symptoms and not the root problem itself.

Deities & Legends

ANANDA

Despite his scandalous associations, Ananda holds a very important place in the historical establishment of Buddhism. Not only was he the Buddha's cousin, but he was also the smartest of the Buddha's ten principle disciples. He was held in high esteem due to his incredible memory, and during the First Buddhist Council that was established to collect and organize all of the Buddha's teachings soon after his death, Ananda's memory played an invaluable part in transferring his late cousin's oral teachings into writings for posterity. However, he is also credited by many to be the Buddha's same-sex lover due to the special closeness and fondness they shared for one another that, to a good number of contemporary onlookers, had an erotic tinge to it.

To backtrack for a second, Ananda was one of the Buddha's closest advisors. He was family, he was incredibly smart, with a phenomenal memory, and the years of growing up together allowed the Buddha to trust him more readily than his other followers, who were originally strangers to him. Thus, in developing his philosophy, Ananda was the person whom the Buddha trusted to bounce ideas off of and talk through things, and he even took advice from him, most famously in the admitting of women into the monastic life of the sangha, a position fiercely advocated by Ananda.

The sexual side of their relationship seems extra salacious to most people nowadays because on top of being gay, it is technically an incestual one. But, remember, 400s BCE India was a very different time. In Indian literature chronicling the Buddha's past lives, collectively known as the *Jataka*, the Buddha always had a male companion with whom he was very compassionately physical, and so to many Indian Buddhists, Ananda was the male lover of the Buddha's final incarnation before enlightenment. In Vajrayana Buddhism he is often portrayed as the archetype for the grieving widow, as evidenced by the scriptures' reference of him as the one who lamented the most and had the hardest time accepting and getting over the Buddha's death, presumably because they were lovers. In Theravada Buddhism Ananda's queerness continues into his later reincarnations, where he is said to have returned as women, transgendered persons, and homosexuals.[158]

AVALOKITESHVARA

Avalokiteshvara is a special gender-bending bodhisattva (ascended master) in Buddhism who has the uniqueness of his gender transformations being the result of his emotional state rather than voluntary will. A crude pop culture comparison would be the Hulk, the superhero whose transformation is involuntarily caused by his emotional anger.

Avalokiteshvara's default gender is generally seen as male, and his constant male state is maintained by this constant, warriorlike protectiveness toward all those who follow him. Nevertheless, whenever he is overcome with compassion for others, especially children, he turns into a female named Guanyin (also spelled Kwan Yin or Quan Yin). Visually, she is portrayed as having one thousand arms (symbolic of the ability to help all). As we'll see when we arrive in East Asia, Guanyin was eventually adopted by Taoists as a stand-alone deity, although to Buddhists she is still the female side of the bodhisattva Avalokiteshvara.[159]

158 Donald L. Boisvert and Jay Emerson Johnson, *Queer Religion Vol.1* (Santa Barbara: Praeger, 2011); Yudit Kornberg Greenberg, *Encyclopedia of Love in World Religions* (Santa Barbara: ABC-CLIO, 2007).

159 Paul Hedges, "Guanyin, Queer Theology, and Subversive Religiosity: An Experiment in Interreligious Theology," in *Interreligious Hermeneutics in Pluralistic Europe: Between Texts and People*, ed. David Cheetham (Amsterdam: Rodopi, 2011).

14

INDIAN SUBCONTINENTAL MAGICAL COMMUNITY

HINDU PUJA RITUAL FOR OUR INNER DIVINE QUEERNESS

Here to help explore Indian queer magic, I have enlisted the help of Ganapati Kamesh, who was named so by Gadadhar Das when he adopted Hinduism as his official religious and spiritual path. He has a long, charitable history of working with his local LGBT+ community, and nowadays Ganapati is a leader of the Shri Ganapatikamesh Matha, which can be found online and whose membership is open to all interested people seeking to learn, explore, and practice Hinduism regardless of race, ethnicity, nationality, sexual orientation, gender identity, economic condition, political affiliation, or any other means by which humanity divides the differences between us. Here as our special guest, Ganapati will be teaching us a Hindu ritual to help us get in touch with, honor, and show love to the divine queerness within us.

Necessary Tools
- *a short table and a cloth*
- *an image (murti); in this case, a mirror*
- *a candle*
- *incense and a holder*
- *fruit and flowers*
- *a plate*
- *a cup of water*
- *a spoon*

Step-by-Step
1. *Place the cloth on the surface of the table.*
2. *Place the mirror in the center top section of the table as the focal point.*
3. *Set the candle to the left of the mirror and the incense holder to the right with incense in it.*
4. *Place the fruit and flowers on the plate and place it in front of the mirror.*
5. *Fill the cup with water and place the spoon in it. Sit it next to the plate.*
6. *Sit in front of the arranged table. Close your eyes, take a deep breath, and then slowly let it out. Begin chanting the mantra "Om Aham Prema" (I Am Love). Do this 12 times. Then say, "Now at this time and on this day in this space I am honored to worship you."*
7. *Light the candle and say, "I am Love offering this light to you."*
8. *Light the incense and wave it clockwise three times in front of the mirror before putting it in the holder and saying, "I am Love offering this incense to you."*

9. With the spoon, put water into it from the cup and move it upward to your reflection in the mirror, saying, "I am Love offering you a sip of cool water to refresh you." Then drink the water from the spoon and place it back in the cup.

10. Take the fruit and hold it before the mirror. Say, "I am Love offering you this fruit, symbolizing the blessings in my life."

11. Take a flower and place it before the mirror, saying, "I am Love offering you this flower, symbolizing the spiritual growth blossoming in my life."

12. Take the spoon and fill with water, repeating step 9.

13. Offer this prayer: "Oh radiant Divinity from which this universe emerges and is sustained, all glories be to you whose very essence is love. May you ever shower me with the blessings of being queer and all that that brings to my life and spiritual progress. May I be true to myself and in so doing be a light shining on others, giving them permission to do the same. May I see you shining in the faces of all who are around me and in every living thing I encounter. Remind me that your light shines in me, too, and that through me you can bring your essence, love, to all. May I never see myself as separate from you. Just like a drop of water in the ocean, so my soul is that drop of water and you are the ocean all around me and in me. Thank you for who I am and for your love and light. Peace, peace, peace."

14. Finish by saying, "Oh God, for I have not been properly instructed on all the rituals and mantras, but please accept this worship as you know my heart and intentions."

—GANAPATI KAMESH

OUT OF THE CLOSET INNER-SELF

Our next special guest came highly recommended to me from a number of people in the know about queer Buddhism. His name is Nikko, and he is a gay cisgender male who has been a practicing Buddhist since the early 1990s, both on his own and with others. But I'll step out of the way now and simply let him tell you more about himself and how Buddhist philosophy helped him accept his inner sacred queerness and come out of the closet.

I grew up feeling awkward, isolated, and different from everyone around me. I was in turn lonely and unable to make meaningful friendships.

I blamed myself for not being accepted by others because, as I convinced myself, I was not good enough. When I hit puberty and realized that I could be also gay, I did everything possible to suppress the feelings. I believed that being LGBT+ would not only make me more ostracized by my peers but also by my family.

Needless to say, I was not a very happy person in the formative years of my youth. I searched for something that could help me.

When I first encountered Buddhist philosophy, I felt that it was something practical. I visited various Buddhist centers and tried different forms of meditation. I found meditation to be hard to do with my restless mind, and the focus I found on eliminating desires also felt like it privileged asceticism, something I wasn't keen on.

After trying several forms of Buddhist practice, I discovered Nichiren Buddhism, which is based on the Lotus Sutra—an ancient Buddhist scripture—as something which could be easily practiced by everyone, no matter their age, sex, or social condition. One of the most impressive teachings of this Buddhism is that everyone has the potential for Buddhahood and is therefore sacred and powerful.

Rather than silent meditation, the main practice of Nichiren Buddhism is the chanting of a mantra out loud (which I will teach you in an upcoming chapter). This chanting practice is like a spiritual workout to help one tap in to their Buddha nature and elevate their life condition with compassion, courage, and wisdom. As Nichiren taught and the Lotus Sutra teaches, this inherent power in everyone can empower individuals to positively transform their karma and lives. Another aspect of Nichiren's teaching is that material desires are not something we need to eliminate but rather transform.

While reading the Lotus Sutra I came across a story about an evil person in the Buddha's time who was described as also having the potential for Buddhahood. Having seen myself as not good enough, this struck me deeply. If evil people have this potential, then so did I, even as a closeted gay person.

I started chanting the mantra consistently on my own in my room in front of a blank wall. I immediately felt better. The more I practiced, the more I began to see positive changes in my life.

Although I had many transformative experiences, one of the most memorable was that I felt my self-esteem strengthen. This led me to finally accept myself as gay, come out to my family and friends, and witness my internalized self-hate and inferiority complexes slowly wither away. Although I still have bouts of these feelings at times, I know that the spiritual workout of chanting the Nichiren Buddhist mantra will reenergize me and enable me to transform sufferings into benefits.

—NIKKO

PART 5

EAST ASIA

Because every portion of the body, mind,
and spirit yearns for the integration of yin
and yang, angelic intercourse is led by the
spirit rather than the sexual organs.
THE HUAHUJING, VERSE 69

Queer East Asia is a paradigm shift away from many of the regions explored thus far. For Westerners, the LGBT+ community is often kept in submissive check through the concept of guilt. A queer person should feel guilty about their sexual orientation and identity because queer acts are personally immoral.

Queer Easterners, however, are kept in check mostly through shame. While guilt is a private, self-negative feeling about personal actions you've done, shame is focused more on feeling bad because of how others perceive you and your personal actions. In the East a person does not necessarily feel guilty about being LGBT+ because queer actions are morally wrong, but rather, they feel ashamed because queerness is socially unacceptable. Thus to be a queer member of an East Asian family is often seen as "bad" because it brings shame upon the family and, consequently, upon those who do business or have associations with the family. So there is a lot of extra familial and external pressure on LGBT+ people to suppress their queerness. But, as we're about to see, not all parts of East Asia at all times felt this way.

15
CHINA

Cultural

China is one of the few nations of the world whose ancient ancestral religions are still practiced by the majority of its modern citizens. Officially, the People's Republic of China is atheist due to communism's Nietzschean preference of science and reason over the perceived superstitions of religion that have been used for centuries by the bourgeoisie to keep the working classes subservient. But that still doesn't stop everyday people from religious practice. For the Chinese, three philosophic schools of thought predominate: Taoism, Confucianism, and Mahayana Buddhism. Most often these are all blended together to form an amalgous hybrid faith, but we'll go through each one individually to highlight their queer implications, starting with what is believed to be the oldest: Taoism.

Taoism is often thought of as being more a philosophy than a religion. Its founder is Lao Tzu, who, being world-weary and jaded from a lifetime of watching humanity fight among itself during the sixth century BCE, was compelled to write down his wisdom before leaving war-torn China for parts unknown. His writings are known as the *Tao Te Ching*, a slim handbook that explains the natural way of things and how to ride the current of life instead of fruitlessly paddling against it and making life difficult for yourself. This natural way of things is known as the Tao; thus, following the Tao is essentially following the natural way of the universe at large.[160]

There are no deities, no discussion of what happens after death, just a focus on the here and now, and how following nature's example is the key to a life of ease. Because of this, there is no mention of queerness or even sexuality. There is even no dictate for what is and is not moral, but rather a warning that straying from the natural flow of the universe will result in bad times. And this is where things get tricky for the LGBT+ Taoist: the interpretation of what constitutes being "natural." Queerness can be witnessed in nature, but the inability to procreate appears to go against how life naturally sustains itself. Since there are no divine mandates, the answer to the "naturalness" of the LGBT+ community really depends upon perspective.

Even the Taoist yin-yang symbol (called the taijitu) has been interpreted as for and against queer "naturalness." We all know the symbol; it's the circle divided into two equal, curved halves, one black (yin) and the other white/red (yang), and within each half there is a smaller circle of the opposite color. Together, the two sides represent the dichotomy of the natural universe and the fact that within each side there exists a bit of the other. Yin is the feminine, passive, emotional, cold, creative side of nature, and yang is the masculine, active, logical, hot, destructive side of

---

160 Derek Lin, *Tao Te Ching: Annotated & Explained* (Woodstock: SkyLight Illuminations, 2006).

nature. Together, they bring balance to the world, and each cannot exist without the other.

To some practitioners, the yin-yang proves that being queer is unnatural since there is a clear division of only two genders, and their union creates the harmonious perfection of life. Yang does not mix with yang, and yin does not mix with yin; each needs its opposite in order to be complete. To other practitioners, however, the yin-yang is proof that being queer is quite natural on two separate levels.

On the first, more superficial level, a same-sex couple is a completion of both yin and yang since there is a passive "bottom" partner and an active "top" partner when making love. Even if both are versatile, the two either take turns being the passive yin and the active yang or they are simultaneously receiving and giving and thus each being the yin and the yang at the same time.

On the more spiritual level, yin and yang are not so much representative of female and male but of the femininity and masculinity of the spirit. The little circles within each half of the yin-yang are the main points of reference for this side of the argument. Individually, a gay man and pre-op transgender female can be seen as a yang body with an inner yin, and a lesbian and pre-op transgender male would be seen as a yin body with an inner yang. An intersex person would be a self-completion of the yin-yang expressed in the self, and a bisexual would be a self-completion of the yin-yang expressed toward others.

To take it a step further, it is argued that the yin-yang is a proponent symbol of being gender fluid since it is representative of the ever flowing and nonstatic nature of all things. And in a certain sense, it subtly asserts that everyone is a little bisexual since both yin and yang are neither pure black nor pure white/red. Each side has a little bit of the other within their center.

Beyond the symbology of the yin-yang, the philosophy of Taoism admits that the true nature of the spiritual Tao is unknowable. The logic is that if humans could fully understand the total spiritual complexity of the Tao, then it wouldn't be the Tao. Since the human mind is limited, and the

Tao is limitless, it is impossible to place any boundaries or labels on what the Tao is or isn't. Human sexuality and identity is akin to the Tao in this way. There is a large, limitless spectrum of possibilities, but no matter how we define or identify ourselves or others, it can never represent the full breadth of possibilities that is human sexuality and identity. Furthermore, our tastes can change, so any answer we give now is never forever permanent.

Still, the philosophy of Taoism eventually led it to grow into a magical practice similar to hermetic alchemy in the West. The more mystical branch of Taoism was often focused on eternal life; for this, male homosexuality was seen as a medicine of sorts, helping to grant immortality (the sexuality of women being seen as unimportant throughout Chinese history until Mao Zedong's establishment of a communist government). In short, a man's semen was seen as his life essence, and if he ejaculated, he was essentially shooting out part of his magic, life-sustaining elixir as "evidenced" by how tired a man would be after rubbing one out. But, of course, that creamy white elixir appeared to only be produced during sexual arousal. Therefore, to produce more life elixir via sexual stimulation without losing any of it via ejaculation was seen as a logical method to lengthen one's life. This was especially so if the arousal was between two men. The yang energy produced by a male lover augmented the yang potency of one's own life elixir—as long as no one ejaculated, of course. [161]

Taoist Takeaway:
GOING WITH THE FLOW OF LIFE

Easily the most immediate takeaway of Taoism is to go with the natural flow of life. Ironically, although this is literally the most natural thing in the world to do, we humans like to complicate things because we either cannot believe that things are that simple or that our problems aren't as unique or as complex as we'd like to think they are.

Queerness is also a natural thing. Too many of us waste precious time and energy fretting "Why am I this way?" or "How can I suppress my

161 Crompton, *Homosexuality and Civilization*.

natural queer tendencies to fit in?" We are how we are for a reason. Trust that you are queer for a reason. Life knows what it's doing, and if you stop suppressing your natural tendencies, you may find out life is easier when you go with the natural flow of the universe.

And think of the art of spellwork, the act of manipulating the natural forces of the world to bring about a specific result. We often don't trust that nature knows what it's doing or don't feel like it's working in our favor, so we have to interfere and change things for our personal benefit. But I'll let you in on a secret: life is *always* working out for the greater good. The more you study magic and the natural sciences, the more you realize that life has a way of working itself out in its own time and on its own accord. The problem is that we want things how we want things when we want them, and sometimes our personal wants are incompatible with the greater good. But the more powerful and wise we become in our magic, we realize that life has everything under control, and we don't have to micromanage everything with magic all the time. Magic can be helpful, but it's never necessary for a healthy, happy life.

So, for this magical activity, try avoiding magic the next time you feel it is a necessary recourse to a specific problem. Yes, magic is a powerful aid, but if we immediately go to it to solve all of our problems all the time, then we lose touch with the universe's natural flow by trying to micro-manage everything. And sometimes coercing a personal win results in the loss of the greater good in ways we cannot see.

Life involves pain. If you never struggle, experience personal loss, or feel pain, then you aren't really experiencing life, you're just living in a bubble separate from the world. So the next time you feel the instinctive need to do magic, hold up a second, stop, and see not only what the problem's existence is trying to teach you, but also how the natural flow of life can solve it for the greater good, without magical manipulation.

CONFUCIANISM

Confucianism was, like Taoism, born from troubling times. Confucius, its eponymous founder, was deeply and personally affected by the endless civil wars ravaging China. However, unlike Lao Tzu, who left society and used nature as a model for harmonious living, Confucius stayed in the thick of things and believed that a rigid social hierarchy that dictated human interactions was the key to harmonious stability. So, as a panacea to the goings-on during his lifetime (551–479 BCE), Confucius established an ethical and moral code that would end the chaos and bring peace back to the land if everyone adhered to it. Its lack of deities, spirituality, discussion of the afterlife, and the Divine make it technically not a religion, even less so than Taoism.

The spread of Confucianism took a while to gain traction, and it contrasted sharply from Taoism. Taoism had a more mystical, laissez-faire, interpretive, and morally ambiguous attitude toward the world, focusing on nature. Confucianism, as an alternative, gave people a direct and straightforward set of conservative social rules to follow and a promise of returning to the good ol' days. As recent times have shown us, this kind of message in uncertain times proved to be very popular.

It should be said, though, that Confucius never lived to see the popularity of his teachings. He died believing himself to be an anonymous failure, and his teachings were never fully compiled until centuries after his death. Coincidentally, in the immediate centuries following Confucius's death, China's internal wars only intensified. Once the Han Dynasty officially came to power in 206 BCE, though, they readily propagated Confucian thought to help normalize peace and order back into society. Confucianism's social conservatism also had the benefit of establishing a pseudo caste system wherein everyone knew their place; in such a society, the Han aristocracy could cement their place at the top.[162]

So, what was Confucius's word on LGBT+ individuals? Nothing. But unlike Taoism's silence toward the queer community generally being

162   Yong Huang, *Confucius: A Guide for the Perplexed* (New York: Bloomsbury Academic, 2013).

interpreted in a positive light, Confucianism's silence has more often been interpreted in a negative light. The reason for this are our old friends shame and the family. Confucius taught that the family was the ideal model for social order, and in addition to outlining every relative's place in the patriarchal family hierarchy, he used it as a metaphor for good government.

So powerfully iconic was Confucianism's use of good government being based upon good family structure that it was used by Justice Anthony Kennedy in the US Supreme Court's majority opinion of the legendary Obergefell v. Hodges decision in 2015 (the one that legalized same-sex marriage throughout the US). Specifically, he wrote: "The centrality of marriage to the human condition makes it unsurprising that the institution has existed for millennia and across civilizations....Confucius taught that marriage lies at the foundation of government."[163]

Ironically, it was this same Confucian logic that pre-Communist China used to suppress LGBT+ rights. A good family was one that did its duties. For the children, it was to unquestioningly obey their parents until they became an adult, at which point they would then marry and produce children of their own, thus adding to the family and strengthening it. If one of those children was queer, then a wrench was thrown into the system by their unwillingness to marry a person of the opposite sex and/or their inability to produce children if they had a same-sex lover. A bisexual child was forced to only marry the opposite sex. Being transgender was simply out of the question since it defied Confucianism's strict, conservative gender hierarchy, where you stay in your place and do not desire to be something else. And, of course, shame was the whip that kept everyone in line.[164]

163 Justice Anthony Kennedy, "Read the Opinion: Supreme Court Rules States Cannot Ban Same-Sex Marriage," *CNN Politics*, June 6, 2015, http://www .cnn.com/2015/06/26/politics/scotus-opinion-document-obergefell -hodges/#document/p8 (accessed Nov. 19, 2016).

164 Martin Weber, "Move Over, Confucius!" *The Huffington Post*, Jan. 30, 2012, http://www.huffingtonpost.com/marten-weber/move-over -confucius_b_1240939.html (accessed Nov. 19, 2016).

Though something shameful, being LGBT+ was not a crime for much of China's history. This all changed after the Opium Wars of the mid-1800s, when it became painfully clear to the defeated Qing Dynasty that China had to modernize if it was to stand any chance of being taken seriously by Western imperial powers. Thus, along with many other things, China adopted then-modern Western morals in an effort to emulate the West and appear equally modern. That meant all things queer would absolutely no longer be tolerated legally, just like in Europe. Homosexuality remained illegal in China until the Communist Party legalized it in 1997 and removed it from the official list of mental illnesses in 2001.[165]

Confucian Takeaway:
PREVENTING CIVIL WAR

Confucianism's original objective for which it was created was as a code of conduct to quell civil war. There's a similar civil war going on in our queer community. We fight among ourselves over everything. Some of the internal complaints are legitimate; some are frivolous. But there is so much infighting from all sides that the frivolous sometimes seems legitimate and the legitimate sometimes seems frivolous.

Civil rights is a long, slow process. The majority of people on this planet are not going to suddenly wake up one day and realize that all queer people are equal in every way to non-queer people. Nowhere in the history of the world has that ever been the case for any social issue. We have to win battle by battle, but fighting each other over how each battle should be fought or could've been better won only creates animosity. We have to appreciate every victory; as long as it is a victory for the queer community, however small and for whatever letter of the LGBT+ acronym, it deserves support and recognition. The goal is to win the war, not just the personal battle that solves the problem for you personally. Total victory is a mara-

---

165 Associated Press, "China Decides Homosexuality No Longer Mental Illness," *South China Morning Post*, Mar. 8, 2001, http://www.hartford-hwp.com /archives/55/325.html (accessed Nov. 19, 2016); Bret Hinsch, *Passions of the Cut Sleeve: The Male Homosexual Tradition in China* (Berkeley: University of California Press, 1992).

thon, not a sprint. It takes time. Until then, every victory counts, and we have to remain united.

The magical community is in similar straits. Certain traditions are so quick to belittle other traditions as not being real magic or as frivolous magic or as being from a tradition that doesn't have ancient or "authentic" roots. Magical practitioners are already a minority maligned by a great number of people. We need to stay united and build each other up. As long as someone's magic is efficacious and works for them, who cares if it's not to your liking or your tradition's standards? Let people live their own lives; promulgating a civil war won't validate your own opinions. Civil wars never change minds, they only eliminate the minds of the losing side.

So, for your next magical activity, pick a magical tradition with which you feel you have issues, and do some unbiased research on it. Find something about that tradition that resonates with you, and then incorporate it into your next spellworking. By finding some common ground and actually proving to yourself the efficacy of a tradition you don't necessarily like, it will help in bridging the divide.

MAHAYANA BUDDHISM

Buddhism was the last of the three major religions to take hold in and greatly influence Chinese culture, arriving during the first century CE from Indian missionaries many centuries after Taoism (sixth century BCE) and the death of Confucius (479 BCE). Specifically, Mahayana Buddhism was the most successful branch of Buddhism. It appealed to heavily populated China because of its emphasis on universal spiritual liberation for all and not simply personal enlightenment, which was seen as merely a means to better help everyone achieve enlightenment.

Since Buddhism was late to the religious party, it met with tough resistance. Its arrival during the pro-Confucianism Han Dynasty made it initially unpopular since Confucianism was all about one's place and duty within society, while Buddhism advocated for an escape from society via personal detachment from societal troubles. The two didn't really mix well, and since Buddhism was a foreign religion, it was associated with barbarism and backwardness. It was, however, more similar to the native-born and former favorite religion of Taoism, as they both had liberal worldviews and an aversion to strict social hierarchies. Thus the Indian missionaries attempted to heighten the similarities between Buddhism and Taoism. This led to Buddhism moving away from its more stoic and godless origins in India and melding into a more mystical tradition with a pantheon of supernatural bodhisattvas who, after attaining enlightenment, forfeited the bliss of nirvana in order to help the masses achieve enlightenment, too.[166]

The vastness of China and its sheer amount of widely different tribes of people forced Buddhism to adapt and change where necessary. This is why there are so many unique takes on Buddhist philosophy throughout the country. In regard to where the LGBT+ community fits into Chinese Buddhism, the answer is everywhere and nowhere. Albeit altered and adapted to Chinese tastes, Mahayana Buddhism has the same fundamental core beliefs and philosophies as originated by the Buddha himself back in India. Everything exists in the mind, and everything outside the mind is just labels we place on our infinite self, including sexuality and gender. We are what we are, and anything more is a labeling of the mind in order to make sense of and interact with the world around us.

Mahayana Takeaway:
FOREGOING NIRVANA

Mahayana Buddhism is by far the most popular of the three Buddhist branches, claiming a little over half of all global adherents. Not surprisingly, it is also the most popular in nations with large urban centers and densely populated living conditions, particularly China and Japan. In such places it's hard to escape from society, and so Mahayana Buddhism's societal focus is relatable.

---

166   Kang-nam Oh, "The Taoist Influence on Hua-yen Buddhism: A Case of the Sinicization of Buddhism in China," *Chung-Hwa Buddhist Journal* 13 (2000), https://web.archive.org/web/20100323000712/http://www.chibs.edu.tw /publication/chbj/13/chbj1338.htm (accessed Nov. 21, 2016).

On a queer level, we, at times, want to go away from the world. We want to escape problematic society and its discrimination and run away to live among our own kind where everyone understands us. But that is impossible. Even highly queer-populated enclaves like West Hollywood and San Francisco's Castro District are neither 100 percent queer nor tolerant.

And so we often isolate ourselves within our community. We go to only queer places, only allow other queer people to be close friends, and only interact with cisgender people at work or when necessary. We fabricate an insulated paradise so we never feel uncomfortable.

But that goes against the universal liberation mindset of Mahayana Buddhism. Unlike other Buddhist branches, the goal of Mahayana is not to escape from the world into a personal paradise, but rather to bring the whole world into that paradise. Being on the frontlines of LGBT+ advocacy and reaching out to heterosociety may not be comfortable, but it is the only way to bring our entire community into a better world. After all, it is because of such people foregoing personal peace to be in the thick of civil rights battles that we have the level of peace and acceptance we enjoy today.

In the magical community, being more in touch with the natural world, there is a common idealized fantasy of running away from the cities and living out among nature, where the problems of heavily populated cities don't exist. Because of this, many of us look down on urban living among nonmagical people as a less idealized way of life that circumstances force us to be in. But that only works against us in our magic. How can we craft a spell with the natural forces around us if we're constantly putting down the natural forces in which we live our everyday lives, the forces of urbanism?

So, for your next magical activity, get in touch with the spiritual deva of the city in which you live, and then begin a relationship with that entity. Understand one another and communicate. Magical practitioners often do the same when entering "natural" places such as forests, deserts, and bodies of water, so why not the city in which you live and spend most of your life? Like any relationship, it'll take time for trust and friendship to develop, but once it does, you'll start noticing that the city and its society will be proactively helping you out with what you need.

Deities & Legends

THE FOX ALCHEMIST

The story of the fox alchemist is an old Chinese folktale with a strong LGBT+ message that combines Taoist and Buddhist philosophies on transcendent love. As the tale goes, an elderly male scholar is visited in his lonely house one night by a man dressed in black asking to make love to him. The scholar is suspicious, but the stranger explains that they were once lovers in a previous life and that he has been searching for his soulmate ever since.

The scholar begins remembering their past-life tragic love—how he had been a young woman and the stranger his young husband. They had vowed to love each other forever, but it was short-lived since they had fallen in love during one of China's civil wars and met with grisly ends while still young. The wife was kidnapped by rebel soldiers and took her own life rather than be raped. The husband joined the rebel soldiers and died in battle.

For each of their deeds, karma awarded them appropriately. The wife, for her loyalty to her husband and emperor in committing suicide before the soldiers could rape her, was allowed to reincarnate as a man—not just any man, but a wise man of letters. (Because, remember, this is ancient China and the patriarchal value of men over women was still very strong.) The man, for his disloyalty to the emperor and willingness to fight for the rebel soldiers, was reincarnated as a lesser animal, a fox.

Even as a fox, the husband still loved his wife and wished to fulfill his vow of loving her forever. So, after discovering she had reincarnated into a male scholar, he studied Taoist alchemy and found the magical concoction that would transform him back into a human so they could be together, the caveat being that the potion's effects would only last one year.

Now with the flood of memories all coming back to the scholar, he recognizes his former husband in the stranger, but he doesn't know how they could possibly make love to each other now that they are both men. The stranger assures the scholar to trust him and tells him that as long as the two love each other, there would always be a way.

The two take advantage of their time and make love each night for 365 consecutive days. Initially after it was over and the stranger had turned back into a fox, the elderly scholar wondered if it had all been a dream, but he remembered his lover had told him that evidence of their love would forever be on the pillars of his home. And so they were: 365 bite marks made during the throes of passion were embedded into the wooden pillars.

Aside from the misogyny in this tale, it's an ancient one of how love knows no boundaries. It is beyond gender, physical age, and even time itself. The concept of one's own spirit is advocated to be gender-fluid, yet love is shown as ever constant.[167]

GUANYIN

Guanyin (also spelled Quan Yin or Kwan Yin) is the bodhisattva of compassion. According to her legend, she had attained enlightenment, but because she had such compassion for humankind, she refused to enter into blissful nirvana until all humans could come with her. She reincarnated as a bodhisattva and dedicated herself to helping end the suffering of people everywhere.

Her place among queer-positive deities comes from her being a transgender female and an icon of the LGBT+ movement in China. Historically, when Indian missionaries spread Buddhism into China, Guanyin was the

---

167 Xiaomingxiong, *GLBTQ Archives*, http://www.glbtqarchive.com/literature/chinese_myth_L.pdf.

female aspect of the male bodhisattva Avalokiteshvara, but this female aspect became more popular among the Chinese, eventually leading to Guanyin becoming her own separate folk bodhisattva. Her transgender identity, however, was supported and maintained by both Taoists and Buddhists, with Taoists seeing Guanyin as a divine harmony of both feminine yin and masculine yang energies, and Buddhists seeing her as a perfection of a male who so accepted his inner compassion and femininity that he achieved full womanhood.

For many centuries Guanyin was an adopted subtle symbol of Chinese lesbians, not only because she was a protectress of women but also because she allegedly advocated against heterosexual marriage in order to pursue a more spiritual life. To the larger queer and feminist movements in China, Guanyin is a symbol of the kind of peace, bliss, and harmony that can be attained if society de-emphasizes its cult worship of masculinity and embraces its self-suppressed femininity as well as love and compassion for all people, regardless of who they are.[168]

THE QUEER EMPERORS

While many Chinese emperors are recorded as having queer tendencies, none have been as legendarily queer as Emperor Wu and Emperor Ai.

Emperor Wu, although a warmonger, was a big proponent of Confucianism, establishing the nation's first official universities in order to teach it to the people. Despite Confucianism's social conservatism, though, Emperor Wu had several male lovers throughout his lifetime. His strongest love was for a former classmate named Han Yun. They began a love affair together while still young, and upon ascension to emperor, Wu granted him prestigious titles and positions in government. The obvious favoritism caused much tension in the court and made him a hypocrite since he was the emperor who had implemented the rule of promoting and bestowing rank based on academic excellence instead of nepotism and

168 Kayla Wheeler, "Women in Religion: Does Gender Matter?" in *Controversies in Contemporary Religion: Education, Law, Politics, Society, and Spirituality*, edited by Paul Hedges (Santa Barbara: Praeger, 2014).

having the right connections. Ultimately, pressure from all sides forced Wu to mandate that Han Yun take his own life, ending the affair and his lover's undue place in government.[169]

The other famously gay monarch of Han China, Emperor Ai, is probably the best known. Ai made no attempt to hide his sexual preference for men and carried out a long-lasting public romance with one of his minor officials, Dong Xian. Their relationship eventually led to the Chinese euphemism of homosexuality being referred to as "the passion of the cut sleeve." This originated from a famous incident wherein, while cuddling together in bed, Emperor Ai wanted to get up, but doing so would risk awakening his lover, who was fast asleep on top of one of his large courtly sleeves. So, rather than take that risk, Ai simply cut off his sleeve.

Like Emperor Wu, though, Ai showed severe favoritism to Dong Xian, promoting him to commander of the armed forces. Unfortunately for his lover, Emperor Ai died suddenly and unexpectedly, leaving Dong Xian as the socially despised top-ranking official in an emperor-less court. He was eventually ousted and forced to commit suicide.[170]

169   Hinsch, *Passions of the Cut Sleeve: The Male Homosexual Tradition in China.*
170   Hinsch, *Passions of the Cut Sleeve.*

16
JAPAN

Cultural

SHINTO

Today's Japan is a healthy mix of native Shinto, Buddhism, and a bit of cultural Christianity. Interestingly, however, Japan is also considered to be the most religious atheist nation in the world. To its devotees, Shinto isn't really seen as a religion but rather as the natural way of the world. Religion is more of a Buddhist or Christian thing in their eyes.[171]

---

171 Matthew Coslett, "Japan: The Most Religious Atheist Country," *GaijinPot*, Feb. 8, 2016, https://blog.gaijinpot.com/japan-religious-atheist-country/ (accessed Nov. 26, 2016).

In general terms, Shinto is a folk religion molded out of the mythologies and native beliefs of the earliest inhabitants of Japan. Its focus is on the divine energies that interplay with the world, both causing events that affect nature and being affected by nature. These divine energies are known as *kami*, which can best be related to in the Western mind as "spirits." The pantheon of kami is endless. They can be invisible beings, shapeshifters, plants, animals, geographic locations, abstract concepts, and natural phenomena such as earthquakes and tsunamis. Technically everything has a kami, but certain objects, places, and natural wonders possess abnormally high levels of energy and are considered sacred.[172]

Because of its deep connection with nature, Shinto, like Taoism, advocates being in harmony with the natural order of the world. For humans, the natural way of things is moral and ethical goodness, but the three main virtues for which a follower of Shinto strive are sincerity, honesty, and purity.[173]

However, the ambiguity of "natural order" and "purity" create the same pitfalls of homophobia that Taoism sometimes experiences. Is queerness natural? Can a queer person be considered pure? Unlike Taoism, though, Shinto has been more of the opinion that being LGBT+ is not natural. Historically, Japan has been much more culturally conservative than China, from where Taoism originated. A factor for this is due to China's multiculturalism and Japan's cultural homogeny. China is composed of many various ethnic groups, each with their own folk beliefs, traditions, and language. So many different people living together requires compromise and cross-cultural understanding. Conversely, the vast majority of Japanese are culturally, ethnically, and linguistically from the same stock, and so cultural differences are at a minimum, as well as the necessity for cross-cultural understanding and the acceptance of differences.

172   Robert Ellwood and Richard Pilgrim, *Japanese Religion: A Cultural Perspective* (New York: Routledge, 1984).

173   Stuart D. B. Picken, *Essentials of Shinto: An Analytical Guide to Principal Teachings* (Westport: Greenwood, 1994).

The fact that the vast majority of people are not LGBT+ as well as the inability for same-sex lovers to procreate are usually the main evidence to Shinto followers that queerness is unnatural. Nevertheless, Shinto doesn't advocate the queer community as bad or evil, simply unnatural, thus contributing to the strange political position of LGBT+ acts and self-expression being neither criminalized nor protected in Japan.[174]

Unsurprisingly, though, as is the case with many world religions that designate the queer community as unnatural, Shinto is filled with stories wherein the kami engage in same-sex eroticism, transgenderism, and queer magic. Tokugawa Era philosophers even wrote that the Divine logically had to be at least bisexual since the first three generations of the gods were all men.[175]

Of all these stories, perhaps the most telling is the tale of the origins of homosexuality. According to legend, the sun goddess Amaterasu had two male servants who fell in love with one another: Shinu No Hafuri and Ama No Hafuri. When Shinu No Hafuri died, Ama No Hafuri was inconsolable and went into a profound depression, ultimately leading to him committing suicide from the overbearing grief. Because the two men were publicly gay lovers, the other kami buried them together in a single grave. The love between these two was the genesis for homosexuality in the world, where humans also have same-sex lovers as these divinities once did.

Unfortunately, the conservativeness of Shinto places a homophobic moral to the end of this tale. Apparently, the sun was so offended by two men being buried together as lovers that it refused to shine, thus bringing starvation and eternal night unto the world. Eventually, the lovers were disinterred from their grave and buried separately, at which point

174   Isaac Stone Fish, "Does Japan's Conservative Shinto Religion Support Gay Marriage?" *Foreign Policy Magazine*, June 29, 2015, http://foreignpolicy.com/2015/06/29/what-does-japan-shinto-think-of-gay-marriage/ (accessed Nov. 26, 2016).
175   Gary Leupp, *Male Colors: The Construction of Homosexuality in Tokugawa Japan* (Los Angeles: University of California Press, 1997).

the sun resumed its normal duties because the egregious wrong had been righted.[176]

Despite whether or not homosexuality was seen as natural in Japan, it was practiced quite often, so much so that the pro-queer minority faction of Shinto practitioners believed that homosexuality had its own Shinto deity, Shudo Daimyojin. Most often, though, homosexuality was practiced in a manner similar to the ancient Greek form of pedagogical pederasty wherein an older established male would take a younger adolescent male under his wing and teach him the ways of sex as well as the ways of manhood and gentlemanly conduct.

Famously, this was practiced in the samurai class of feudal Japan wherein a young man would gain a military education by being the apprentice and lover of an older, more experienced samurai. Among these warriors, though, this older-younger relationship was seen as a sacred bond and therefore monogamous. Also, it is worth mentioning that in this relationship, the benefit to the older man in exchange for his tutelage wasn't just sex with a younger man. The real benefit to the older man was seen as him becoming an even better warrior, adhering to the universal maxim of "you learn more through teaching."[177]

Outside of the warrior class, though, the eccentrically lavish and opulent court life of the Japanese aristocracy was another hotbed of queer libertines. Artistic writings and diaries were popular hobbies in the royal court, and references to queer acts in these writings are many. One of the most famous examples comes from what is considered the world's first novel, *The Tale of Genji*. Within the first chapters of the eleventh-century story, the eponymous protagonist is rebuffed by a female for whom he has the hots. So, in a show of passive-aggressive vengeance and desperation to get laid that evening, he, being an infamous lothario, sleeps with

176   John Dececco and Ronald Long, *Men, Homosexuality, and the Gods: An Exploration into the Religious Significance of Male Homosexuality in World Perspective* (New York: Routledge, 2004).

177   Gregory M. Pflugfelder, *Cartographies of Desire: Male-Male Sexuality in Japanese Discourse, 1600–1950* (Berkeley: University of California Press, 2007).

the girl's younger brother.[178] More intriguingly, Murasaki Shikibu—the author of *The Tale of Genji* and a lady-in-waiting at the imperial court—kept a hodge-podge diary of random thoughts and writings in which she reveals her more-than-platonic interest in other women and poeticizes the lesbian crushes and same-sex trysts she had had.[179]

Even among the common people throughout Japan's history, queerness was everywhere (though, again, we are mostly aware of gay queerness among commoners since Japan is a severely patriarchal society, and only aristocratic educated women like Murasaki Shikibu knew how to write about their own experiences). Impoverished parents often sold their sons and daughters to brothels. At these houses of ill repute, gay clientele could request a male or a male dressed as a woman to either "top" or "bottom" him. Still, the best place to find gay sex was at kabuki theaters. Much like Shakespearean *chefs-d'oeuvre*, all the roles in Japanese theater were played by men (though originally all roles were played by women until their participation in public theater was made illegal in the mid-1600s), and the female roles often went to the younger, more effeminate males in the troupe. And much like elsewhere, traditional Japanese theater also had higher-than-average proportions of gay men in them. So, in this era before gay bars and discreet dating apps, the theater was the understood place to go to meet someone for a gay rendezvous. And since theater troupes didn't make much money, hustling on the side to closeted groupies was a lucrative side job.[100]

After the centuries of feudal infighting was quelled by the establishment of the Tokugawa Shogunate in the early 1600s, domestic peace allowed the middle class to expand, and this expansion led to disposable income. Artists like the great Hokusai and Hiroshige capitalized on the public's taste for the scandalous and transgressive by painting erotic ukiyo-e style

---

178 Murasaki Shikibu, *The Tale of Genji*, trans. Edward G. Seidensticker (New York: Alfred A. Knopf, 2006).

179 Murasaki Shikibu, *The Diary of Lady Murasaki*, trans. Richard Bowring (New York: Penguin Classics, 1996).

180 Leupp, *Male Colors*.

artwork known as shunga, much of which depicted same-sex, transvestite, and transgender acts of eroticism. Gay and bisexual main characters as well as same-sex subplots were even written into mass-market books of the time as a form of shock-value marketing, and they sold well.[181]

Shinto Takeaway:
PURITY

Arguably, one of most unique lessons from Shinto is the sacredness of purity. With today's sexual liberation, the notion of purity (in a sexual sense) seems outdated, a relic from the prudish past. While this is true, there is something to be said for purity. I'm not talking about virginal purity but purity in the sense of not contaminating oneself.

Many of us in the LGBT+ community have had a rough time growing up, and we often utilize sex as a form of substitution for the love we lacked in our earlier years. To be made to feel special, desired, and wanted, if even just for one night, is a powerful aphrodisiac. Our need to escape loneliness and feel "loved" makes many of us take on undesirable, shady, and unsavory people as lovers.

But sex is a magical act. It is an exchange of energies even at its most emotionally detached. If we become physically intimate with someone, their energy mixes with ours, so if we allow ourselves to have sex with a disrespectful, rude, and uncaring person, then their toxic energy becomes entangled in our own, tainting our energetic purity. Now, I'm not saying don't have a lot of sex; I'm saying maintain standards and be selective. Ask yourself, "Do I really want this person's energy mingled into my own?" The more tainted energy we allow in, the less efficacious our magic will be and the darker life will become.

So, for your next magical activity, do a self-purifying ritual specifically to eradicate the remnant energy of unsavory sexual partners. Dedicate yourself to being more spiritually selective the next time you want to get intimate.

---

181 Joshua S. Mostow, Normal Bryson, and Maribeth Graybill, *Gender and Power in the Japanese Visual Field* (Honolulu: University of Hawai'i Press, 2003).

JAPANESE BUDDHISM

Although Japan was an isolated archipelago at the edge of the known world, it was also fairly close to the cultural powerhouse of the region known as China. Japan was no exception to humankind's fascination for the foreign and the exotic, so all things Chinese became an obsession to those who could afford them. The high price of imported goods all the way from China, as well as the fact that China was, for most of Sino-Japanese history, technologically more advanced than Japan, meant Chinese products and culture were received well and considered refined taste, thus leading to their adoption by the Japanese aristocracy, literati, and intelligentsia. And following the wealthy's example, Japanese society began to adapt Chinese culture into their everyday lives.

Of all the imported customs from China, one of the more mystical was Buddhism. Granted, Buddhism was originally from India, but by the time its Mahayana branch reached the shores of Japan in mid-500s CE, it had gone through about a half millennium of Chinese and then Korean appropriation, and, in turn, the Japanese appropriated it to create their own unique forms of the religion.

In regard to the Japanese queer community, Buddhism formed to be very LGBT+ accepting. Even the infamously stoic and minimalist form of Japanese Buddhism known as Zen (of "If a tree falls in the woods and no one is around, does it make a sound?" fame) believed that queerness was not a bad thing since in all of the Buddha's teachings, never once did he make a point to let everyone know that being queer was somehow immoral.[182] Arguably, the sects of Mahayana Buddhism as practiced in Japan are perhaps the most LGBT+ accepting of this major world religion, not just because they don't condemn queerness, but because they actively advocate for and promote it.

---

182 Robert Aitken Roshi, "Robert Aiken Roshi on Gay Marriage: A Zen Buddhist Perspective," *The Jizo Chronicles*, March 27, 2013, https://jizochronicles .com/2013/03/27/robert-aitken-roshi-on-gay-marriage-a-zen-buddhist -perspective/ (accessed Nov. 28, 2016).

Of course, this isn't to say that *all* Japanese Buddhists were universally so progressively minded, but there is a good amount of evidence that indicate the majority of them were. This was especially so among the leading monks and priests throughout the islands. In fact, when one particularly homophobic Buddhist priest of the Tendai sect named Genshin began going on public tirades against homosexuality, the consensus among his fellow Tendai monastics was that he was just upset because he couldn't attract a male lover himself.[183]

Even outside of those who knew him and among the various other Buddhist sects in Japan, it seemed that Genshin's opinion was very much in the minority. Commonplace among Buddhist monasteries in Japan was the practice of pederasty, similar to that of the samurai. Also just like the samurai, the sex between the older and younger men was expected to be monogamous, but in the monastic setting, the elder man had to officially write a formal vow of fidelity to his young acolyte.[184]

Such rampant homosexuality by Japanese Buddhist monks wasn't only accepted by those of the cloth, but also among the Buddhist laypersons of Japan. In the 1600s a leading scholar of the time on Japanese Buddhism, Kitamura Kigin, argued that the Buddha himself advocated for the homosexuality of monks. The crux of his argument was that since the Buddha expressly forbade heterosexual sex for his monks and nuns, and since the Buddha was a wise man painfully aware of the natural desires of humans, sex with one's own gender was implied as a safe and preferred alternative. Moreover, since there were obviously gays and lesbians in all social classes, Buddhist monks and nuns were no exception, therefore making homosexuality natural.[185]

The queerness of Buddhist monks was so well-known and observed that it became a running joke in pre-modern pop culture Japan. The trials

---

183 Leupp, *Male Colors.*

184 Margaret H. Childs, "Chigo Monogatari. Love Stories or Buddhist Sermons?" *Monumenta Nipponica* 35:2 (1980).

185 Kitamura Kigin, "Wild Azaleas," in *Paintings at Dawn: An Anthology of Gay Japanese Literature* (12th–20th Century), ed. Stephen D. Miller, trans. Paul Gordon Schalow (San Francisco: Gay Sunshine Press, 1996).

and tribulations between same-sex monks or the audaciously public liaisons the monks had with same-sex prostitutes became common plotlines in the arts.[186]

And, of course, as mentioned earlier, the mass market of Japanese readers and art aficionados *loved* buying homoerotic-themed works. Among men, at least, open bisexuality and homosexuality was perfectly acceptable. It might be frowned upon by Shinto culture, but there was little to no shame in being a queer Japanese Buddhist of olden times. In fact, when Europeans finally made contact with Japan and the Portuguese Jesuit priest Francisco Cabral arrived to convert the natives to Catholicism, he wrote extensively and vehemently about how commonplace, accepted, and honorable homosexuality was there, especially among the most religious Buddhists, the monks.[187]

Japanese Buddhist Takeaway:
FOCUS ON THE BIGGER PICTURE

Arguably Japan's most famous sect of Buddhism is Zen Buddhism. Zen often emphasizes not obsessing over teachings, but rather keeping your mind on the ultimate goal of enlightenment. The focus is not the teacher or the lesson because they are only conduits to help you see the bigger picture. The Zen analogy for this, popularized by Bruce Lee in his film *Enter the Dragon*, describes a sage pointing to the moon but the students simply focus and concentrate on the sage's finger, forgetting to look at the moon to which it's pointing.

Too often, as queer people, we focus on others' opinions on what it means to be queer and how to be queer that we lose sight of our own unique queerness. All those teachings, documentaries, and books—even this book—are nothing but insights to help you live your own queer life to the fullest. By obsessing over the teachings, you miss out on the greater

---

186   Mostow, Bryson, and Graybill, *Gender and Power in the Japanese Visual Field.*

187   Jonathan D. Spence, *The Memory Palace of Matteo Ricci* (London: Faber and Faber, 1985).

lesson and the main objective. As queer people, just being ourselves is a form and expression of queerness.

So, for your next magical activity, go out and teach a tenet of your magical tradition to a non-believer/skeptic whom you know. This will exercise your "bigger picture" muscles because you can't use or rehash the exact teachings from which you've learned since your student will not see anything special from those sources. That method would be like teaching Buddhists the importance keeping kosher via pointing to where it says so in the Torah; it just carries no effect since Buddhists don't hold the Torah as sacred or believe in the Hebrew God to follow his rules just because he said them. You have to teach not from your point of view but from the point of view of the understanding of the student.

This activity will force you to think outside the box and find a new way to express the bigger picture to someone else. And if you can't explain the bigger picture in a simple way without using past teachings as a crutch, then you simply don't grasp the bigger picture as well as you think.

Deities & Legends

AMATERASU

Amaterasu, the sun goddess, is one of the most popular and major deities in Shinto. With her stature and preeminence, she is involved in many legends, but the one that most concerns us is the legend of her cave hideout since it reveals her bisexual fascination for other women. As the legend goes, her brother, Susa-No-O (god of sea and storms), was jealous of her supreme power and began challenging her. In response to his chaotic havoc, Amaterasu retreated to a cave out of fear and as a way to regroup her energy. Being the sun goddess, her self-cloistering meant that the sun never shone all the while she was in the cave, leading to even more chaos and havoc on the earth. Despite pleas from both mortals and gods, Amaterasu refused to exit the cave.

However, Ame-No-Uzume (goddess of the dawn, mirth, and revelry) tried a different approach. She stood just outside the cave and performed a sexualized, bawdy dance that so attracted Amaterasu and caught her fascination that she unwittingly came out of the cave to get a better view. Once outside, the transgender female deity Ishi-Kore-Dome-No-Kami (goddess of masonry) invented the mirror, which she gave to Amaterasu, who was, in turn, so fascinated by her own radiant beauty that she didn't even notice the other gods sealing up the cave behind her.

Unable to continue hiding, Amaterasu then dresses as a male warrior and frightens Susa-No-O with an aggressive, masculinized battle dance, based off of Ame-No-Uzume's dance outside the cave. This energetic combination of Ameterasu's masculinity and femininity allowed her to overcome her brother and reign supreme once more. Because of this dual-gendered victory, she is also considered, in some circles, to be a patroness of intersex individuals.[188]

Nevertheless, let's not forget that this is the same goddess who reviled same-sex lovers being buried together from another Japanese folktale. Most people attribute this contradiction to the fact that Amaterasu is so popular that both queer-positive and queerphobic people have utilized her through the years to teach whatever moral lesson to which they personally espouse. Still, some others see Amaterasu as a bit of a hypocrite deity wherein something is okay for her to do, but it's wrong if other people do it—a trait not uncommon in the "down-low" queer community.

In worship, her correspondences are the sun, rice, chickens/roosters, brass, gold, saffron, and warm colors.

KITSUNE

Kitsune is the Japanese word for "fox," but in this sense, kitsune is in reference to the magical, seductive foxes common in Shinto folktales. Similar to many Native American traditions, kitsune are seen as trickster spirits that are morally ambiguous and teach valuable lessons in a roundabout way through trickery. Like Amaterasu, they are involved in a great number of folktales and legends, but one common myth about kitsune in particular

---

188 Connor, Sparks, and Sparks, *Cassell's Encyclopedia of Queer Myth, Symbol, and Spirit.*

revolves around their homosexual lust for lonesome men. The myth pops up in a lot of stories, but the plotline is generally the same: a male wayward traveler becomes lost in unfamiliar territory, he comes across a beautiful and desirable woman who provides him with shelter and sex, and the woman transforms back into her true form of a fox after completing his sexual conquest of the man.

The kitsune were usually male, though they always shapeshifted into seductive women in order to lure men. The popularity of these kitsune tales peaked during Japan's feudal era, when people rarely ventured beyond the borders of their villages. The erotic ruse of the kitsune was used as a kind of boogeyman story to keep the needed male populace from leaving the village and to scare them from having an affair with strange women, since that woman could quite possibly be a male kitsune.[189]

SHIRABYOSHI

Shirabyoshi is the name of specific Shinto deities and of a specific type of entertainer in Japanese society. The deity shirabyoshi were kami that were half humanoid and half serpent and were often transgender females. They were prominent spiritual patrons of transgender individuals and those who portrayed the opposite gender in the arts and entertainment.

The human shirabyoshi were cross-dressing performers who were called as such due to the spiritual shirabyoshi's patronage of them. These performers were biologically female, but they sang and danced and acted in plays dressed as men. Essentially, they were drag kings of eighth–twelfth century Japan. Even queerer was their notorious ability to arouse the sexual appetites of male members of the Imperial Court while performing plays and dances as men. Within time, it became commonplace for aristocratic men to pay to have sex with these women in male drag, although the shirabyoshi's main financing came from their drag shows and not from being solicited by their audience.[190]

---

189 Royall Tyler, *Japanese Tales* (New York: Pantheon, 1987).
190 Connor, Sparks, and Sparks, *Cassell's Encyclopedia of Queer Myth, Symbol and Spirit*.

17
SHAMANISM

Cultural

Shamanism is a tricky spiritual tradition to talk about. It is spread out into many pockets of the world, each with their own traditions, practices, and worldviews. To make it more complicated, because it is such a general term, not even anthropologists fully agree on how to classify and define shamanism into a single definition. Nevertheless, shamanism is a necessary topic for us to explore because many forms of it from many parts of the globe share a common pattern of having outwardly unabashed queer elements to them. Even more so, LGBT+ individuals are commonly leaders in these global shamanic traditions. Still, despite many indigenous people who practice shamanism, to talk about them all would be a book unto itself—for now, since we'll explore Native American shamanic traditions when we cross the Pacific, I'll center our exploration of queer shamanism to the other region of the world from where it is most famous and celebrated in pop culture: Siberia and Mongolia.

Before we get into the queer specifics of shamanism, though, let's try to define it so that we're all on the same page of what we're talking about. Yes, the anthropological community cannot come to an agreed definition of shamanism, but out of the sake of necessity I'll just define a shaman the way the *Oxford English Dictionary* does: "A person regarded as having access to, and influence in, the world of good and evil spirits, especially among some people of northern Asia and North America. Typically such people enter a trance state during a ritual, and practice divination and healing."[191]

One of the most important roles of a shaman is as mediator. He or she is in constant fluidity and lacks the rigid confines of labels. The shaman travels freely into the spiritual world, works with spirits, works with male and female energies, and helps both men and women. This natural ability to go beyond the binary of gender roles and paint with all the colors in the crayon box is a necessity for the shaman and an inherent gift of LGBT+ individuals.

The shaman doesn't label him/herself and is thus free to be anything since he/she is not any one thing in particular. Because of this, shamanism has often caught the romantic eye of Westerners who, in an effort to "fit in" and "belong" somewhere, feel themselves limited and restricted, rarely realizing that these limits and restrictions are the natural result of "fitting in" and "belonging" to a definite group. The shaman, however, belongs nowhere and thus belongs everywhere. Is the shaman a person of the spirit realm? A person of the physical realm? A shaman is both because he/she is neither.

Of course, the people of Siberia and Mongolia are not all shamans. It is a calling and ability of a very select few. Interestingly, but unsurprisingly, many of these shamans are LGBT+ individuals who, being aware of not belonging, own their personal ambiguity and differentness.

191 *Oxford English Dictionary*, https://en.oxforddictionaries.com/ (accessed July 29, 2017).

In far eastern Siberia, near the Bering Sea, there is a shamanic people known as the Chukchi. The strongest and most powerful of all the Chukchi shamans were proud queer individuals known colloquially as "soft men." These soft men were biological males who dressed and styled their hair like females, yet did not adopt fully feminine behaviors. They even married cisgender men, and these husbands retained their full masculinity and were not seen as any different from any other husband of female wives. Nevertheless, the soft men were regarded with great contempt among the other Chukchi shamans who were envious of their mighty power that stemmed from their gender fluidity to be both man and woman and neither all at the same time. Rarely did the heteronormative shamans lash out at the soft men, though, since they feared the spiritual wrath of the soft men even more so than they despised them.[192]

The idea of queerness and spiritual power went hand in hand in Siberia. Showing queer tendencies in one's early years as a child was a sign that the child was destined to be a shaman. Unlike many other cultures around the globe, the people of Siberia, particularly the Chukchi, the Kamchadal, and the Koryak, did not force or train their children to behave in a prescribed manner that would facilitate them fitting into the category of "male" or "female." Instead, children were allowed to express themselves as they truly felt they were, and oftentimes the gender-fluid ones, like the soft men who chose to not define themselves at all, developed the greatest shamanic abilities. In adulthood, however, not fitting in led to much derision from their fellow tribesmen, but the spiritual freedom and powers of being without label were seen as worthwhile exchanges for being an outsider.[193]

Not all queer shamans, however, were born that way. A number of gender-fluid individuals were told by the spirit world to break away from the confines of their traditional gender in order to further develop their shamanic prowess. To help them with the transformation, these selected

192   Neil Price, *The Archaeology of Shamanism* (New York: Routledge, 2001).
193   Raven Kaldera, *Wightridden: Paths of Northern-Tradition Shamanism* (Hubbardston: Asphodel Press, 2007).

shamans married spiritual entities who would be their life companion in developing their magic and in embracing characteristics of the opposite sex. These spiritual spouses existed only in the spirit world and could either be a same-sex lover who would force the shaman to be the more butch or effeminate partner (whichever he/she needed to learn), or they were an opposite-sex lover who would teach by example rather than role domination. And regardless if the shaman was married beforehand or found a human spouse after their spiritual marriage, it was understood that the spiritual spouse was the #1 husband/wife, outranking the human spouse.[194]

A little farther south in what is now Mongolia, the shamans there were similar in their queerness, yet uniquely different from their more northern counterparts. Today, the majority of Mongolians are Buddhists (of the Vajrayana type mostly), but shamanism still ranks high as the belief system of choice among a good percentage of the people. For most of Mongolia's history, stretching back into prehistoric times, shamanism was the staple practice of the people. Although introduced to the Mongols when Kublai Khan conquered China, Buddhism didn't really take hold here until the 1600s, when the aristocratic classes attempted to use it as a common force to unite the various tribes that had splintered off after the fall of the Mongol Empire. After all, if the Mongols became a large empire again, the aristocracy would have more influence, power, and luxury, so their intentions to promote Buddhism weren't really that of a bodhisattva nature.

Pre-Buddhist Mongolia, however, which included its golden age of the Great Khans (1206–1368 CE), was centered on shamanism. Mongolian shamanism, though, was a lot less freeform and more hierarchical and divisional. Still, many of the leading shamans throughout Mongolian history were queer individuals, as in Siberia. Their queerness was nurtured and seen as a sign of great spiritual ability. Around the ages of ten to twelve was the time when a Mongolian would begin training as a shaman. Not coincidentally, this was around the time of puberty, when one's sexual and expressional differentness could be undeniably seen.

---

194   Kaldera, *Wightridden.*

It was this differentness that experienced shamans looked for when choosing who to train, and the most popular sign of differentness was the innate ability to intermingle between the masculine and feminine worlds (such as an effeminate boy or a butch girl). These children defied the gender binary of male and female, and thus were seen as naturally gifted to travel between the spiritual and physical realms. More so than in Siberia, though, biologically female shamans were just as numerous and respected as biologically male ones, and oftentimes they, too, were gender fluid. They dressed like men and had masculine hairstyles, married women or men, and yet were never seen as any less of a woman because of it.[195]

Unfortunately, modern queer Mongolian shamanism is in a precarious position. Beyond it being certainly minority religion of the people, Mongolia's recent pendulum-swinging history of LGBT+ rights and setbacks creates an air of uncertainty for the future. Back in the times of the Great Khans, homosexuality was punishable by death unless practiced by or with a shaman.[196] After Mongolia became a communist nation, the communists decriminalized homosexuality in 1961 (in comparison, it was federally decriminalized in the US in 2002).[197]

Mongolia hasn't been a communist nation since the 1990s, and since that time, extreme rightist sentiment has grown and violence toward queer people has risen dramatically. In fact, things have gotten so bad recently that in 2015 the Mongolian Parliament had to adopt a new criminal code that defines violence toward a person due to sexual orientation or gender identity as a hate crime.[198]

195　Tris Reid-Smith, "From Shamans to Gay Bars: Booming Mongolia's LGBT People," *Gay Star News*, April 5, 2013, http://www.gaystarnews.com/article/shamans-gay-bars-booming-mongolia%E2%80%99s-lgbt-people050413/#gs.dOei=Is (accessed Dec. 4, 2016).

196　Urgunge Onon, *The Secret History of the Mongols: The Life and Times of Chinggis Khan* (Oxford: Routledge-Curzo, 2001).

197　Mary Bernstein, Anna-Maria Marshall, and Scott Barclay, *Queer Mobilizations: LGBT Activists Confront the Law* (New York: NYU Press, 2009).

198　Lila Seidman, "LGBT Centre Executive Director N. Anaraa Talks LGBT Rights Then and Now," *The Ulaanbaatar Post*, May 18, 2016, http://theubpost.mn/2016/05/18/lgbt-centre-executive-director-n-anaraa-talks-lgbt-rights-then-and-now/ (accessed Dec. 5, 2016).

Shamanic Takeaway:
LIVE BEYOND LABELS

The shamanic virtue of living beyond labels is often too uncomfortable for people. It is much easier and more comfortable to find someplace where you fit in so as to see that you are not alone. But to not be alone in this sense is to not be yourself. Our LGBT+ community is starting to run into this problem. On the one hand, there is a rising tide of the queer community wanting to fit in with mainstream society to the point where we want to be viewed as exactly the same as the rest of the world. And on the other hand, the same tide is wanting mainstream society to notice how different and unique we are compared to the rest of the world. Then when the world outwardly recognizes us as unique and different, we get upset at how they are not seeing us as exactly the same as them. And when they outwardly recognize us as being just the same as them, we get upset at how they are not seeing us as specially unique and different from them.

Infighting also abounds. Every letter in the LGBT+ acronym wants to be recognized as unique and different, further labeling themselves with their own unique sub-group under the queer umbrella. Then exclusionary sub-sub-groups develop for the same reasons. Are you a gay twink? A gay jock? A gay leather daddy? Are you a lipstick lesbian? A chapstick lesbian? A butch lesbian? Are you a comedy drag queen? A pageant queen? A fishy queen? And so on.

We have to learn from our shamanic brothers and sisters that labels divide us more than they unite us. By not having labels and not belonging to a specific group, we belong everywhere. So, for your next magical activity, you're going to do a spell without paying attention to its tradition or labels. Go to a library or bookstore's esoterica section, close your eyes, and pick out a book at random. Then open to a random "how-to" spellworking page, and do that spell. Ignore the labels of what tradition it is and who wrote it. The point is to release your mind from self-restricting and biased labels that you place on everything. And you don't have to actually get the book; just take a photo of how to do it and give it an honest try. This exercise frees you from all the labeling divisions (and personal prejudices) within the magical community that you have built up inside your head. See beyond labels and judge the teaching based on one criteria only: "Does it work?"

18
EAST ASIAN
MAGICAL COMMUNITY

THE TAO OF OPPOSITE UNDERSTANDING

For a more hands-on approach to Taoist thought, I'll be your special guest. If you've read other books of mine, you might be surprised to see me as the Taoism representative since my approach to the spiritual is more eclectic and a patchwork of the best of what's around. But just between us, since we've spent so much time together on this global trek, I'll let you in on a little secret: at the core level of my spirituality, I'm actually more of a Taoist than anything. Yes, I adhere to Hermetic philosophy, have a devotion to la Santa Muerte, and participate in eclectic practices from various traditions, but Taoism is what keeps me grounded and acts as my base perspective from which I view all of this and the world around me. So here's some LGBT+ Taoist philosophy that I've used and hope you'll try out at least once.

Like the Tao, both gender and identity are fluid and impermanent. You might consider yourself masculine, but that's all relative since some people might be considered more masculine or less masculine than you. So if masculinity is not even able to be definitively pinpointed, the pursuit of masculinity is, by its very nature, an absurd and impossible task. The same goes for femininity. How can anyone really call themselves masculine or feminine when those ideals exist only in comparison to their opposite, which, in turn, only exist in comparison to those initial ideals?

Still, we live in a world where labels are a necessity. Life is a lot easier when we can point at something and immediately know what it is and what it is not. By comparing what it is not, we understand what it is. Masculinity is such because it's not feminine, and femininity is such because it's not masculine. But what about everything in between? And what is masculinity/femininity anyway? Well, Taoism has a unique approach to understanding extremes and the spaces between.

Chapter 36 of the Tao Te Ching *expounds on this idea of achievement through seemingly opposite action:*

> If one wishes to shrink it
> One must first expand it
> If one wishes to weaken it
> One must first strengthen it
> If one wishes to discard it
> One must first promote it
> If one wishes to seize it
> One must first give it
> This is called subtle clarity
> The soft and weak overcome the tough and strong.[199]

Applying this lesson in practice, the best way to understand our own gender identity is to first understand the opposite. So, in order to become more masculine, you have to first become more feminine and vice versa. I

---

199   Lin, *Tao Te Ching.*

know it sounds ridiculous at first, but if you think about it, it's true. Think of the ideal man, a man who knows how to treat a woman right on all levels: emotionally, socially, sexually. He can only be this ideal man because he understands the wants and needs of a woman. Being the ideal woman is the same; she understands the wants and needs of a man. When you truly understand the psyche of the opposite sex, you know how to approach them and thus be the ideal of a true man or woman in their eyes.

Most people don't understand the opposite sex because they don't take the time to think outside the box of their own gender identity. So, the Taoist exercise for you is to spend time being the opposite sex. On a day off from work, live a day in the life. If you consider yourself masculine, get up earlier to do your hair a special way, apply make-up, wear feminine clothing if you have access to it, watch a "chick flick," and go out and visit stores and locales stereotyped as feminine (in/out of drag, depending on your comfort level and safety).

If you consider yourself feminine, spend the day doing stereotypically masculine things: sit with your legs open and your long hair hidden under a hat, watch a cheesy action movie, go out to a basketball court or batting cage to play some sports, etc. Yes, these are all stereotypes, but that's the point. By living out the ridiculous extremes of the other gender, all the other differences begin to seem less ridiculous in comparison.

And if your immediate reaction is "I'm not gonna do that," then I ask you: Why not? Is there something wrong with being feminine or being masculine? What exactly is it about you that is so against this activity? If you consider yourself open-minded, then this is the moment to walk your talk.

After all, the important thing to remember is that this is more than doing drag and playing pretend. To see how the other half lives, truly try to embody the opposite sex in mind and spirit, not in a mocking way but in a deeply psychoanalytical way that promotes understanding. Once you truly experience femininity, you will understand masculinity, and once you truly experience masculinity, you will understand femininity. Until then, you're really just guessing.

—Tomás Prower

NICHIREN BUDDHIST MANTRA CHANT

Back to give another example is Nikko, our resident queer Buddhist. You already know about how Buddhism was a transformative force for the better in his life as a gay man. Here he is going to share a Japanese Buddhist mantra chant for us to practice on our own that may lead us to greater enlightenment.

> The mantra of Nichiren Buddhism is "Nam-myoho-renge-kyo," also known as daimoku. Chanting daimoku is the primary practice of millions of Nichiren Buddhists worldwide. This practice, together with studying the writings of the tradition, is said to help practitioners in their quest to transform their lives and attain enlightenment.
>
> This form of Buddhism was started by a thirteenth-century Japanese priest named Nichiren. It was Nichiren's quest to establish a practice that would be easily accessible for all people, no matter their class, occupation, level of education, or sex. Nichiren based his teachings on the Lotus Sutra, an ancient Buddhist scripture.
>
> Chanting daimoku is like a spiritual workout to tap in to one's Buddha nature. Our Buddha nature can be seen as our inherent potential characterized by an energized life condition with increased courage, compassion, and wisdom.
>
> There are many layers of meaning to the phrase "Nam-myoho-renge-kyo." For the sake of brevity, it can be translated as "I dedicate my life to the wonderful law of cause and effect"—which leads to Buddhahood—or "I dedicate myself to the teaching of the Lotus Sutra"—which is that we all have the Buddha nature.
>
> Curious seekers interested in testing the practice can follow the steps listed below:
>
> 1. Make a list of goals you want to accomplish. (Nichiren Buddhism takes into account the reality in which regular laypersons find themselves. Desires are not seen as something to be eliminated but rather faced and transformed.)

2. *Choose a place where you can relax and chant comfortably out loud. You can be seated in a chair, kneeling, or sitting cross-legged; it is up to you. Just be comfortable.*

3. *Choose a focus point on a blank wall slightly above eye level. Keep your eyes open and focus on the selected point.*

4. *Hold your hands with palms facing in and touching each other (an often-seen prayer position) in front of your chest.*

5. *Keep your back as straight as possible while still being comfortable.*

6. *There is no need to empty your mind or visualize anything in particular. Be yourself and focus on your hopes and prayers.*

7. *Begin to chant "Nam-myoho-renge-kyo." The words are pronounced as follows:*
   - *Nam (Nahm, Namu) = Nahm-moo*
   - *Myoho = Mee-yoh-hoh*
   - *Renge = Rain-gay*
   - *Kyo = Kee-oh*

8. *The recommended pace of recitation is vigorous and quick.*

Commit to chanting for 5 to 10 minutes twice a day every day for a few weeks. The chanting sessions should be done in the morning and the evening. Establishing a twice-daily rhythm is important. You can also do extra chanting whenever you have spare time or are being faced with a problem.

Let the words and their vibrations go deep into your life. Allow them to bring forth your wisdom and to reenergize you with the strength to not be defeated and to overcome your problems and afflictions. After a few days or weeks, note how the chanting has helped you achieve your goals or transformed them into a more constructive reality.

To really take advantage of the practice to its fullest, you'll want to read, study, and apply the writings of Nichiren and the Lotus Sutra. These can be found online via various Nichiren Buddhist organizations.

—Nikko

PART 6

OCEANIA

*When you find that place in yourself to acknowledge
both male and female aspects within and accept
the capacity to embrace both…that is where
the māhū exists and true liberation happens.*
—KAUMAKALWA KANAKA'OLE

Oceania is a vast and varied geopolitical zone of the world generally consisting of Australia, New Zealand, and the islands of the Pacific. With the world's largest ocean serving as its personal moat and being far removed from the exploration craze of sixteenth-century Europe, this world region was one of the last to be encountered, influenced, and colonized by Westerners. But by the time they came, European explorers and missionaries had become experts in religious conversion.

Nowadays Oceania is highly Christianized, to the point where Christianity is considered one and the same with some native cultures. Time has a funny way of normalizing the unusual, and while Christianity is the majority faith in most Oceanic nations, the people's Christian values, especially toward the queer community, are quite diverse.

Ironically, the truly native spiritual traditions and precolonial customs of these Oceanic peoples were highly queer positive. So let's follow the trade winds and explore the Pacific to rediscover the queer history of these southern islands, starting with the closer and larger landmass from our East Asian departing point: Australia.

19

ABORIGINAL AUSTRALIA

Cultural

Modern Australia is largely a product of European immigration, and as such, its religious heritage is largely that of Europe. However, that is not the case for *all* Australians. The indigenous people, known regionally as Aboriginals, have their own unique spiritual traditions and belief systems dating back well before James Cook ever landed in Botany Bay.

The biggest impediment to learning about Australian Aboriginal history, let alone its queer history, is the fact that there are no first-hand written documents. Most of the documentation that we have comes from European explorers and colonists, which is highly skewed. Furthermore, Australia is *huge*. Naturally, with so much land, there doesn't exist one sole Aboriginal tribe with a unifying culture. Like the Native North Americans, there are numerous Aboriginal tribes, all with their own unwritten spiritual histories and cultural dispositions to LGBT+ persons.

With much of the Aboriginals' history being passed down via oral tradition, its history is only as true and valid as the previous generation and the way in which they told it. Unfortunately, Christian missionaries were forcefully influential to these native people, so Aboriginal history has become blurred with Christian ethics and values. Among most tribes nowadays, the firm assertion that queerness of any kind has never existed among their people is the de facto belief. If any of their own turns out to be queer, then it is because of the influence of the West, who has corrupted their youth because it is assumed not to be natural throughout their people's history. (The irony of how Christianity used to justify such beliefs as also a Western import is lost amidst the homophobia.) Because of this, queer Aboriginals face profound derision and mistreatment from their own people.[200]

If we look at Aboriginal history from an objective, nonreligious vantage point, we can ascertain that there *must've* been queer people among their indigenous tribes. LGBT+ persons have existed in all societies all over the world, so one can safely presume that the same is true for Australian Aboriginals. One tribe that we know to be queer-inclined was the Aranda tribe. Located in what is now the modern state of South Australia, homosexual displays within the context of playing was encouraged from an early age. Common children's games involved Aranda youths mimicking homosexual acts, albeit unaware of their significance. One Aranda game, common among children everywhere, was playing house, wherein a group of kids pretend to be a family and imitate the roles that they saw their families doing. Among this tribe, however, the roles of mother and father were not strictly divided by gender, and so little boys could pretend to be

200 Troy-Anthony Baylis, "The Art of Seeing Aboriginal Australia's Queer Potential," *The Conversation*, April 15, 2014, http://theconversation.com /the-art-of-seeing-aboriginal-australias-queer-potential-25588 (accessed Dec. 9, 2016).

the mother and little girls could pretend to be the father without anyone, young or old, seeing it as odd.

However, Aranda children would take it a step further and mimic everything they saw their parents doing, including having sex, an act never hidden in privacy from children. Of course, being kids, they didn't know what sex was, and even if they did, they didn't have the biological maturity to actually do it or the cultural impression that it was something dirty and taboo. As long as siblings and cousins didn't play pretend sex, the adults of the tribe were cool with it. In fact, they even applauded their children for simulating sex since sexuality was seen as a natural and admirable part of life. And since the parental roles were not gender specific, two girls or two boys could be mother and father while pretending to have sex. The little girls playing the father, in particular, were known for using sticks as dildos in order to enhance the imaginative realism.

When Aranda youths reached that awkward age where they were barely biologically mature enough to have sex, yet were still considered kids in the eyes of society, they took playing house, or rather playing bedroom, to the next level. If two gay boys were playing together, the one playing the father would insert his penis in between the thighs of the one playing the mother and effectively have sex that way because they could get away with it via the ambiguity of it being a children's game. If two girls were playing, the one playing the father would use her fashioned dildo as an actual sex toy and insert it into the vagina of the one playing the mother. Even among adult lesbians of the tribe, the use of fashioned dildos was well-known and popular.[201]

However, the Aranda are probably better known for their boy-wives. Just as with girls, young boys, too, could be promised to older men. These boys effectively served as temporary wives by doing domestic chores, helping the "husband" with the hunt, and having conjugal sex (but only after the boy became sexually mature). Unlike girls, though, around

---

201 R. Aldrich, "Peopling the Empty Mirror: The Prospects for Gay and Lesbian Aboriginal History," *Gay Perspectives II* (Sydney: University of Sydney Australian Centre for Gay and Lesbian Research, 1993).

their mid-teens these boy-wives would become emancipated from their arranged marriages since they were now considered adults. During the marriage, the "husband" was expected to teach the younger man the ways of manhood, essentially preparing him for adulthood by the time he was emancipated. The actual sex, itself, though, was very unique and would probably be seen as too painful even for the most hardcore masochistic fetishist in today's dungeon scenes.

In Aranda culture (and in other Aboriginal cultures in central and northwestern Australia), ritual subincision of the penis was commonly practiced. Before you search online for images of subincision, know it's the slicing of the penis from the tip of the urethra down the bottom of the shaft to the base, halfway bisecting the penis the same way a worm is dissected in science class. The blood from this ritual mutilation was considered sacred and used in a host of spiritual workings, but between male lovers a subincised penis could conveniently form a makeshift vagina. The younger male would wrap the older male's subincised flesh around his own penis (like a hotdog bun) and masturbate into the open urethra of his husband. The act of anal sex, however, was considered off-limits between boy-wives and their husbands.[202]

With the arrival of Europeans, much of anything the Aboriginals did that could be perceived as homoerotic was heavily suppressed. Along with the explorers came colonists, and with colonists came Christian society, which, to a large extent, is the dominant spiritual ideology of Australia and its native people today.

Aboriginal Australian Takeaway:
LET THE CHILDREN BE

As shown by the Aranda, there is great power in letting kids be free to play with gender and identity and be themselves. Many of us in the queer

---

202 Bob Hay, "Boy Wives of the Aranda," *Bob Hay Online Resources* (Canberra: University of the Third Age, 2006), http://bobhay.org/_downloads/_homo /NHH%2007%20Boy%20Wives%20of%20the%20Aranda%20-%20The%20 Pre-History%20of%20Homosexuality%20I.pdf (accessed Dec. 9, 2016).

community grew up under our parents' expectations of being straight and were often told to act more like how our biological gender is "supposed" to act. As adults we try to not do this, but we inadvertently do it in other ways. We might not expect our kids to be straight, but we pressure them in other expectative ways: you have to go to college, don't go into the arts because it won't pay the bills, girls should be less promiscuous than boys, do things this way, don't do things that way, etc.

So, for your next magical activity, do a deep meditation focusing on the expectations you have or had of your children; if you don't have children, imagine that you did or substitute younger relatives. In the stillness of your heart, examine where you've pressured or pushed your kids with certain expectations, good or bad. Why those particular expectations? Do they stem from issues or baggage from your own past? Is it unconscious copying of how things have always been done in your family without a particular reason? Are they based on your worldview of how to survive in this modern society? Is that worldview the only worldview? Is your worldview your children's maturing worldview? Do they have to interact with the world exactly how you did or would've done? And so on.

Only nothing comes from nothing. There is a source for why you push your kids with certain expectations. Get to the root source of those expectations and objectively see if they truly are for the child's greater good or if they are for other motives unresolved or unknown.

Deities & Legends

MIMI SPIRITS

According to the Aboriginal Australians of northern Australia, the Mimi were fairylike spirits who lived alongside humans in an alternate dimension where genders didn't exist. They are described as being extremely tall and thin and spent most of their time in rock crevices since even a moderate wind could snap their fragile, elongated frame. They're also credited with teaching the native people how to hunt, use fire, cook meat, and paint.

However, the Mimi were also notorious for being very dangerous and fatally attacking people if they felt they were being approached in an incorrect manner. Because they existed in this other dimension, though, they were thought to be genderless. The indigenous people of northern Australia never enquired further into the sexual identity of the Mimi, instead allowing them to exist in sexual ambiguity, living in an alternate dimension where singular gender/sexuality is agreed to be beyond human comprehension.[203]

203 Baylis, *The Conversation*, http://theconversation.com/the-art
     -of-seeing-aboriginal-australias-queer-potential-25588.

20
POLYNESIA

Cultural

By far, New Zealand's North Island and South Island are the largest of the Polynesian islands. In fact, New Zealand makes up about 87 percent of all the land in Polynesia. The native people of this 87 percent majority are the Maori, and just like modern New Zealand, they have very permissible and welcoming attitudes toward their LGBT+ tribespeople. Because they didn't have a written language, though, the only physical evidence we have of precolonial Maori attitudes toward queer persons is of cave artwork depicting homosexuality as an accepted orientation, along with hetero-sexuality.[204] Like most indigenous cultures who didn't have a written

---

204 Chris Brickell, "Gay Men's Lives," in *Te Ara: The Encyclopedia of New Zealand* (Wellington: Manatū Taonga Ministry for Culture and Heritage, 2005), http://www.teara.govt.nz/en/gay-mens-lives (accessed Dec. 13, 2016).

language, a lot of the documented evidence we have on the Maori comes from the writings of colonizing Christian Europeans. British missionaries, in particular, made special notice to write about how homosexual relationships between men, between women, and between the gods was a normal part of life for these people.[205]

Sexuality in general, though, was much more liberalized among the Maori than the British, who would eventually colonize them. Sex and physical intimacy were not seen as sinful or shameful, and there was no perceived value in virginity. Even for women, there was no stigma in being promiscuous and taking on multiple lovers. Premarital sex was the accepted norm, and bastard children were accepted as no different or less than children born in wedlock. The only societal restraint on sexuality was the expectation of being faithful once married, extending to polygamous marriages.[206]

Such accessibility to sex without social stigma often proved too tempting to the British settlers, sailors, and missionaries who would come to the islands. They would often "go native" and take part in the pleasures all around them, including the pleasures of homoeroticism. The Reverend William Yate is New Zealand's most infamous example of this through his longtime relationships with Maori males. Despite his actions and orientation being accepted by the natives he was trying to convert, his Christian counterparts greatly disapproved, leading to his banishment back to Britain in disgrace.[207]

The Maori also had a healthy sense of humor when it came to sexual orientation. Although they accepted homosexuality the same as heterosex-

---

205 Steven Eldred-Grigg, *Pleasures of the Flesh: Sex and Drugs in Colonial New Zealand 1840-1915* (Wellington: A.H. & A.W. Reed Ltd., 1984).

206 Clive Aspin, "Hōkakatanga—Māori Sexualities," in *Te Ara: The Encyclopedia of New Zealand* (Wellington: Manatū Taonga Ministry for Culture and Heritage, 2011), http://www.teara.govt.nz/en/node/168875 (accessed Dec. 13, 2016).

207 Judith Binney, "Yate, William," in *Te Ara: The Encyclopedia of New Zealand* (Wellington: Manatū Taonga Ministry for Culture and Heritage, 1990), http://www.TeAra.govt.nz/en/biographies/1y1/yate-william (accessed Dec. 13, 2016).

uality, they were aware of their differences and how different people liked different things. They were also aware of how different their laissez-faire outlook on sexual orientation was from the arriving British. A famous example of this was a scam the Maori played on one of the horny sailors aboard Capt. James Cook's ship the *Endeavour*.

In his log, the ship's scientist wrote about how one of the sailors paid a Maori family to have sex with one of their beautiful daughters. When he brought the maiden back to the ship to get his money's worth of action, it was discovered that he had actually bought one of their sons in drag. So the sailor went back to the family and paid for another daughter, the family complied, clothes came off, and again the sailor realized that the family had given him another pretty male in drag. When he went to complain about these ruses, the Maori family just laughed, amused at the profitable practical joke they were able to pull off multiple times thanks to their playfulness in playing with gender identity.[208]

Across the waters in Samoa, homosexuality was not so tolerated as among the Maori, which is especially interesting since queerness plays an important role in Samoan society. This nonheteronormative norm centers on the *fa'afafine* and still continues to this day. The fa'afafine are people of a third gender recognized by the native Samoans. These are biological males who behave and look like women. As in most Polynesian cultures, Samoans' concept of family goes beyond the nuclear parents and children to include larger, extended communal clans. In these family groups, the fa'afafine are a great asset because they do domestic chores along with the women, albeit with the physical strength of men.[209]

Fa'afafine were spotted in early childhood. Little boys who displayed effeminate characteristics were recognized as future fa'afafine, and their femininity was nurtured by their families since fa'afafine and their help with women's work were a welcome blessing to any household. In fact,

208 Aspin, *Te Ara: The Encyclopedia of New Zealand*, http://www.teara.govt.nz/en/node/168875.
209 Saleimoa Vaai, *Samoa Faamatai and the Rule of Law* (Apia: The National University of Samoa: Le Papa-I-Galagala, 1999).

if a family had too many sons and not enough daughters to get all of the domestic work done, it was traditional that families train one of their sons to become a fa'afafine to be sure they had enough people to do all the necessary female labor. [210]

It is important to remember, though, that the fa'afafine of Samoa are not considered gay since traditional Samoan culture doesn't acknowledge homosexuality as a real thing among their people. Rather, they are seen as a distinct third gender, and as such, they are free to have sexual relations with and be married to men and women. Fooling around with other fa'afafine as well as marrying them, however, is off-limits. Importantly, a small percentage choose to live their life as men, yet because they are fa'afafine, they are allowed to be effeminate men since they are not categorized as "males." [211]

Island-hopping to the south, the conservative Christian Kingdom of Tonga has their own version of the Samoan fa'afafine known as *fakaleiti*. The fakaleiti are biological males who live and act as females. Their traditional role in Tongan society was as reliable helping hands, greatly esteemed since they were taller and stronger than female servants and were considered more reliable. Despite their prestige as servants to kings and the gentry, fakaleiti often come from the lower, poorer classes. [212]

When it comes to having sex, fakaleiti do it almost exclusively with men. The men who have sex with them, though, are never considered gay since not only does traditional Tongan culture not recognize homosexuality, but the fakaleiti aren't even considered men, so their sexual partners technically aren't having sex with another man. Still, though, life as a faka-

---

210 Hazy Pau Talauati, *"Fa'afafine—Samoan Boys Brought Up as Girls,"* *Australian Broadcasting Corporation*, 2005, http://www.abc.net.au/ra/pacific/people/hazy .htm (accessed Dec. 13, 2016).

211 Yvette Tan, "Miss *Fa'afafine*: Behind Samoa's 'Third Gender' Beauty Pageant," *British Broadcasting Corporation*, Sept. 1, 2016, http://www.bbc.com/news /world-asia-37227803 (accessed Dec. 13, 2016).

212 Peter Munro, "Transgendered Tongan 'Leitis' Finding Their Way in the Conservative Country," *Sydney Morning Herald*, Aug. 28, 2015, http://www .smh.com.au/world/transgendered-tongan-leitis-finding-their-way-in-the -conservative-country-20150820-gj48qw.html (accessed Dec. 13, 2016).

leiti is not an easy one. They are often the victims of sexual abuse, violent hate crimes, and dangerous circumstances fueled by the extreme Christian conservatism that predominates modern Tonga, even despite the annual fakaleiti beauty pageant competition "Miss Galaxy" sponsored by the Tongan government and local businesses.[213]

In the Society Islands, particularly the largest and most famous island of Tahiti, the *māhū* are their version of third-gender individuals. They're regarded as having magical powers and thus were historically very well respected. To have a māhū in the family brings along with it great prestige, and because of this it was historically fairly common for parents to nudge and raise their firstborn son to become one. To them it isn't seen as losing a son but rather as gaining a child who had the energies of both genders as well as that of the Divine. Although born males, these māhū dress, live, work, and act like women. Of particular note, they're seen as the best people to raise children in these communal "it takes a village" societies of the Society Islands, and they're highly sought out to be babysitters and caretakers.[214]

The Tahitians also have another, special group of queer individuals in addition to the māhū known as *rae-rae*. Unlike māhū, rae-rae are not a specialized third gender unto themselves, but rather biological males who dress and act like women and are regarded as women, similar to modern transgender women. They were historically seen as having a divine aptitude toward hospitality, and so even today, the rae-rae are prized as highly sought-after and elite service industry professionals who are employed at the most posh and luxurious resorts on the island.[215]

213 Brian Favorite, "My Friends, the *Fakaleitis* of Tonga," *Lesbian, Gay, Bisexual, Transgender Returned Peace Corps Volunteers*, Nov. 2, 2006, https://lgbrpcv .org/2006/11/02/my-friends-the-fakaleitis-of-tonga/ (accessed Dec. 13, 2016).

214 Trevor Bormann, "Tahiti Mahu," *Australian Broadcasting Corporation*, March 23, 2005, http://www.abc.net.au/foreign/content/2005/s1330291.htm (accessed Dec. 15, 2016).

215 Ian Lloyd Neubauer, "A Week with Tahiti's Transexual *Rae-Rae*," *CNN Travel*, May 14, 2012, http://travel.cnn.com/explorations/escape/transsexuals -tahiti-887006/ (accessed Dec. 15, 2016).

Nowadays the word *māhū* in Tahiti has fallen out of favor, and the word *rae-rae* has come to encompass all effeminate men who live as women regardless of whether they are considered a third gender or a transgender woman. Nevertheless, a third term has come into vogue called *petea*, who are males that live their lives as men but spend their nights dressed as women, either for work or for personal sexual kicks, like modern drag queens and transvestites, respectively.

Up in Hawai'i, the third-gender māhū are similar to their Tahitian counterparts, and they, too, are still flourishing in the Aloha State. To the Hawaiian natives, the belief is that every person possessed both male and female energies. What makes a man a man and a woman a woman is based on if they have more male energy or female energy. Māhū, however, are seen as individuals having a close balance of male and female energy. In practice, they are biological males who live as women, yet are seen as both man and woman in their perfectly balanced third sex. Not considered homosexuals, they represent a gender/sexual identity beyond the binary of man/woman gay/straight.

An interesting fact about the Hawaiian māhū is that they were the sacred keepers of the arts, including the hula. When Christian missionaries came to the islands, they were appalled by hula dancing since to them it was a sinfully erotic pagan dance often taught by perverted men who pretended to be women. Because of this, the hula was high priority on things that had to be abolished on the islands. During those times of persecution, it was the māhū who continued to teach the sacred dance and pass it along the generations, thus allowing it to survive to modern times. [216]

The Kingdom of Hawai'i was also a place that was quite tolerant of homosexuality. Special homoerotic relationships here were called *aikāne*, which translates best to "kept male lover," though there is reported evidence of it taking place between women as well. Aikāne relationships were

216 Kalikiano Kalei, "Hawaiian Sexuality and the 'Mahu' Tradition," *Authors Den*, March 7, 2009, http://www.authorsden.com/categories/article_top .asp?catid=62&id=46603 (accessed Dec. 15, 2016).

seen as normal, and they were a part of everyday life even among people who were already in heterosexual relationships. The great unifier of the Hawaiian Islands, King Kamehameha I, had aikāne lovers, and Kamehameha III co-ruled his kingdom with his half-Tahitian same-sex lover Kaomi. [217]

The nobles of Hawai'i were especially notable for partaking in aikāne, particularly the chiefs. To be an aikāne to a chief was an honor because it was a way to increase one's inherent status and spiritual power, known as *mana*. Men who were particularly graced with good looks or were particularly gifted in the arts of dance or chanting were selected by the tribal chiefs to be their personal aikāne. In this way, the chief would add the mana of this beautiful and talented youth to his own, and the youth would add the mana of the sacred chief to his own.

To many modern scholars, the Kingdom of Hawai'i was a perfect example of a naturally sexually fluid culture. Sexuality was simply accepted as fluid, and while there were defining labels such as men and women, those labels were subject to change without any negative social stigma. Queerness was neither reprehensible nor praiseworthy; it simply was a mundane status quo reality of life. Nowadays, the lingering effects of the Christian missionaries still affect the mindsets of a number of native Hawaiians who consider queerness as "not natural" to native culture and an unwanted import from Western colonizers, but for the most part, LGBT+ persons are welcome and accepted. Hawai'i being one of the most liberal states in the US, the queer community enjoys full privileges and protections as well as a laid-back, permissive atmosphere of out and proud acceptance wherein all people are considered part of the *ohana* of the islands. [218]

217   Michelle Broder Van Dyke, "A Brief History of Sexual Identity in Hawaii," *Buzzfeed*, Nov. 12, 2013, https://www.buzzfeed.com/mbvd/a-brief-history-of-sexual-identity-in-hawaii?utm_term=.vo9DVqx4a#.fbDnPBYd5 (accessed Dec. 15, 2016); Alan Robert Akana, *The Volcano Is Our Home: Nine Generations of a Hawaiian Family on Kilauea Volcano* (Carlsbad: Balboa Press, 2014).

218   Paul Canning, "Polynesia's Ancient Same-Sex Acceptance," *LGBT Asylum News*, Sept. 12, 2010, http://madikazemi.blogspot.com/2010/09/polynesias-ancient-same-sex-acceptance.html (accessed Dec. 15, 2016).

Polynesian Takeaway:
DE-SHAME YOUR STEREOTYPE

A look through Polynesia shows a trend in queer stereotyping. For the third gender (usually male-to-female) individuals, they are homemakers, hospitality experts, keepers of the arts, dancers, and so on. From a modern Western perspective, some might dismiss this as an unfortunate stereotyping of them. But in the native perspective, these "stereotypes" are talents that queer people are divinely blessed with. It isn't seen as pigeonholing LGBT+ people, but rather acknowledging their divine gifts that their straight/cis counterparts generally lack.

In the Western world, we queer people are in every profession, but it is undeniable that certain professions have a higher concentration of us, professions that we freely choose because that is where our interests lie, and there is no shame in this. Oftentimes, in a desperate bid to fit in or run away from our queerness, we avoid queer stereotypes that we personally enjoy. So what if a lesbian is interested in construction, if a gay man is a hairdresser, if a genderqueer person is a performance artist, or if you like to watch reality shows about drag queens? If it brings you happiness, then avoiding it because it is a "stereotype" only means that you are depriving yourself of that happiness. Again, people like what they like, and if what you like is a stereotype of your identity, who cares? Live your own life.

So, for your next magical activity, you're going to assess whether or not you're living your own divine truth. Go to your closest friends and ask them to describe you with brutal honesty. If this makes you feel anxious, then that's even more reason why you need to do this. Ask them to describe how they see you and how you come across as if you two weren't friends, as if they're a non-involved observer. Does what they say resonate with your inner truth? If not, then why not? Are you wearing a mask and trying to fit in so you don't stand out or seem too much like a stereotype, even though that's where your natural interests/talents lie?

If your best friend doesn't see the you that you feel you are on the inside, the true you, then you're not living your own life true to you.

Remember, how we feel we are and how we actually live our lives are two different things. Until your outward self reflects your inner self, you're suppressing yourself. Use this exercise to examine how aligned you're living your life to your own divine truth.

Deities & Legends

HI'IAKA

In Hawaiian mythology Hi'iaka is the goddess of the hula, chanting, medicine, magic, and Hawai'i itself. In terms of sexuality she would be considered bisexual or pansexual, yet she is more renowned for her retinue of female lovers. Her most infamous queer stories involve her love-hate relationship with her sister Pele (creator goddess of fire, volcanoes, lightning, wind, and the Hawaiian Islands). Much like her dominion, Pele is a jealous and temperamental deity, and on one legendary occasion her wrath had runneth over onto Hi'iaka.

There are various versions of the legend, but the general story goes as follows. Pele falls in love with the bisexual young chief of Kaua'i named Lohiau, but through her own jealous paranoia, she convinces herself that her sister Hi'iaka is trying to seduce Lohiau for her own and is off having trysts with him. To get back at her sister for these imagined offenses, Pele murders Hi'iaka's most favored female aikāne lover, Hopoe, by covering her in an avalanche of lava flow. Understandably, Hi'iaka is devastated, and through trying to comfort her, Lohiau actually does become intimate with his lover's sister and falls in love with Hi'iaka. Thus, Pele's self-fulfilling prophecy becomes realized due to her own paranoid actions. In some versions this sobers her into remorse, while in others she remains too blinded by jealousy to see the truth.

Ironically, despite her murdering her sister's lesbian companion (and her ridicule of male-male anal sex, as we'll talk about in an upcoming story), Pele has, in modern times, gained a large lesbian and feminist following due to her independence, strength, athletic prowess, and power of creation through destruction. Of all the Hawaiian deities, Pele is arguably the most well-known and seen in modern pop culture.[219]

HINEMOA & TUTANEKAI

One of the most famous legends in Maori mythology, the tale of Hinemoa and Tutanekai shares similarities with Shakespearean works and the ancient Greek tragedy of Hero and Leander, except this native New Zealand tale is much queerer and has a happy ending. As the story goes, the young maiden Hinemoa falls in love with the brave male hero Tutanekai, who lives on an island in the middle of a vast lake. But there's a problem in that Tutanekai is well-known for only being interested in other men. So Hinemoa disguises herself as a man and seduces him to become her "gay" lover. The ruse works, and Tutanekai is soon head-over-heels for the "male" Hinemoa. Such a secret between lovers couldn't be kept forever, though, and Tutanekai eventually finds out that his boyfriend is actually his girlfriend. But by then it doesn't matter; he had fallen in love with Hinemoa regardless of her real gender.

The young couple's parents vehemently disapprove of the relationship, however, and forbid the two lovers to carry on their romance. To be sure that the infatuation would be put to an end, Hinemoa's father, as chief of the island, decrees that no canoes be given to his daughter to help her travel to Tutanekai's island in the middle of the vast lake. All seems lost, but one day Hinemoa hears the music of Tutanekai's flute from way across the waters. Fueled by love and determination, she swims across the radius of the lake, guided by her lover's music, and the two reunite and live happily ever after.[220]

---

219 From http://sacred-texts.com (accessed Aug. 20, 2016).
220 Maria Pallotta-Chiarolli, *Women in Relationships with Bisexual Men: Bi Men By Women* (Lanham: Lexington Books, 2016).

KAMAPUA'A

Hawaiian demigod child of Hine (goddess of the moon) and Kahiki-ula (chief of O'ahu), Kamapua'a possessed the unique physique of half-pig, half-man. Likened to the ancient Greek god Pan, he is seen as a wild, pansexual, lascivious personality who cannot be tamed and pursues life's more basic pleasures. Because of this, he is considered the god of sexuality, battle, rain, divination, and agriculture, and he is often associated with Lono, who is also a bisexual deity of the same domains.

Like Hi'iaka, he is often at odds with Pele, who frequently ridicules the way Kamapua'a can only have anal sex with his male partners as opposed to more "normal" vaginal sex as with his female partners. This is especially insulting considering that Kamapua'a prefers anal sex regardless of his partner, so much so that his derrière has its own nickname that translates to "Gaping Above." Nevertheless, Kamapua'a is deeply attracted to the beautiful Pele and relentlessly attempts to woo and bed her. Numerous are the romantic misadventures between Pele and Kamapua'a, some where they are actual lovers and some where the love is one-sided, but their queerest story together is one where there is no love between them.

According to the legends, Kamapua'a and Pele are in an ongoing feud with each other that turns physically violent. Each engagement ends in a stalemate, and so to gain an advantage, Pele sends two of her brothers to rough up Kamapua'a before their next fight. The plan fails, however, because Kamapua'a counters by sending Lonoikiaweawealoha (god of love) to seduce her familial thugs. So effective is this counterstrategy that Pele's brothers, after multiple orgies between themselves and Lonoikiaweawealoha, completely forget what they were originally sent to do. And thus Kamapua'a remains in full ability for his next bout against Pele thanks to his ingenious plan of interceptive distraction via an impromptu gay orgy.[221]

221 Ruchika Singhal, "Gay Gods in Mythology," *Speaking Tree*, Nov. 28, 2012, http://www.speakingtree.in/blog/gay-gods-in-mythology (accessed Aug. 20, 2017).

21

OCEANIC MAGICAL COMMUNITY

FIELD TRIP TO A PLACE IN THE MIDDLE

Our regular example of a fellow modern-day member of the queer tribe giving us first-person insight into their lives, magic, and spirituality will be a bit different for this leg of our global trek. We've come a long way already, and as we relax here in the Oceanic isles, let me explain how this "field trip" is going to work.

Originally, when researching information on queer Oceania, I came across the documentary film *Kumu Hina*,[222] which I later learned won the GLAAD Media Award for Outstanding Documentary in 2016. Far and away it was one of the best, most well-rounded, and truthfully empathetic

---

222 *Kumu Hina*, directed by Dean Hamer and Joe Wilson (2014, Haleiwa: Qwaves, 2016), Netflix (accessed Feb. 5, 2017).

pieces on the queer community I had ever seen. Every medium has its own magic; there are things books can do that the movies cannot, and there are things that the movies can do that books cannot. When it comes to truly showing visceral reality of life as a māhū in modern-day Hawai'i and all the joys, challenges, struggles, and personal victories that come with it, *Kumu Hina* is a class unto its own.

I began contacting various people involved with the documentary, including the directors and eponymous title character, in order to invite them to be the featured contributing authors for this Polynesian section of the book. And while everyone was very receptive and wondrously helpful and supportive to contribute their stories and experiences to this book, it became more and more obvious that this was something that had to be seen rather than read. A certain magic of this documentary and what it has to teach us would get lost in translation if it was converted to short personal written excerpts.

That leads us back to our field trip. While I stay here and restock on supplies for our sail eastward to the Americas, go watch the documentary *Kumu Hina* and allow her to not just tell you what it's like being a native third-gender māhū in contemporary Hawai'i, but also show you how she overcomes and lives her truth as a person the Western world cannot define, yet the ancient Hawaiians have for centuries. There's a reason it won so many prestigious awards, and I do not make recommendations lightly. Support the queer arts and support our tribe; watch *Kumu Hina* and let her show you firsthand the magic of being māhū.

PART 7

THE AMERICAS

…if nature puts a burden on a man by making him different, it also gives him a power.
JOHN FIRE LAME DEER,
SIOUX MEDICINE MAN

The Americas cover a vast swath of land stretching from pole to pole, dividing the Atlantic and Pacific Oceans. "Discovered" by Europeans on accident, these terrains of the Western Hemisphere were already well populated before colonization by the Old World. From Patagonia to the Yukon, the Americas were home to numerous peoples, each with their own histories, cultures, and beliefs.

The spiritual traditions and cultures here in the New World are as numerous as the indigenous peoples themselves. But in terms of queer spirituality and tradition, there are two general categories. First, there is Latin America, where the largest and mightiest empires of the Americas once existed, though the Catholic Church now reigns supreme. Then there is North America (for our purposes, the lands above Mexico), inhabited by tribes of Native Americans, famed for their prolific acceptance of "two-spirit" people.

For our queer trek across the Americas, we'll follow the course of history to plot our route. Beginning in Latin America, where the first empires fell, we'll transition northbound toward the Native American tribes and end in the great white north of the Arctic Circle.

22

LATIN AMERICA

Cultural

Latin America is an interesting place due to it being such a seemingly contradictory region of the globe. It was the first part of the Americas to be conquered by Europeans, and yet it is still revealing "new" and previously uncontacted tribes of indigenous peoples. It is the strongest and largest bastion of the Catholic Church and is where the majority of the world's Catholics live, yet it is one of the most socially progressive global regions wherein many LGBT+ rights and protections were first legalized. And it is a region where the people are fiercely proud to be natives, yet what is considered "native" is actually imposed ideology from colonial times (Catholicism, Spanish language, mestizos) while true natives are often shunned (their indigenous languages, religions, and skin colors).

Since we already talked about Catholicism when we were back in Europe, we'll stick to exploring indigenous queerness here in Latin America, starting with the Aztecs. Most of what we know about Aztec history comes from artwork and written accounts by Spanish colonizers. Unfortunately, Spanish Catholicism during the time of the New World conquest was experiencing hyperzealotry and fervor, so accounts of LGBT+ activity and persons in their entries should be taken with grains of salt.

To modern historians, it is generally agreed that the Aztecs—whom we'll call by their original name of Mexica since Aztec is a modern word referring to the empire of the ethnic Mexica people—were just as intolerant of homosexuality and queerness as their Spanish conquerors. The Mexica were a very bellicose society who valued hypermasculinity in all its forms: warfare, aggression, violence, and strength. It was this extreme alpha-male mindset that led them to be the most powerful tribe in the region, subjugating their neighbors by brute force. Because of their cult of masculinity, anything seen as feminine, especially within a biological male, was reviled. Sodomy between men was seen as a grave offense to Mexica culture because it meant a man lowering himself to that of a woman. The punishment for being caught having homosexual relations was death. The male "top" was to be impaled on a stake, the male "bottom" was to have his intestines pulled out through his offending anus, and lesbians were to be strangled.[223]

While many other militaristically inclined civilizations have also placed a high value on masculinity, the unusual and extreme levels to which the Mexica despised and persecuted homosexuality is not 100 percent understood. Different academics have different theories, but the consensus seems to be that homoerotic activity was seen as something "others" do, while true Mexica were virile heterosexuals. There is much credence to this majority opinion, considering that most of the surrounding people whom

---

223 Bernarda Reza Ramirez, "Propuesta Para Abatir el Delito en el Estado de Veracruz—Llave," *Acontecer Jurídico*, vol. 2, Aug. 26, 2012, https://issuu.com /acontecerjuridico/docs/www.acontecerjuridico.com (accessed Dec. 21, 2016).

the Mexica conquered and subjugated into their Aztec Empire were very tolerant of homosexuality. In fact, the Spanish wrote extensively on the liberal queerness of these subjugated people, especially the cross-dressing and male-prostitution-accepting cultures in the modern-day state of Veracruz.[224]

The most notable and telling people in the region who celebrated homosexuality, though, were the Toltecs. The Toltecs were the reigning people of what is modern Mexico before the Mexica conquered them. Their rivalry could be likened to that of the city-states of Sparta and Athens in ancient Greece. The Mexica and Spartans were an aggressive, warlike people who valued physical might, while the Toltecs and Athenians were more artistic and philosophical people who valued logic, reasoning, and mental might. As in much of world history, though, the intellectual Toltecs (and Athenians) were eventually overcome by the military superiority of the aggressive Mexica (and Spartans).

Having proven that might is right, the Mexica associated the ideals of the defeated Toltecs as something negative, which included their acceptance of homosexuality. The Aztec cosmology further cemented this idea through the myth of the Four Worlds. In brief, it tells the history of the Mexica people up until their then-modern glory as hegemon of the region. The world just previous to this golden age, however, was described in this myth as dominated by people who had grown weak and feminine due to a life too easy from constant peace and lack of war. This previous world was governed by strong devotees of Xochiquétzal and Xochipilli—the gods of, among other things, homosexuality—and they celebrated nonheterosexual relations among their people. This myth of the Four Worlds never mentions the Toltecs by name, but its description of the previous world is quite historically accurate of the Toltecs who ruled the region just before the Mexica.[225]

224   Stephen O. Murray, *Latin American Male Homosexualities* (Albuquerque: University of New Mexico Press, 1995).
225   Ibid.

To the east of the Aztec Empire (and predating it by thousands of years) existed a civilization much different from the Mexica and much more accepting of queerness: the Mayans. Historical knowledge about Mayan life is some of the most authentic we have today in all the region, owing greatly to the fact that the Mayans had invented a fully developed writing system, the only civilization to do so in the pre-Columbian Americas.

From their own accounts, we know that the Mayans were very tolerant of queerness. Same-sex orgies and orgies wherein all sexualities and orientations participated were acceptable means of pleasure. There even still exist Mayan cave paintings of same-sex couples locked in embrace, rubbing genitals together. To the Mayans, one's sexuality and sexual identity were non-issues; nevertheless, anal sex was illegal and punishable by death, specifically by being thrown into a pit of fire. So whether you were a hetero- or homosexual couple, all acts of carnal pleasure were fair game, as long as everyone abstained from using the back door.[226]

Homosexuality was also seen by the Mayans as spiritual. Not only would shamanic priests engage in ritualized homoerotic activity with their patients as a form of medicine, but they would also spiritually engage in it with their gods. On a more earthly level, homosexuality was also seen as a status symbol of the idle rich. The gentry of Mayan society, as well as those who could afford it, would customarily buy male sex slaves for their teenage sons. To purchase such an expensive "toy" of leisure for an adolescent showed that you were a family of privilege since most male slaves were used for labor rather than pleasure, thus justifying their expensive cost. To gift your queer son with a male sex slave was essentially a flashy show of wealth to society, kind of like a modern sixteen-year-old's parents giving them a Rolls Royce as their first car.[227]

226 Lens Evans, "Chronology of Gay Mexican History," *Fifty Gay Years in the Greater Sacramento Area 1950–2000*, Oct. 2002, http://gayinsacramento.com /Chron-Mex.htm (accessed Dec. 21, 2016).

227 Peter Herman Sigal, *From Moon Goddesses to Virgins: The Colonization of Yucatecan Maya Sexual Desire* (Austin: University of Texas Press, 2000).

Traveling further down into South America, the Inca Empire also had their own ideas about queerness. The Incas had a very liberal attitude toward sex. In addition to homosexuality, they encouraged premarital sex and held no special honor for a female to be a virgin. The first Spanish conquistadors to the region wrote at length about such rampant sin and held special contempt for the Moche and Chimu cultures within the empire, who decorated their pottery with gay men and lesbians engaging in homoerotic and anal sex.[228]

Unique to the Incas, lesbians were regarded with much high esteem. Although men held social dominance over women, a lesbian was allowed to have the same privileges as a man while still being considered a woman. Permitted the full privileges of manhood, Incan lesbians were allowed to join the army and fight in combat, be promiscuous and engage in extramarital affairs, and have their voices heard in council. Additionally, among the jungle tribes who paid tribute to the Incas, many were led by fierce warrior women who engaged in lesbianism and permitted it within their tribes. The language of the Incas even referred to these jungle tribes with lesbian terms. When the Europeans penetrated into these jungle lands, such a mix of open lesbianism, female chieftains, and women in the military led them to name these regions of the Inca Empire after the fierce fighting women of ancient Greek mythology, the Amazons.[229]

Outside of these big three pre-Columbian empires, smaller tribes have also exhibited a range of LGBT+ acceptance and spirituality. One of the more enduring is the Tapirapé tribe of the Amazonian jungle. Full contact was only made with them around the 1950s, and they are thought to be a surviving example of human society as it was in prehistoric times. This is positive news for the queer community because the Tapirapé exhibit quite a liberal attitude toward queerness and sexuality. In their society,

228 Paul Mathieu, *Sex Pots: Eroticism in Ceramics* (New Brunswick: Rutgers University Press, 2003).

229 Eduardo Ramon Lopez, "El Rostro Oculto de los Pueblos Precolombinos," *Ecuador Gay*, Oct. 2004, https://web.archive.org/web/20051216191923 /http://www.islaternura.com/APLAYA/HOMOenHISTORIA/Pueblos%20 precolombinos%20Octubre%202004.htm (accessed Dec. 21, 2016).

two people of the same sex can make love together and marry each other alongside heterosexuals. Even more revolutionary is how they do not assign gender roles to these same-sex couples wherein the "bottom"/ femme is expected to be the woman of the relationship, and the "top"/ butch is expected to be the man. Part of this support for same-sex couples comes from the Tapirapé's strict family planning policies of three children maximum in order to prevent overpopulation beyond their means to support everyone sufficiently. [230]

Nowadays in Latin America there is a new pro-queer spirituality that is taking the region by storm. It is the devotion to Death, personified as a female grim reaper called la Santa Muerte (which best translates to "Holy Death"). I won't go on at length here about it since I previously wrote an entire book in English and another in Spanish on this pro-LGBT+ underground cult, but because of how accepting it is of the queer community, it definitely deserves a mention here as well.

The short version is that devotees of la Santa Muerte usually come from groups who are ostracized and maligned by Mexican Catholic society. These often include criminals, prostitutes, the working poor, self-empowered women, and LGBT+ individuals. Not feeling like they belong in the Catholic Church yet still culturally raised in a Catholic tradition, they turn to Death to be their intercessor.

I know it sounds odd, but from a Catholic theological view, it makes sense. According to the Gospels, Jesus died on the cross and rose from the dead three days later, on Easter Sunday. Though each Santa Muerte devotee has their own beliefs, a good majority believe that during those absent days, Jesus learned from Death the final defining human experience: mortality. Without death, Jesus never would have experienced the totality of what it is to be human, thus allowing God to finally fully empathize with humankind. Moreover, God so highly favored Death that he trusted his only son to her as his final teacher.

---

230   Hinsch, *Passions of the Cut Sleeve.*

Devotion to la Santa Muerte is Catholic enough to where the outcasts of Mexico can feel comfortable and familiar, yet it has a very big difference: it practices magic and *brujería* (witchcraft). While a lot of Mexican Catholics engage in various forms of folk magic, what sets la Santa Muerte magic apart is that she doesn't care about your intentions or the consequences of your desires.

Death accepts everyone equally, regardless of age, religion, race, income, sexuality, or personal morality. So if you do a magical working for something that the social majority deems "immoral," la Santa Muerte will help get you what you want, ethics be damned. This augments the affinity outcasts have toward her: narcos will pray to her to help smuggle drugs, prostitutes will do a spell for a profitable night, and so on. But more often these are crimes of necessity wherein socioeconomic circumstances grant no other avenue for survival outside of moral ambiguity.

On a queer level, this makes her the de facto spiritual patroness of modern LGBT+ people in Latin America. Queerness in any form is seen as "wrong" in Catholic Latin American society, and therefore God won't help the queer community. But since Death accepts everyone and doesn't judge, the queer community turns to her for divine intercession. Queer love spells, self-empowerment/self-love amulets, protection prayers, and much more are all extremely popular among Death's devotees. Additionally, the Santa Muerte community is a community of "others," so not only do LGDT+ people find spiritual acceptance with la Santa Muerte, but they also find an oasis of communal acceptance where they can safely be themselves and find support, much like what Vodou and Santería are to the Caribbean queer communities.

There's so much more queer lore and magic in the Santa Muerte community, too much to go on about here. But if you're curious enough to learn more about it and how it's revolutionizing Mexican queer acceptance and spirituality, then check out my other books on it: *La Santa Muerte: Unearthing the Magic & Mysticism of Death* and the Spanish-language version *La Santa Muerte: La exhumación de la magia y el misticismo de la muerte.*

Latin American Takeaway:
UTILIZE YOUR DARK EMOTIONS

We all have grand darkness inside of us. We can be as socially progressive and New Agey "white light" as we want, but all of us are capable of unspeakable horrors. In the Santa Muerte tradition, being able to accept your darkness is a prerequisite for being able to do Santa Muerte magic. But we don't like to acknowledge our dark emotions because they make us uncomfortable. As queer people and spellworkers, though, how can we expect to combat the darkness of others who wish to do us harm if we can't even face the darkness in ourselves?

So, for your next magical activity, you're going to acknowledge and allow yourself to feel the darkness in your heart. Think back to the Mexica, their hatred of queer culture, and how they mercilessly treated our queer brothers and sisters. Listen to songs that tell about true-story hate crimes against our queer community such as Rod Stewart's groundbreaking "The Killing of Georgie" and Melissa Etheridge's infamous "Scarecrow" about the murder of Matthew Shepard, a student who, because he was gay, was pistol whipped and left to die alone in the rural Wyoming cold. Watch films featuring true-story violence to people like us such as the visceral Academy Award winner *Boys Don't Cry*. Read news stories about the state-sponsored genocide of queer people going on in Chechnya, about the legal daily death sentences of LGBT+ people all over the world, about how yet another trans brother/sister has been murdered on the street, and about how queer people were also victims of Nazi genocide, forced to return to their prisons after the fall of the Third Reich. Focus on the pain, the anger, and the sorrow all this makes you feel. Allow yourself to fester in these dark emotions. Know that you, too, are capable of being victimized as well as victimizing others in this same way.

Once you've allowed yourself to feel these negative, dark emotions, do something with them. Don't lose your temper; *use* your temper. The Stonewall uprising of our people only came about because the poorest and most marginalized of the queer community were angry, sad, and hurting to the point where they stood up and used their dark emotions to fuel positive action against the darkness of others. All progressive achievements throughout the world have come about only once marginalized people, fueled by their dark emotions, stood up against the darkness of others. The enemy will not perish of itself, and sometimes we have to gaze into our own darkness in order to fuel the fire within, finally say *enough*, and take action.

Deities & Legends

CHIN

Chin is the Mayan god of homosexuality. According to Mayan cosmology, Chin was a generic demon who developed a special attraction to a fellow male demon. Instigated by Chin, the two began fooling around and developing ways in which people of the same sex could enjoy one another physically, thus introducing homosexuality into the world. Originating from a spiritual being, the Mayans thus regarded homosexual sex as something more spiritual and magical than heterosexual sex. Bartolomé de las Casas, noted as being the most humane and empathetic of the Spanish missionaries in the New World, even wrote about how young men were instructed in the ways of male-male intercourse in Chin temples as if it was a holy sacrament.[231] Subsequently, such pomp and circumstance involved with homosexuality helped it to become associated with the wealth, elitism, and luxury in Mayan culture.[232]

TLAZOLTÉOTL

Tlazoltéotl is an Aztec underworld deity who is known as the goddess of purification, lust, adultery, transgression, vice, and life and death. The common name for her is "Eater of Filth," but the "filth" she eats is symbolic of what we would nowadays call "sin." She has a dual nature to her wherein she simultaneously encourages you to live without inhibitions

---

231 Bartolomé de las Casas, *Apologética Historia Sumaria*, vol. 2, ed. Edmundo O'Gorman (Mexico City: UNAM, 1967), c. 1559.

232 Grant D. Jones, *The Conquest of the Last Maya Kingdom* (Palo Alto: Stanford University Press, 1998).

and push boundaries while also being the one who both forgives and punishes you for having no self-restraint and taking things too far. Appropriately, the Mexica believed she was the deity who cursed people by giving them sexually transmitted diseases, and it was she to whom they would turn to help rid themselves of those same diseases.[233]

The reason Tlazoltéotl makes an appearance here in our travels is because she was seen as a refuge deity for the Mexica queer community. As previously discussed, being queer in the Aztec Empire was not an easy thing. Of the many spiritual powers Tlazotéotl possesses is that of transforming suffering into prosperity. This attribute is thought to have attracted LGBT+ individuals who believed that through her intercession, their daily suffering would one day pay off somehow in the future. Moreover, specifically for the ladies, she (along with Xochiquétzal) is one of the two mother goddesses of the lesbian and transgender female priestesses of the Huastec indigenous people (who were subjugated by the Mexica into the Aztec Empire). Lastly, Tlazotéotl also possesses the title "Goddess of the Anus" and was associated with anal sex.[234]

Known sacred correspondences to Tlazotéotl included cotton, seeds, dirt, brooms, and human excrement. Taking part in lechery and sexual fetishes as well as cleaning, bathing, and acts of self-purification were activities sacred to her.

XOCHIPILLI

Of all the Latin American deities associated with the queer community, Xochipilli is probably the most flamboyant. He is the god of flowers, beauty, dance, song, and the arts, all of which have strong stereotypical gay associations even today. His name best translates to "Prince of Flowers," and surviving archeological artefacts depict him in psychedelic bodily ecstasy. Descriptions of him reveal that he is a peaceful deity whose rituals

---

233 Mary Ellen Miller and Karl A. Taube, *The Gods and Symbols of Ancient Mexico and the Maya: An Illustrated Dictionary of Mesoamerican Religion* (New York: Thames & Hudson, 1993).

234 Christopher Penczak, *Gay Witchcraft*.

and celebrations forbade human sacrifice and who was the chief deity of the Toltecs.

Because of him being the ruling deity during the Toltec era, the Mexica conquerors of the Toltecs viewed him as the embodiment of the weak, peace-loving virtues of the Toltec people that led to their downfall. This especially included their tolerance and celebration of homosexuality. Thus, to the Mexica, Xochipilli was the quintessential deity of male weakness as exemplified by his queerness. To modern researchers of Mexica culture, Xochipilli is often considered to be a hippie archetype due to his affinity for flowers, peace, entheogenic highs, communal song and dance, and liberal attitude toward sex and sexuality.[235]

Known sacred correspondences to Xochipilli included flowers, corn, mushrooms, dancing, mother-of-pearl, teardrop shapes, and earth elements. Taking part in artistic endeavors as well as psychotropic trips were activities sacred to him.

235 Greenberg, *The Construction of Homosexuality.*

23
NATIVE NORTH AMERICA

Cultural

For those of us in the United States, the most frequent references to queer-accepting spiritualities and societies are from Native American traditions. And while their queer cultures certainly aren't at the vibrancy they once were before the West was won (rarely fairly) by the United States government, they are nevertheless still here and need to be heard.

Anyone who has done even the slightest of research into LGBT+ Native American culture is familiar with the term "two-spirit." A two-spirit person is someone who has both male and female energies within them. And while in a cosmic sense everyone has masculine and feminine energies in them, what makes a person stand out as two-spirit is having the proportions in unusual equilibrium or having a disproportionately larger amount of the energy that is opposite one's biological sex.

For many tribes, the two-spirit individual was seen as sacred and possessing a certain magic. Native American tribes are also shamanic, and so reverence toward those who can transcend the binary of male/female were often also thought to be able to transcend boundaries on all levels, including the barrier between the physical and spiritual worlds.

The phenomenon of the two-spirit person is a concept pervasive throughout North America and goes by many different names. Some of the more well-known ones include the *winkte* of the Lakota, the *nádleehí* of the Diné, the *boté* of the Crow, the *ikwekanaazo* and *ininiikaazo* of the Ojibwe, the *lhamana* of the Zuni, and the *he'eman* and the *hetaneman* of the Cheyenne. Most famously, though, the Cheyenne's version was popularized to non-indigenous moviegoers in 1970 via the character of Little Horse in the Dustin Hoffman Western epic film *Little Big Man*, argued by film historians to be the first major motion picture to depict gender-variant people in a natural, respectful, and matter-of-fact way.[236]

Despite the hundreds of extant Native American tribes, the popularity of the pan-Indian word "two-spirit" in place of each tribe's own term for LGBT+ individuals is a purposeful and conscious effort by the modern Native American queer community. By using a universal term rather than hundreds of different ones, queer Native Americans consolidate their identity into a singular force, thus making their queerness easier to discuss, be recognized by the general public, and advocate for in courts of law. It also unifies the indigenous queer community of North America into a larger minority with more political sway while still maintaining themselves as separate and distinct from non-indigenous LGBT+ persons. In fact, modern consensus among queer Native Americans says that only Native Americans should be labeled as "two-spirit," and others who

236 "Two-Spirit Terms in Tribal Languages," *Native OUT*, http://nativeout.com /twospirit-rc/two-spirit-101/two-spirit-terms-in-tribal-languages/ (accessed Dec. 28, 2016).

identify as two-spirit should use their own indigenous terms for labeling themselves.[237]

In regard to the specifics of various two-spirit identities of various tribes, we'll start with the wínkte. Among the Lakota, a wínkte is a biological male who works, acts, and lives as a traditional female. While some accounts describe them as being sacred individuals in Lakota society, other accounts speak of them as regular people no more special than anyone else, just different as men and women are different from each other.

Regardless of whether they were treated as divine intercessors or regular Joes, a curious similarity that almost all wínkte share is their preference for masculine men, specifically married masculine men. As is controversially common in the modern gay community of widespread preference for masculine (or non-effeminate) men as being the most desirable sex partner, the desires of the wínkte were the same. Sexual relations among the Lakota were seen as a union of masculine and feminine energies. Two men together, two women together, or two wínkte together was seen as unnatural. A wínkte with a heterosexual male, however, was seen as an appropriate and natural balance of sexual energies. Having sex with a wínkte did not make a man gay, as "gay" was seen as two cisgender men having sex with each other. Because of all this, in the psychology of a wínkte, a male who exudes masculinity is the best lover to complement their own self, which exudes femininity.[238]

In modern times, the Lakota community is divided in regard to their affinity toward wínkte. Like many indigenous cultures of Africa, Oceania, and Latin America, Christian missionaries have had a profoundly lasting effect. The Lakota, similar to many Native American tribes, were brutally forced to convert to Christianity as their sole religion, and as generation after generation has come and gone, Christian culture has become the

237 Mary Annette Pember, "'Two Spirit' Tradition Far from Ubiquitous Among Tribes," *Rewire*, Oct. 13, 2016, https://rewire.news/article/2016/10/13/two-spirit-tradition-far-ubiquitous-among-tribes/ (accessed Dec. 28, 2016).

238 Evelyn Blackwood, *The Many Faces of Homosexuality: Anthropological Approaches to Homosexual Behavior* (New York: Routledge, 1986).

dominant norm. And what was once normal, such as gender variance, is now regarded as unnatural. Of course, not all Lakota see wínkte as abominations, but a not-so-small percentage of contemporary Lakota do.[239]

Over in the deserts of the Southwest, the Navajo are of queer interest due to their nuanced spectrum of gender and sexual identities. The preferred title for the Navajo people is Diné, and so for the rest of our trek, we will refer to them as such. There are four separate, recognized genders in Diné society. *Asdzaan* are biological females who are effeminate and live as traditional women. *Dilbaa* are biological females who are masculine and live as traditional men. *Hastiin* are biological males who are masculine and live as traditional men. *Nádleehí* are biological males who are effeminate and live as traditional women.[240]

The Diné also practiced their own spiritual versions of same-sex marriages long before and after contact with any Europeans. In 2005, however, that changed when the Diné Nation overwhelmingly passed a tribal law called the Diné Marriage Act that legally defined marriage as between one biological male and one biological female. So, despite same-sex marriage being legalized throughout the United States in 2015, on Diné lands it remains illegal, which is ironic since historically it was the other way around.[241]

Even more nuanced than those of the Diné, the Cree up in modern-day Canada have eight different gender classifications. Aside from the two uni-

239   Beatrice Medicine, "Directions in Gender Research in American Indian Societies: Two Spirits and Other Categories," *Online Readings in Psychology and Culture*, vol. 3 (Bellingham: Western Washington University Center for Cross-Cultural Research, 2002), https://web.archive.org/web/20030330115133 /http://www.ac.wwu.edu/~culture/medicine.htm (accessed Dec. 31, 2016).

240   Dr. Zuleyka Zevallos, "Rethinking Gender and Sexuality: Case Study of the Native American 'Two Spirit' People," *The Other Sociologist*, Sept. 9, 2013, https://othersociologist.com/2013/09/09/two-spirit-people/ (accessed Dec. 31, 2016).

241   Jorge Rivas, "Gay Marriage Is Still Illegal for the Navajo. This Man Is Trying to Change That," *Fusion*, July 7, 2015, http://fusion.net/story/161887/gay -marriage-is-still-illegal-for-the-navajo-this-man-is-trying-to-change-that/ (Jan. 1, 2017).

versally traditional genders of masculine males and feminine females, the other six are recognized as follows: a *napêw iskwêwisêhot* is a biological male who dresses as a traditional woman, an *iskwêw ka napêwaya* is a biological female who dresses as a traditional man, an *ayahkwêw* is a biological male who lives as a traditional woman, an *înahpîkasoht* is a biological female who lives as a traditional man, an *iskwêhkân* is an effeminate, biological male, and a *napêhkân* is a butch biological female. It should be said, though, that even among the contemporary Cree there exist disagreements over the exact definitions of these various genders and if some ever existed at all, though the latter argument seems to be based on conservative denial, an unfortunately common theme of the oppressed adopting the ways of the oppressor and calling them their own.[242]

Back down in the Southwest, the Zuni are a Native American tribe of special mention. Like many other tribes indigenous to North America, the Zuni have a separate third gender of biological males who live and take on the traditional gender roles of females. They are called *lhamana*, and they are tasked with performing the most difficult female-assigned labors in the tribe in addition to being the tribe's premier artists, mediators, and keepers of spiritual wisdom. Unlike other tribes, though, the Zuni believed that gender was not determined at birth; rather, it was a personal choice each tribe member made upon puberty. The general protocol would be to allow a child to act like whichever gender they chose, even if it meant weaving in and out as the years went by. Then, upon puberty, the child would be asked which of the genders they identified with so as to prepare and train them appropriately for their growth into sexualized adulthood.

As an added tidbit, the Zuni also had a less publicized lhamana-like alternate gender for biological females who lived and acted as traditional males. They were called by slang terms such as *katsotstsi* (girl-man) and *otstsi* (manly), and it's a sad but unsurprisingly common example of the

242 Harlan Prudan and Se-ah-dom Edmo, "Two-Spirit People: Sex, Gender & Sexuality in Historic and Contemporary Native America," *National Congress of American Indians Policy Research Center*, http://www.ncai.org/policy-research -center/initiatives/Pruden-Edmo_TwoSpiritPeople.pdf (accessed Jan. 1, 2017).

patriarchal old boys' club that is academia that not much about them is known as compared to their biological male counterparts, and only one female anthropologist, Elsie Clews Parson, has done any major research on them, with later research being mostly based on her findings.[243]

The last Native American tribe of our world tour takes us to the arctic north where queer mythology abounds among the Inuit. In Inuit culture homosexuality was very common among women and men, and it was given the names "two soft things rubbing together" for female homosexuality and "two hard things rubbing together" for male homosexuality. Both same-sex and polyamorous relationships were normal up in the taiga and tundra of modern Alaska and Canada.

Nowadays, however, like in many parts of the globe, colonialism and Christian missionaries have had a dire lasting effect upon the native peoples. Many Inuit individuals identify so strongly with Christianity, to the point where Christianity and Inuit identity are now almost one and the same. The hallmarks of Inuit society, such as remoteness and isolation, further add to the homophobia that is now so prevalent among them. Nevertheless, times are changing, and there is a bourgeoning queer-acceptance movement being led by the younger generations to return to their traditional roots of widespread love and acceptance of all Inuit tribe members, regardless of sexual identity or orientation.[244]

243 Will Roscoe, *The Zuni Man-Woman* (Albuquerque: University of New Mexico Press, 1991).

244 Miles Kenyon, "Documentary Shines Spotlight on Experience of LGBT Inuit," *The Toronto Star*, May 28, 2016, https://www.thestar.com/news/insight/2016/05/28/documentary-shines-spotlight-on-experience-of-lgbt-inuit.html (accessed Jan. 3, 2017).

Native American Takeaway:

UNION

Despite their differences, Native American tribes have a history of uniting different factions together to combat a singular powerful enemy. Just like their ancestors, modern queer Native Americans are uniting together to form a singular unit. For each individual tribe, let alone each version of queerness within each tribe, to go up against the overwhelming enemy of public opinion and of the US justice system is practically impossible. The hard truth is that great masses of average Americans have no time or desire to learn about and support all these types of queerness. They can barely support and learn about the basic queerness of the LGBT+ among their own race/culture as it is.

However, by putting personal differences aside and sacrificing a little bit of individuality, they are coming together under the banner of two-spirit people. Yes, two-spirit doesn't fully explain the totality of nuances in Native American queerness, but it's a strategic move. It is a singular identity easier for outsiders and the general American public to understand, empathize with, and support. Getting people talking is the first step, and the united two-spirit banner is a way for the majority to understand such a minority. In a democracy the minority can never implement lasting change without the voting support of the majority.

So, for your final magical activity, unionize with the magical queer community. Yes, this means actually going out there and contacting other people. I know solitary practice is easier and more convenient, but just like voting, the more people involved in support of a singular cause, the more likely it is that that cause will manifest. Online is your best resource for this. Check out if there are any local groups or individuals around with whom you can team up. If there's no one nearby, find someone open to doing a spell together via live chat. United in community, our whole is greater than the individuals making up its parts. If we stay divided and keep only to our individual selves, then we are easier to conquer, just as a single small stick is easier to snap than a large bundle of small sticks united together. Many of us are often called bundles of sticks, so let's show the world just how strong such a tight union can be.

Deities & Legends

SEDNA

Inuit lesbian goddess of the sea, animals, hunting, heaven, destiny, life, and death, she is represented as a gynandromorph (bilaterally divided half-male, half-female). There are many myths associated with her, but one of her more salacious ones involves her attempted murder by her father. According to this myth, Sedna is sexually uninterested in men and dismissive of all the suitors that her father brings to her. To mock him, she jokingly marries a dog, an act that enrages her father to the point that he attempts to kill her and dump her body in a lake during a boat ride à la *The Godfather: Part II*. Ever after that incident, she lives in the depths of the ocean with a lesbian lover, controlling the life and death of humans by providing or withholding from them the bounty of the sea (the Inuit people's main food source). Her head priests and priestesses were often also queer shamans.[245]

VILLAGE OLD WOMAN OF THE HIDATSA

The Hidatsa are a Native American tribe in present day North Dakota, and in their mythology Village Old Woman is one of the three creator deities of the world. She's also patroness of the *miati*, Hidatsa third-gender individuals of biological males who live and act like traditional females. In order to become a miati, a young male must first be visited by Village Old Woman in a dream and be directly instructed by her to forego masculine norms and embrace female stereotypes. According to legend, if a male receives such a dream of Village Old Woman and obstinately refuses to embrace his femininity, she would send spirits to slowly drive him insane until he embraces his destiny.

---

245 Penczak, *Gay Witchcraft: Empowering the Tribe* (San Francisco: Red Wheel/ Weiser, 2003).

Fully initiated miati were treated as an exalted class of spiritual leaders who specialize in the healing of mental illnesses, paralysis, and complications associated with childbirth. So sought after and valued were these healing gifts that the miati, along with a number of elderly women, formed a kind of guild often referred to as the Holy Women Society, named in honor of their patroness, Village Old Woman. The power held by the miati inspired envy among many wannabes and pretenders who had no spiritual connection with Village Old Woman yet wanted to be one of her devotees in order to gain social influence. Being highly visible people of great spiritual power also made the miati a target by the US government in their westward conquest as well as the Hidatsa chiefs themselves in strategic power plays.[246]

WE'WHA

We'wha was a Zuni lhamana who, despite her tragic end, was arguably one of the most internationally famous and beloved third-gender Native Americans of the nineteenth century. Having a childhood unusual to a lhamana, We'wha was first initiated into the male mysteries of the Zuni, but soon after was initiated into the female mysteries due to her latent lhamana energy. Once We'wha was in her thirties, then-President Grant sent Protestant missionaries to Christianize the Zuni in an effort to assimilate them into "American" culture rather than forcibly move them onto reservations. We'wha's intellect, charisma, and adeptness in learning languages made her the primary intermediary of these missionaries.

We'wha's networking and connections with the movers and shakers of white colonists in the New Mexico Territory brought her into close friendship with ethnologist célèbre Matilda Coxe Stevenson, who was studying the Zuni. Being the featured subject of Stevenson's literary writings and research, We'wha gained prestige among the educated elite of American society, eventually leading her to be hired to create Zuni religious pottery for the Smithsonian Museum in Washington, DC, where she moved in

---

246 Robert A. Schmidt and Barbara L. Voss, *Archaeologies of Sexuality* (New York: Routledge, 2000).

with Stevenson and became something of an exotic curiosity/Zuni cultural ambassador.

While in the American capital, she was labeled and assumed to be an "Indian Princess," allowing her to circulate amongst the highest levels of the US government. However, all throughout We'wha's rise to influence among the United States' most politically powerful, nobody knew We'wha was a biological male, predating *M. Butterfly* and *The Crying Game* by over 100 years. Yes, everyone—including Stevenson and then-President Cleveland—thought We'wha was a biological woman the entire time.[247]

It wasn't until years later that Stevenson found out about We'wha, making a special note of it in her diary, writing of how she would always regard We'wha as a woman in her eyes and continue to treat her as such.[248] We'wha, however, didn't encounter such open-minded white people again after moving back to the New Mexico Territory. Tensions grew between the non-assimilating Zuni and the US government, leading to the arrest of We'wha and other high-profile Zuni leaders. They were all accused of witchcraft and sent to prison. At the age of forty-seven, We'wha died of heart failure. Nevertheless, her story and pottery still live on in the Smithsonian as preserved artifacts of Zuni culture.[249]

247 Roscoe, *The Zuni Man-Woman*.

248 Matilda Coxe Stevenson, *The Zuni Indians: Their Mythology, Esoteric Fraternities, and Ceremonies* (Charleston: BiblioBazaar, 2010).

249 Chuck Stewart, *Proud Heritage: People, Issues, and Documents of LGBT Experience*, 3rd ed. (Santa Barbara: ABC-CLIO, 2014).

24

AMERICAN MAGICAL COMMUNITY

SANTA MUERTE PROTECTION SPELL

For our concluding voyage through the Americas, I have here a friend of mine and a Santa Muerte devotee, Anthony Lucero. He is a gay witch/sorcerer whom I met at Phoenix Pagan Pride Day during my *Santa Muerte* book tour. Anthony is a co-founder of the magic shop Toad and Broom and started working with la Santa Muerte back in 2011. Before that he had experienced a lot of negativity that often comes from being a young, out of the closet, gay Latino in a small Catholic town in New Mexico. Many of you may have had or be in similar straits, and being LGBT+ isn't always safe everywhere you go, so he's going to share a protection spell you can use while partnering with la Santa Muerte, whom he affectionately calls "la Niña" (the Girl).

Necessary Tools

- *holy water*
- *white copal or rose incense*
- *a pendant with her image (you can substitute a rosary)*
- *one white candle dressed with frankincense oil, graveyard dirt, and rose petals*
- *an image of la Niña Blanca and a glass of water*

Ritual Spell

1. *Wash the rosary with holy water and put the frankincense oil, graveyard dirt, and some of the rose petals on the candle. Light the incense.*

2. *Breathe in the water and tell it that it is an offering to la Niña, and now make the sign of the cross, saying:*
   "In the name of la Niña Blanca, la Roja, y la Negra, I pray to you, the sweetest, most loving Death; you who protect all who walk the earth, you who protect the hopeless and downtrodden, the outcasts and those who walk the night. I pray that you empower this pendant/rosary so that as I wear it I am wrapped in your cloak of protection, that I am protected from harm by your powerful scythe, that I be protected as I go about my days and nights. Oh Holy Queen, I pray that you will do this for me and in exchange for keeping me safe physically, spiritually, and emotionally, I will (state your promise of what you will do, such as bringing her red apples, assisting those in need, or a form of public thanks to her)."

3. *Make the sign of the cross, then say:*
   "In the name of la Niña Blanca, la Roja, and la Negra."

4. *Pray three "Our Fathers."*

5. *"Amen."*

6. *Lay the pendant/rosary around the candle or on her image and repeat the spell for three days, then carry the necklace and fulfill your promise.*

—ANTHONY LUCERO

SOUTHWESTERN SAGE RITUAL

Our final special guest for our global trek is my friend Brian Simpson. He is a gay Native American of the Diné/Navajo tribe living in Phoenix, Arizona, and is co-founder of the magic shop Toad and Broom. He is here to conclude our journey by telling us a little bit about growing up gay on the reservation and giving us a sage ritual to help neutralize the negativity around and within us.

For a while in my late teens I had issues with identifying as gay, mostly because of family and the way they spoke about gays and lesbians in general. Several of them attended church on a regular basis. I myself never really resonated with church. I tried but never felt a spiritual connection to it. So when I came out of the closet, I had a few cousins tell me, "Don't act like you normally do; my mom and dad are here."

This obviously had a negative effect on me and made me question several things and want to try to fit in so it wasn't an inconvenience to others. Around this time my mother had noticed I had been a bit depressed and kept asking me what was wrong, and I refused to talk about it. So she did the next best thing she could think of, which was to call a local medicine man and have a ceremony done to help me.

My mother called a family friend who I was comfortable with and who would later become my spiritual mentor and brother. He sat me down with his traditional ceremonial tools set up in front of us. On a little makeshift altar was a quartz crystal the size of the palm of my hand, flanked by two feathers and a bowl of burning cedar greens in the east. He looked into his crystal and explained to me what was going on and not to feel bad. "Don't worry about what they say; be yourself. Get some sage and cedar and pray about it. Don't let the negativity bother you. You're going to be okay."

Then he did a prayer in our traditional Diné language and was done. After that each day for a week I did as he suggested, and I noticed I felt better and their negativity didn't bother me so much—the next time they said it to me I just simply told them, "I can only be me. If they don't like me, they don't have to talk to me."

Sage Ritual Tools
- *dried white sage*
- *lighter or matches*
- *fireproof container or bowl you can put the sage in*
- *feather or fan (or use your hand)*

Ritual Spell

1. *Light your sage and blow it or fan it out so it smokes. If you have a bowl, then place it in there now. If you're using another cleansing herb or resin such as copal or frankincense and myrrh, add it now. Make sure you use a fire-safe container that can withstand the heat.*

2. *Wave the smoke to yourself three or four times and say:*
   "I cleanse and purify myself of all negativity, fear, and anger."

3. *Fan the smoke to the east three or four times and say to yourself or aloud:*
   "I call on my helping spirits who dwell in the (name direction),
   to cleanse the (direction) of all negativity and impurities, and
   remove fear, anger, and all stagnate energies that are present."

4. *Do this in each direction, changing the words to fit the appropriate direction: north, east, south, and west.*

5. *Return to the center space, wave the smoke to the ground, and say:*
   "Great Mother on whom we dwell, cleanse this
   space of all negativity and impurities."

6. *Wave the smoke above you and say:*
   "Great Father who is above us, I ask that you cleanse this
   space of all negativity and impurities that reside here."

7. *Wave the smoke to yourself again a few times and say*
   a personal prayer to be cleansed of negativity.

—BRIAN SIMPSON

DEBARKATION

People should fall in love
with their eyes closed.
ANDY WARHOL

And now we have finally returned home. As we pull back into port, you can see in the distance the familiar skyline of the familiar territory, with all the familiar faces of home waiting for your return to your familiar life. Little do they know, though, that that's impossible. The you that existed when we first set sail on our global trek is not the same person reading these pages now. Those familiar faces won't recognize it at first, but you've changed. You've found your tribe, learned about your history, heard the tales from modern magical community members, discovered new magic, and have gotten in touch with the queer divine that exists both out there and within you.

And now that you know all this, you can never un-know it. What you do with this knowledge will set the course for further adventures in your life. You can share it and be a beacon of light for fellow members trying to find their tribe. You can use it as comforting self-assurance when all the world seems to tell you that you are something that you really are not. You can start a movement, bringing ideas and faiths from the past back into the modern era. It'll be you at the helm from now on, guiding the voyage.

And as you look into your passport, wishing you could have had the time to learn more than our fast-paced expedition's schedule would allow, you can always go back. This globe trek was not the be-all and end-all of queer magic, cultures, and faiths; it was just a taste of all that is out there.

So if any culture, religion, magical tradition, or form of gender expression resonated strongly with you, book a trip to the library or surf the high seas of the world wide web. By learning more about them, you learn more about yourself, for all knowledge leads to self-knowledge. And who knows, your self-identity when we first embarked on our expedition may not be the same now after having seen more of the infinite spectrum of queerness in our world. And it may change again in the future as you discover more of the variety that life offers.

Oh, and remember...should you at any time wish to re-embark on our trek across the globe, I'll be right here at the harbor, waiting for you to pick up the book again and come with me once more. You can even bring a friend, if you like, to open their eyes to the world that exists out there, though each time you go, you'll be different, and with different eyes you'll see different things in a different way, even the familiar. There are worlds awaiting you out there with people to meet and things to do. Come back again; your LGBT+ family has always been here, and we'd love for you to join in on our queer magic anytime.

BIBLIOGRAPHY

Abel, Ernest L. *Death Gods: An Encyclopedia of Rulers, Evil Spirits, and Geographies of the Dead*. Westport: Greenwood Press, 2009.

Adair, Jamie. "Dracula: Impalement, Punishment By Proxy of His Brother's Lover?" *History Behind Game of Thrones*. March 6, 2014. http://history-behind-game-of-thrones.com/historical-periods /draculaimpale (accessed Oct. 13, 2016).

Ahmed, Shahab. "Ibn Taymiyyah and the Satanic Verses." *Studia Islamica* 87 (1998): 67–124.

Akana, Alan Robert. *The Volcano Is Our Home: Nine Generations of a Hawaiian Family on Kilauea Volcano*. Carlsbad: Balboa Press, 2014.

Alchin, Linda. "Hapi, God of Egypt." *Egyptian Gods: The Mythology of Ancient Egyptian Gods and Goddesses for Kids*. March 2015. http:// www.landofpyramids.org/hapi.htm (accessed Aug. 18, 2017).

Aldrich, R. "Peopling the Empty Mirror: The Prospects for Gay and Lesbian Aboriginal History." *Gay Perspectives II*. Sydney: University of Sydney Australian Centre for Gay and Lesbian Research, 1993.

Ali, Kecia. "Same-Sex Sexual Activity and Lesbian and Bisexual Women." *The Feminist Sexual Ethics Project*. December 10, 2002. https://www.brandeis.edu/projects/fse/muslim/same-sex.html (accessed Oct. 12, 2016).

Alimi, Bisi. "If You Say Being Gay Is Not African, You Don't Know Your History." *The Guardian*. September 9, 2015. https://www .theguardian.com/commentisfree/2015/sep/09/being-gay-african -history-homosexuality-christianity (accessed Oct. 25, 2016).

Allen, Andrea Stevenson. *Violence and Desire in Brazilian Lesbian Relationships*. New York: Palgrave Macmillan, 2015.

Alpert, Rebecca T. *Like Bread on the Seder Plate: Jewish Lesbians and the Transformation of Tradition*. New York: Columbia University Press, 1997.

al-Tabari, Muhammad ibn Jarir. *The History of al-Tabari, Vol. 9: The Last Years of the Prophet*. Translated by Ismail K. Poonwala. Albany: State University of New York Press, 1990.

Alvarez, Sandra. "Intersex in the Middle Ages." *Medievalists*. January 9, 2015. http://www.medievalists.net/2015/01/09/intersex-middle -ages/ (accessed Sept. 19, 2016).

Appiah, Anthony Kwame, and Henry Louis Gates Jr. *Encyclopedia of Africa*. Oxford: Oxford University Press, 2010.

Aspin, Clive. "Hōkakatanga—Māori Sexualities," in *Te Ara: The Encyclopedia of New Zealand*. Wellington: Manatū Taonga Ministry for Culture and Heritage, 2011. http://www.teara.govt.nz/en /node/168875 (accessed Dec. 13, 2016).

Associated Press. "China Decides Homosexuality No Longer Mental Illness." *South China Morning Post*. March 8, 2001. http://www .hartford-hwp.com/archives/55/325.html (accessed Nov. 19, 2016).

Asthana, Sheena, and Robert Oostvogels. "The Social Construction of Male 'Homosexuality' in India: Implications for HIV Transmission and Prevention." *Social Sciences & Medicine* 52:5 (2001).

Aveela, Ronesa. "Samodivi—Witches of Darkness or Thracian Goddesses?" *Mystical Emona*. June 22, 2015. http://mysticalemona .com/2015/06/22/samodivi-witches-of-darkness-or-thracian -goddesses/ (accessed Sept. 16, 2016).

Baker, Carolyn. "Men, Women, Collapse and Conflict." *Transition Voice*. June 2013. http://transitionvoice.com/2013/06/men-women -collapse-and-conflict/ (accessed Oct. 25, 2016).

Barber, Malcolm. *The Trial of the Templars*. 2nd ed. Cambridge: Harvard University Press, 2002.

Barford, Vanessa. "Iran's 'Diagnosed Transsexuals." *British Broadcasting Corporation*. February 25, 2008. http://news.bbc.co.uk/2 /hi/7259057.stm (accessed Oct. 11, 2016).

Barry, Kieren. *The Greek Qabalah: Alphabetic Mysticism and Numerology in the Ancient World*. Newbury: Samuel Weiser, 1999.

Bassey, Udee. "Yoruba Orishas: Erinle, Orisha of Natural Forces." *Beudeeful*. February 5, 2015. http://beudeeful.com/orisha-erinle/ (accessed June 11, 2017).

Bawden, C. R. *Modern History Mongolia*. New York: Routledge, 2013.

Baylis, Peter, and New South Wales Supreme Court. *Unfit for Publication: NSW Supreme Court and Other Bestiality, Buggery and Sodomy Trials 1727–1930*. Balmain: P. de Waal, 2007.

Baylis, Troy-Anthony. "The Art of Seeing Aboriginal Australia's Queer Potential." *The Conversation*. April 15, 2014. http://theconversation .com/the-art-of-seeing-aboriginal-australias-queer-potential-25588 (accessed Dec. 9, 2016).

Bearman, P., Th. Bianquis, C. E. Bosworth, E. van Donzel, and W. P. Henrichs. *The Encyclopaedia of Islam*. Leiden: Brill, 1983.

Bernstein, Mary, Anna-Maria Marshall, and Scott Barclay. *Queer Mobilizations: LGBT Activists Confront the Law*. New York: NYU Press, 2009.

Best, Richard Irvine. *The Book of Leinster: Formerly Lebar na Núachongbála*. Dublin: Dublin Institute for Advanced Studies, 1954.

Bieber, Irving, Toby B. Bieber, Harvey J. Dain, Paul R. Dince, Marvin G. Drellich, Henry G. Grand, Ralph R. Gundlach, Malvina W. Kremer, Alfred H. Rifkin, and Cornelia B. Wilbur. *Homosexuality: A Psychoanalytic Study of Male Homosexuals*. New York: Basic Books, 1962.

Bihar News. "Supreme Court's Third Gender Status to Transgenders Is a Landmark." April 15, 2014. http://news.biharprabha .com/2014/04/supreme-courts-third-gender-status-to -transgenders-is-a-landmark/ (accessed Nov. 8, 2016).

Binney, Judith. "Yate, William," in *Te Ara: The Encyclopedia of New Zealand*. Wellington: Manatū Taonga Ministry for Culture and Heritage, 1990. http://www.TeAra.govt.nz/en/biographies/1y1/yate-william (accessed Dec. 13, 2016).

Blackwood, Evelyn. *The Many Faces of Homosexuality: Anthropological Approaches to Homosexual Behavior*. New York: Routledge, 1986.

Boisvert, Donald L., and Jay Emerson Johnson. *Queer Religion*, vol.1. Santa Barbara: Praeger, 2011.

Bolich, G. G. *Transgender History & Geography: Crossdressing in Context*, vol. 3. Raleigh: Psyche's Press, 2007.

Bormann, Trevor. "Tahiti Mahu." Australian Broadcasting Corporation. March 23, 2005. http://www.abc.net.au/foreign/content/2005/s1330291.htm (accessed Dec. 15, 2016).

Boswell, John. *Same-Sex Unions in Pre-Modern Europe*. New York: Vintage, 1995.

Bottéro, Jean. *Everyday Life in Ancient Mesopotamia*. Translated by Antonia Nevill. Baltimore: Johns Hopkins University Press, 2001.

Bourcier, Nicolas. "Brazil Comes to Terms with Its Slave Trading Past." *The Guardian*. October 23, 2012. https://www.theguardian.com/world/2012/oct/23/brazil-struggle-ethnic-racial-identity (accessed Nov. 2, 2016).

Brickell, Chris. "Gay Men's Lives," in *Te Ara: The Encyclopedia of New Zealand*. Wellington: Manatū Taonga Ministry for Culture and Heritage, 2005. http://www.teara.govt.nz/en/gay-mens-lives (accessed Dec. 13, 2016).

British Broadcasting Corporation. "Candomblé at a Glance." September 15, 2009. http://www.bbc.co.uk/religion/religions/candomble/ataglance/glance.shtml (accessed Nov. 2, 2016).

Broder Van Dyke, Michelle. "A Brief History of Sexual Identity in Hawaii." *Buzzfeed*. November 12, 2013. https://www.buzzfeed.com/mbvd/a-brief-history-of-sexual-identity-in-hawaii?utm_term=.vo9DVqx4a#.fbDnPBYd5 (accessed Dec. 15, 2016).

Brooten, Bernadette J. *Love Between Women: Early Christian Responses to Female Homoeroticism*. Chicago: University of Chicago Press, 1996.

Brown, David H. *Santería Enthroned: Art, Ritual, and Innovation in an Afro-Cuban Religion*. Chicago: University of Chicago Press, 2003.

Browne, Kath, and Sally R. Munt. *Queer Spiritual Spaces: Sexuality and Sacred Places*. New York: Routledge, 2010.

Brunner-Traut, Emma. *Altägyptische Märchen: Mythen und andere volkstümliche Erzählungen*, 10th ed. Munich: Diederichs, 1991.

Burgess, Ann Wolbert, Albert R. Roberts, and Cheryl Regehr. *Victimology: Theories and Applications*. Burlington: Jones & Bartlett Learning, 2009.

Calame, Claude. *Les Chœurs de jeunes filles en Grèce archaïque*. Rome: L'Ateneo & Bizzarri, 1977.

Canning, Paul. "Polynesia's Ancient Same-Sex Acceptance." *LGBT Asylum News*. September 12, 2010. http://madikazemi.blogspot.com/2010/09/polynesias-ancient-same-sex-acceptance.html (accessed Dec. 15, 2016).

Card, Claudia. *Lesbian Choices*. New York: Columbia University Press, 1995.

Carroll, Rory. "She Who Must Be Surveyed." *The Guardian*. April 14, 2003. https://www.theguardian.com/world/2003/apr/14/worlddispatch.southafrica (accessed Oct. 27, 2016)

Chadwick, Nora. *The Celts*. London: Folio Society, 2001.

Childs, Margaret H. "Chigo Monogatari. Love Stories or Buddhist Sermons?" *Monumenta Nipponica* 35:2 (1980).

Ciklamini, Marlene. "The Old Icelandic Duel." *Scandinavian Studies* 35:3 (1963): 175–194.

Clarke, John R. *Looking at Lovemaking: Constructions of Sexuality in Roman Art 100 B.C.–A.D. 250*. Berkeley: University of California Press, 2001.

Clover, Carol J. "The Politics of Scarcity: Notes on the Sex Ratios in Early Scandinavia." *Scandinavian Studies* 60 (1988): 147–188.

Conkin, Dennis. "Dalai Lama Urges 'Respect, Compassion, and Full Human Rights for All,' Including Gays." *Bay Area Reporter*. June 19, 1997. http://quietmountain.org/links/teachings/gayrites.htm (accessed Nov. 14, 2016).

Conner, Randy P. *Blossom of Bone*. San Francisco: HarperCollins, 1993.

———. "Gender and Sexuality in Spiritual Traditions," in *Fragments of Bone: Neo-African Religions in a New World*, edited by Patrick Bellegarde-Smith. Champaign: University of Illinois Press, 2005.

——— and David Hatfield Sparks. *Queering Creole Spiritual Traditions: Lesbian, Gay, Bisexual, and Transgender Participation in African-Inspired Traditions in the Americas*. Binghampton: The Haworth Press, Inc., 2004.

Conner, Randy P., David Hatfield Sparks, and Mariya Sparks. *Cassell's Encyclopedia of Queer Myth, Symbol, and Spirit*. London: Cassell & Co., 1997.

Coslett, Matthew. "Japan: The Most Religious Atheist Country." *GaijinPot*. February 8, 2016. https://blog.gaijinpot.com/japan-religious-atheist-country/ (accessed Nov. 26, 2016).

Crompton, Louis. *Homosexuality and Civilization*. Cambridge: Harvard University Press, 2003.

Danielou, Alain. *The Complete Kama Sutra*. Rochester: Park Street Press, 1994.

Davies, Simon E. "The Orisha; Gods of Yoruba Mythology." *Ancient Code*. https://www.ancient-code.com/orisha-gods-yoruba-mythology/ (accessed June 11, 2017).

Dececco, John, and Ronald Long. *Men, Homosexuality, and the Gods: An Exploration into the Religious Significance of Male Homosexuality in World Perspective*. New York: Routledge, 2004.

de la Cruz, Juana Inés. *A Sor Juana Anthology*. Translated by Alan S. Trueblood. Cambridge: Harvard University Press, 1990.

de las Casas, Bartolomé. *Apologética Historia Sumaria*, vol. 2, edited by Edmundo O'Gorman. Mexico City: UNAM, 1967 [c. 1559].

Des hommes et des dieux (DVD). Directed by Anne Lescot, and Laurence Magloire. 2002. Port-au-Prince: Digital LM, 2003.

Dhammika, S. *The Buddha and His Disciples*. Singapore: Buddha Dhama Mandala Society, 2005. http://www.buddhanet.net/pdf_file/bud -disciples.pdf (accessed Nov. 11, 2016).

Dharma, Krishna. *Mahabharata: The Greatest Spiritual Epic of All Time*. Imperial Beach: Torchlight Publishing, 1999.

Dhwty. "The Ancient Tradition of Whirling Dervishes of the Mevlevi Order." *Ancient Origins*. April 23, 2015. http://www.ancient -origins.net/history/ancient-tradition-whirling-dervishes-mevlevi -order-002943 (accessed Aug. 18, 2017).

Dollinger, André. "King Neferkare & General Sasenet." *An Introduction to the History and Culture of Pharaonic Egypt*. October 2006. http:// www.reshafim.org.il/ad/egypt/texts/sasenet.htm (accessed Sept. 30, 2016).

Donham, Donald L. *Work and Power in Maale, Ethiopia*. New York: Columbia University Press, 1994.

Dover, K.J. *Greek Homosexuality*. Cambridge: Harvard University Press, 1978.

Driberg, Jack Herbert. *The Lango: A Nilotic Tribe of Uganda*. London: T. Fisher Unwin, Ltd., 1923.

Dumézil, Georges. *From Myth to Fiction: the Saga of Hadingus*. Chicago: University of Chicago Press, 1970.

Dynes, Wayne. *Encyclopaedia of Homosexuality*. New York: Routledge, 1990.

Eldred-Grigg, Steven. *Pleasures of the Flesh: Sex and Drugs in Colonial New Zealand 1840–1915*. Wellington: A.H. & A.W. Reed, Ltd., 1984.

Ellwood, Robert, and Richard Pilgrim. *Japanese Religion: A Cultural Perspective*. New York: Routledge, 1984.

Encarnación, Omar G. "Why Is Latin America So Progressive on Gay Rights?" *The New York Times*. January 29, 2014. http://www .nytimes.com/roomfordebate/2014/01/29/why-is-latin-america -so-progressive-on-gay-rights (accessed Dec. 22, 2016).

Epprecht, Marc. *Heterosexual Africa? The History of an Idea from the Age of Exploration to the Age of AIDS (New African Histories)*. Athens: Ohio University Press, 2008.

Evans, Lens. "Chronology of Gay Mexican History." *Fifty Gay Years in the Greater Sacramento Area 1950–2000*. October 2002. http:// gayinsacramento.com/Chron-Mex.htm (accessed Dec. 21, 2016).

Evans-Pritchard, E. E. "Sexual Inversion Among the Azande." *American Anthropologist* 72:6 (1970).

Favorite, Brian. "My Friends, the *Fakaleitis* of Tonga." *Lesbian, Gay, Bisexual, Transgender Returned Peace Corps Volunteers*. November 2, 2006. https://lgbrpcv.org/2006/11/02/my-friends-the-fakaleitis -of-tonga/ (accessed Dec. 13, 2016).

Feinberg, Leslie. *Transgender Warriors: Making History from Joan of Arc to RuPaul*. Boston: Beacon Press, 1996.

Fernando de Oviedo y Valdés, Gonzalo, and Amador De Los Ríos. *Historia General y Natural de Las Indias: Islas y Tierrafirme del Mar Océano*. Charleston: Nabu Press, 2014.

Fish, Isaac Stone. "Does Japan's Conservative Shinto Religion Support Gay Marriage?" *Foreign Policy Magazine*. June 29, 2015. http:// foreignpolicy.com/2015/06/29/what-does-japan-shinto-think -of-gay-marriage/ (accessed Nov. 26, 2016).

Fox, Robin Lane. *The Search for Alexander*. Boston: Little Brown & Co., 1980.

Freeman, Philip. *War, Women, and Druids: Eyewitness Reports and Early Accounts of the Ancient Celts*. Austin: University of Texas Press, 2008.

Geen, Jessica. "UN Passes Gay Rights Resolution." *Pink News*. June 17, 2011. http://www.pinknews.co.uk/2011/06/17/un-passes-gay -rights-resolution/ (accessed Oct. 10, 2016).

Gilmour-Bryson, Anne. "Sodomy and the Knights Templar." *Journal of the History of Sexuality*. 7:2 (1996).

Goldman, Jason. "Subjects of the Visual Arts: St. Sebastian." *GLBTQ Archive*. 2002. http://www.glbtqarchive.com/arts/subjects_st _sebastian_A.pdf (accessed Sept. 21, 2016).

Grant, Preston. *Gay, Explained: History, Science, Culture, and Spirit*. San Francisco: Guide Media, 2016.

Greenberg, David F. *The Construction of Homosexuality*. Chicago: University of Chicago Press, 1990.

Greenberg, Yudit Kornberg. *Encyclopedia of Love in World Religions*. Santa Barbara: ABC-CLIO, 2007.

Haggerty, George, and Bonnie Zimmerman. *Encyclopedia of Lesbian and Gay Histories and Cultures*. New York: Taylor & Francis, 2015.

Hanson, Victor Davis. *The Western Way of War: Infantry Battle in Classical Greece*. Oakland: University of California Press, 1994.

Harvey, Peter. *An Introduction to Buddhist Ethics*. New York: Cambridge University Press, 2000.

Hay, Bob. "Boy Wives of the Aranda." *Bob Hay Online Resources*. Canberra: University of the Third Age, 2006. http://bobhay. org/_downloads/_homo/NHH%2007%20Boy%20Wives%20 of%20the%20Aranda%20-%20The%20Pre-History%20of%20 Homosexuality%20I.pdf (accessed Dec. 9, 2016).

Hedges, Paul. "Guanyin, Queer Theology, and Subversive Religiosity: An Experiment in Interreligious Theology." In *Interreligious Hermeneutics in Pluralistic Europe: Between Texts and People,* edited by David Cheetham. Amsterdam: Rodopi, 2011.

Herdt, Gilbert H. "Ritualized Homosexuality in Melanesia." *Studies in Melanesian Anthropology* vol. 2. Berkeley: University of California Press, 1993.

Herdt, Gilbert. *Sambia Sexual Desire: Essays from the Field*. Chicago: Chicago University Press, 1999.

Hinsch, Bret. *Passions of the Cut Sleeve: The Male Homosexual Tradition in China*. Berkeley: University of California Press, 1992.

Horner, Thomas Marland. *Jonathan Loved David: Homosexuality in Biblical Times*. Louisville: Westminster John Knox Press, 1978.

Huang, Yong. *Confucius: A Guide for the Perplexed*. New York: Bloomsbury Academic, 2013.

Hussain, Ishtiaq. *The Tanzimat: Secular Reforms in the Ottoman Empire*. Faith Matters, 2011. http://faith-matters.org/images/stories/fm-publications/the-tanzimat-final-web.pdf (accessed Oct. 13, 2016).

Iaccino, Ludovica. "Gay Ugandan King Proves that Homosexuality Is African." *International Business Times*. January 30, 2014. http://www.ibtimes.co.uk/gay-ugandan-king-proves-that-homosexuality-african-1434416 (accessed Oct. 20, 2016).

International Gay and Lesbian Human Rights Commission, and SEROvie. *The Impact of the Earthquake, and Relief and Recovery Programs on Haitian LGBT People*. 2011. http://www.iglhrc.org/sites/default/files/504-1.pdf (accessed Oct. 28, 2016).

Jackson, Peter. "Thai Buddhist Accounts of Male Homosexuality and AIDS in the 1980s." *The Australian Journal of Anthropology* 6:3 (1995). http://ccbs.ntu.edu.tw/FULLTEXT/JR-EPT/anth.htm (accessed Nov. 14, 2016).

Jeyakumar, Krish. "Ardhanarishvara." *Beyond the Binary*. September 12, 2016. http://beyondthebinary.co.uk/ardhanarishvara/ (accessed Aug. 19, 2017).

Jochens, Jenny. *Women in Old Norse Society*. Ithaca: Cornell University Press, 1995.

Jones, Grant D. *The Conquest of the Last Maya Kingdom*. Palo Alto: Stanford University Press, 1998.

Kaldera, Raven. *Wightridden: Paths of Northern-Tradition Shamanism*. Hubbardston: Asphodel Press, 2007.

Kalei, Kalikiano. "Hawaiian Sexuality and the 'Mahu' Tradition." *Authors Den*. March 7, 2009. http://www.authorsden.com /categories/article_top.asp?catid=62&id=46603 (accessed Dec. 15, 2016).

Kalende, Val. "Africa: Homophobia Is a Legacy of Colonialism." *The Guardian*. April 30, 2014. https://www.theguardian.com /world/2014/apr/30/africa-homophobia-legacy-colonialism (accessed Aug. 18, 2017).

Kelly, Fergus. *A Guide to Early Irish Law*. Dublin: Dublin Institute for Advanced Studies, 2005.

Kendall, K. Limakatso. "Women in Lesotho and the (Western) Construction of Homophobia." In *Female Desires: Same-Sex Relations and Transgender Practices Across Cultures*, edited by Evelyn Blackwood and Saskia Wieringa. New York: Columbia University Press, 1999.

Kennedy, Anthony. "Read the Opinion: Supreme Court Rules States Cannot Ban Same-Sex Marriage." *CNN Politics*. June 6, 2015. http://www.cnn.com/2015/06/26/politics/scotus-opinion -document-obergefell-hodges/#document/p8 (accessed Nov. 19, 2016).

Kenyon, Miles. "Documentary Shines Spotlight On Experience of LGBT Inuit." *The Toronto Star*. May 28, 2016. https://www.thestar .com/news/insight/2016/05/28/documentary-shines-spotlight-on -experience-of-lgbt-inuit.html (accessed Jan. 3, 2017).

Kiama, Wanjira. "Homosexuality Takes Root in Kenya." *Daily Nation*. June 24, 1998. http://archive.globalgayz.com/africa/kenya/gay- kenya-news-and-reports-199-2/#article1 (accessed Oct. 20, 2016).

Kinross. *Ottoman Centuries: The Rise and Fall of the Turkish Empire*. New York: Harper Perennial, 1979.

Kitamura, Kigin. "Wild Azaleas." In *Paintings at Dawn: An Anthology of Gay Japanese Literature (12th–20th Century)*, edited by Stephen D. Miller, translated by Paul Gordon Schalow. San Francisco: Gay Sunshine Press, 1996.

Kumu Hina. Directed by Dean Hamer and Joe Wilson. 2014. Haleiwa: Qwaves, Netflix, 2016. (accessed Feb. 5, 2017).

Lambert, Royston. *Beloved and God: The Story of Hadrian and Antinous.* London: George Weidenfeld & Nicolson, 1984.

Leupp, Gary. *Male Colors: The Construction of Homosexuality in Tokugawa Japan.* Los Angeles: University of California Press, 1997.

Lin, Derek. *Tao Te Ching: Annotated & Explained.* Woodstock: SkyLight Illuminations, 2006.

Lopez, Donald. *Buddhist Scriptures.* New York: Penguin Classics, 2004.

Lopez, Eduardo Ramon. "El Rostro oculto de los pueblos precolombinos." *Ecuador Gay.* October 2004. https://web.archive .org/web/20051216191923/http://www.islaternura.com/APLAYA /HOMOenHISTORIA/Pueblos%20precolombinos%20Octubre%20 2004.htm (accessed Dec. 21, 2016).

Lyon, Alissa. "Ancient Egyptian Sexuality." *Archaeology of Ancient Egypt.* October 23, 2014. http://anthropology.msu.edu/anp455 -fs14/2014/10/23/ancient-egyptian-sexuality/ (accessed Sept. 30, 2016).

Manwell, Elizabeth. "Gender and Masculinity," in *A Companion to Catullus,* edited by Marilyn B. Skinner, 118. Hoboken: Blackwell Publishing, 2011.

Mark, Monica. "Nigeria's Yan Daudu Face Persecution in Religious Revival." *The Guardian.* June 10, 2013. https://www.theguardian .com/world/2013/jun/10/nigeria-yan-daudu-persecution (accessed Oct. 25, 2016).

Mathieu, Paul. *Sex Pots: Eroticism in Ceramics.* New Brunswick: Rutgers University Press, 2003.

Mbugguss, Martha. *Same Gender Unions: A Critical Analysis.* Nairobi: Uzima, 2004.

McAlister, Elizabeth A. *Rara!: Vodou, Power, and Performance in Haiti and Its Diaspora.* Berkeley: University of California Press, 2002.

Medicine, Beatrice. "Directions in Gender Research in American Indian Societies: Two Spirits and Other Categories." *Online Readings in Psychology and Culture*, vol. 3. Bellingham: Western Washington University Center for Cross-Cultural Research, 2002. https://web .archive.org/web/20030330115133/http://www.ac.wwu .edu/~culture/medicine.htm (accessed Dec. 31, 2016).

Metal Gaia. "Homosexuality Once Accepted in Pre-Christian Africa— But Now Persecuted." January 28, 2014. https://metal-gaia.com /tag/rain-queen/ (accessed Oct. 27, 2016).

Miller, Mary Ellen, and Karl A. Taube. *The Gods and Symbols of Ancient Mexico and the Maya: An Illustrated Dictionary of Mesoamerican Religion.* New York: Thames & Hudson, 1993.

Minkowitz, Donna. "Religiously Queer." *The Huffington Post.* June 29, 2013. http://www.huffingtonpost.com/donna-minkowitz /religiously-queer_b_3520142.html (accessed Sept. 18, 2016).

Moores, D. J. *The Ecstatic Poetic Tradition: A Critical Study from the Ancients through Rumi, Wordsworth, Whitman, Dickinson and Tagore.* Jefferson: McFarland, 2014.

Most, Glenn W. "Reflecting Sappho." *Bulletin of the Institute of Classical Studies* 40.1 (1995) 15–38.

Mostow, Joshua S., Normal Bryson, and Maribeth Graybill. *Gender and Power in the Japanese Visual Field.* Honolulu: University of Hawai'i Press, 2003.

Munro, Peter. "Transgendered Tongan 'Leitis' Finding Their Way in the Conservative Country." *Sydney Morning Herald.* August 28, 2015. http://www.smh.com.au/world/transgendered-tongan-leitis -finding-their-way-in-the-conservative-country-20150820 -gj48qw.html (accessed Dec. 13, 2016).

Murray, Jacqueline. "Twice Marginal and Twice Invisible: Lesbians in the Middle Ages," in *Handbook of Medieval Sexuality*, edited by Vern L. Bullough and James A. Brundage. New York: Garland Publishing Inc., 1996.

Murray, Stephen O. *Homosexualities*. Chicago: University of Chicago Press, 2002.

———. *Latin American Male Homosexualities*. Albuquerque: University of New Mexico Press, 1995.

——— and Will Roscoe. *Islamic Homosexualities: Culture, History, and Literature*. New York: NYU Press, 1997.

Murray, Stuart. *The Library: An Illustrated History*. Chicago: Skyhorse Publishing 2009.

Nadel, Siegfried Frederick. *The Nuba: An Anthropological Study of the Hill Tribes in Kordofan*. London: Oxford University Press, 1947.

Nanda, Serena. "Hijra and Sadhin," in *Constructing Sexualities*, edited by S. LaFont. Upper Saddle River: Pearson Education, 2002.

Native OUT. "Two Spirit Terms in Tribal Languages." http://nativeout.com/twospirit-rc/two-spirit-101/two-spirit-terms-in-tribal-languages/ (accessed Dec. 28, 2016).

Neubauer, Ian Lloyd. "A Week with Tahiti's Transexual *Rae-Rae*." *CNN Travel*. May 14, 2012. http://travel.cnn.com/explorations/escape/transsexuals-tahiti-887006/ (accessed Dec. 15, 2016).

Oh, Kang-nam. "The Taoist Influence on Hua-yen Buddhism: A Case of the Sinicization of Buddhism in China." *Chung-Hwa Buddhist Journal* 13 (2000). https://web.archive.org/web/20100323000712/http://www.chibs.edu.tw/publication/chbj/13/chbj1338.htm (accessed Nov. 21, 2016).

O'Neil, Dennis. "Homosexuality." *Sex and Marriage: An Introduction to The Cultural Rules Regulating Sexual Access and Marriage*. August 3, 2007. http://anthro.palomar.edu/marriage/marriage_6.htm (accessed Dec. 9, 2016).

Onon, Urgunge. *The Secret History of the Mongols: The Life and Times of Chinggis Khan*. Oxford: Routledge-Curzo, 2001.

Ovid. *Metamorphoses*, translated by A. D. Melville. Oxford: Oxford University Press, 2009.

Oxford Classical Dictionary, 3rd rev. ed. Oxford: Oxford University Press, 2005.

Pallotta-Chiarolli, Maria. *Women in Relationships with Bisexual Men: Bi Men By Women*. Lanham: Lexington Books, 2016.

Palmo, Tenzin. *Reflections on a Mountain Lake: Teachings on Practical Buddhism*. Ithaca: Snow Lion Publications, 2002.

Paprocki, Joe. "What Does St. Paul Say About Homosexuality?" *Busted Halo*. August 27, 2010. http://bustedhalo.com/questionbox/what -does-st-paul-say-about-homosexuality (accessed Sept. 19, 2016).

Parkinson, Richard. "Homosexual Desire and Middle Kingdom Literature." *The Journal of Egyptian Archaeology* 81 (1995): 57–76.

Pattanaik, Devdutt. *The Man Who Was a Woman and Other Queer Tales from Hindu Lore*. New York: Routledge, 2012.

Pau Talauati, Hazy. "*Fa'afafine*—Samoan boys Brought Up As Girls." Australian Broadcasting Corporation, 2005. http://www.abc.net .au/ra/pacific/people/hazy.htm (accessed Dec. 13, 2016).

Paz, Octavio. *Sor Juana Inés de la Cruz o las Trampas de la Fe*. Ciudad de México: Fondo de Cultura Económica, 1982.

Pember, Mary Annette. "'Two Spirit' Tradition Far from Ubiquitous Among Tribes." *Rewire*. October 13, 2016. https://rewire.news /article/2016/10/13/two-spirit-tradition-far-ubiquitous-among -tribes/ (accessed Dec. 28, 2016).

Penczak, Christopher. *Gay Witchcraft: Empowering the Tribe*. San Francisco: Red Wheel/Weiser, 2003.

Pflugfelder, Gregory M. *Cartographies of Desire: Male-Male Sexuality in Japanese Discourse, 1600–1950*. Berkeley: University of California Press, 2007.

Picken, Stuart D. B. *Essentials of Shinto: An Analytical Guide to Principal Teachings*. Westport: Greenwood, 1994.

Pollini, John. "The Warren Cup: Homoerotic Love and Symposial Rhetoric in Silver." *Art Bulletin* 81.1 (1999) 21–52.

Price, Neil. *The Archaeology of Shamanism*. New York: Routledge, 2001.

Pritchard, James B. *Ancient Near Eastern Texts Relating to the Old Testament.* Princeton: Princeton University Press, 1969.

Prower, Tomás. *La Santa Muerte: Unearthing the Magic & Mysticism of Death.* Woodbury: Llewellyn Worldwide, 2015.

———. "Royal Queerness: Gay Monarchs of the World." *Dandy Dicks.* May 30, 2016. https://dandydicks.com/blog-entry/royal-queerness -gay-monarchs-of-the-world (accessed Oct. 26, 2016).

Prudan, Harlan, and Se-ah-dom Edmo. "Two-Spirit People: Sex, Gender & Sexuality in Historic and Contemporary Native America." National Congress of American Indians Policy Research Center. http://www.ncai.org/policy-research-center/initiatives/Pruden -Edmo_TwoSpiritPeople.pdf (accessed Jan. 1, 2017).

Reid-Smith, Tris. "From Shamans to Gay Bars: Booming Mongolia's LGBT People." *Gay Star News.* April 5, 2013. http://www.gaystarnews.com/article/shamans-gay-bars -booming-mongolia%E2%80%99s-lgbt-people050413 /#gs.dOei=Is (accessed Dec. 4, 2016).

Reza Ramirez, Bernarda. "Propuesta para abatir el delito en el estado de Veracruz—Llave." *Acontecer Jurídico,* vol. 2. August 26, 2012. https://issuu.com/acontecerjuridico/docs/www.acontecerjuridico .com (accessed Dec. 21, 2016).

Rivas, Jorge. "Gay Marriage Is Still Illegal for the Navajo. This Man Is Trying to Change That." *Fusion.* July 7, 2015. http://fusion.net /story/161887/gay-marriage-is-still-illegal-for-the-navajo-this -man-is-trying-to-change-that/ (Jan. 1, 2017).

Roscoe, Will. *Queer Spirits: A Gay Men's Myth Book.* Boston: Beacon Press, 1995.

———. *The Zuni Man-Woman.* Albuquerque: University of New Mexico Press, 1991.

Roshi, Robert Aitken. "Robert Aiken Roshi on Gay Marriage: A Zen Buddhist Perspective." *The Jizo Chronicles*. March 27, 2013. https://jizochronicles.com/2013/03/27/robert-aitken-roshi -on-gay-marriage-a-zen-buddhist-perspective/ (accessed Nov. 28, 2016).

Rowson, Everett K. "The Effeminates of Early Medina." *Journal of the American Oriental Society* 111:4 (1991): 671–693.

Royalark. "The History and Life of Kabaka Mwanga II." http://www .royalark.net/Uganda/buganda7.htm (accessed Oct. 20, 2016).

Santagi, Adriana. "Buenos Aires, nueva capital del turismo gay de Sudamérica." *Clarín*. November 1, 2003. http://edant.clarin.com /diario/2003/11/01/h-05015.htm (accessed Dec. 22, 2016).

Schmidt, Robert A., and Barbara L. Voss. *Archaeologies of Sexuality*. New York: Routledge, 2000.

Schmitt, Arno, and Jehoeda Sofer. *Sexuality and Eroticism Among Males in Moslem Societies*. New York: Routledge, 1992.

Seidman, Lila. "LGBT Centre Executive Director N. Anaraa Talks LGBT Rights Then and Now." *The Ulaanbaatar Post*. May 18, 2016. http://theubpost.mn/2016/05/18/lgbt-centre-executive-director -n-anaraa-talks-lgbt-rights-then-and-now/ (accessed Dec. 5, 2016).

Shah, Parin. "Homosexuality and the Hindu Society." Random Rants. February 6, 2016. https://parinvshah.wordpress.com/2016/02/06 /homosexuality-and-the-hindu-society/ (accessed Feb. 12, 2017).

Shankbone, David. "Dalai Lama's Representative Talks About China, Tibet, Shugden and the Next Dalai Lama." Wikinews. November 14, 2007. https://en.wikinews.org/wiki/Dalai_Lama%27s _representative_talks_about_China,_Tibet,_Shugden_and_the _next_Dalai_Lama (accessed Nov. 14, 2016).

Shikibu, Murasaki. *The Diary of Lady Murasaki*, translated by Richard Bowring. New York: Penguin Classics, 1996.

———. *The Tale of Genji*, translated by Edward G. Seidensticker. New York: Alfred A. Knopf, 2006.

Sigal, Peter Herman. *From Moon Goddesses to Virgins: The Colonization of Yucatecan Maya Sexual Desire*. Austin: University of Texas Press, 2000.

Singh, Reverend Severina KM. "Haitian Vodou and Sexual Orientation," in *The Esoteric Codex: Haitian Vodou*, edited by Garland Ferguson, 50-53. Morrisville: Lulu Press, Inc., 2002.

Singhal, Ruchika. "Gay Gods in Mythology." *Speaking Tree*. November 28, 2012. http://www.speakingtree.in/blog/gay-gods-in-mythology (accessed Aug. 20, 2017).

Skinner, Marilyn B. *Introduction to Bisexuality in the Ancient World*, 2nd ed. by Eva Cantarella, translated by Cormac Ó Cuilleanáin, xi–xii. New Haven: Yale University Press, 2002.

Spence, Jonathan D. *The Memory Palace of Matteo Ricci*. London: Faber and Faber, 1985.

Statius. *Silvae*, translated by D. R. Shackleton Bailey. Cambridge: Harvard University Press, 2003.

Steiner, Kristóf Yosef. "Confessions of a Gay Kabbalist." *White City Boy*. October 15, 2014. http://whitecityboy.com/2014/10/15/confessions-of-a-gay-kabbalist/ (accessed Oct. 6, 2016).

Stevenson, Matilda Coxe. *The Zuni Indians: Their Mythology, Esoteric Fraternities, and Ceremonies*. Charleston: BiblioBazaar, 2010.

Stewart, Chuck. *Proud Heritage: People, Issues, and Documents of LGBT Experience*, 3rd edition. Santa Barbara: ABC-CLIO, 2014.

Sturluson, Snorri. *The Poetic Edda*, translated by Lee M. Hollander. Austin: University of Texas Press, 1986.

Tacitus. *The Annals*, translated by Alfred John Church and William Jackson Brodribb. Internet Classics Archive. http://classics.mit.edu/Tacitus/annals.html (accessed Sept. 13, 2016).

Tamale, Sylvia. "Homosexuality Is Not Un-African." *Aljazeera America*. April 26, 2014. http://america.aljazeera.com/opinions/2014/4/homosexuality-africamuseveniugandanigeriaethiopia.html (accessed Oct. 20, 2016).

Tan, Yvette. "Miss *Fa'afafine*: Behind Samoa's 'Third Gender' Beauty Pageant." British Broadcasting Corporation. September 1, 2016. http://www.bbc.com/news/world-asia-37227803 (accessed Dec. 13, 2016).

Teece, Geoff. *Religion in Focus: Islam*. London, Franklin Watts Ltd., 2003.

Téllez-Pon, Sergio. *Un Amar Ardiente: Poemas a la virreina*. Madrid: Flores Raras, 2017.

Tencic, Natalie. "Papua New Guinea's Gay and Transgender Community Finds Safety in Hanuabada Village." Australian Broadcasting Corporation. October 7, 2014. http://www.abc.net .au/news/2014-10-08/living-gay-in-papua-new-guinea/5796236 (accessed Dec. 9, 2016).

Thompson, James C. "Women in Sparta." *Women in the Ancient World*. http://www.womenintheancientworld.com/ (accessed Jan. 30, 2017).

Thumma, Scott, and Edward R. Gray. *Gay Religion*. Walnut Creek: Altamira Press, 2004.

Titsingh, M. Isaac. *Nipon o daï itsi ran ou Annales des empereurs du Japon*. Paris: Royal Asiatic Society Oriental Translation Fund of Great Britain and Ireland, 1834.

Tyler, Royall. *Japanese Tales*. New York: Pantheon, 1987.

Vaai, Saleimoa. *Samoa Faamatai and the Rule of Law*. Apia: The National University of Samoa: Le Papa-I-Galagala, 1999.

Vasey, Michael. *Strangers and Friends: A New Exploration of Homosexuality and the Bible*. London: Hodder & Stoughton, 1995.

Vidal-Ortiz, Salvador. "Sexual Discussions in Santería: A Case Study of Religion and Sexuality Negotiation." *Journal of Sexuality Research & Social Policy* 3:3 (2006). http://www.academia.edu/1953070 /Sexuality_discussions_in_Santer%C3%ADa_A_case_study _of_religion_and_sexuality_negotiation (accessed Nov. 1, 2016).

Wafer, Jim. *The Taste of Blood: Spirit Possession in Brazilian Candomblé*. Philadephia: University of Pennsylvania Press, 1991.

Walker, Brian. *Hua Hu Ching: The Unknown Teachings of Lao Tzu.* San Francisco: HarperOne, 2009.

Weber, Martin. "Move Over, Confucius!" *The Huffington Post.* January 30, 2012. http://www.huffingtonpost.com/marten-weber/move-over-confucius_b_1240939.html (accessed Nov. 19, 2016).

Wheeler, Kayla. "Women in Religion: Does Gender Matter?" in *Controversies in Contemporary Religion: Education, Law, Politics, Society, and Spirituality,* edited by Paul Hedges. Santa Barbara: Praeger, 2014.

Wilford, John Noble. "A Mystery, Locked in Timeless Embrace." *New York Times,* December 20, 2005.

Wilhelm, Amara Das. "Hindu Deities and the Third Sex (2)." *GALVA-108: Gay & Lesbian Vaishnava Association,* 2014. http://www.galva108.org/single-post/2014/05/04/Hindu-Deities-and-the-Third-Sex-2 (accessed Aug. 19, 2017).

———. "India's Slow Descent into Homophobia." GALVA-108: Gay & Lesbian Vaishnava Association, 2014. http://www.galva108.org/single-post/2014/05/09/Indias-Slow-Descent-Into-Homophobia (accessed Aug. 19, 2017).

Williams, Carolyn D., *Boudica and Her Stories: Narrative Transformations of a Warrior Queen.* Newark: University of Delaware Press, 2009.

Williams, Craig. *Roman Homosexuality.* Oxford: Oxford University Press, 1999.

Wolff, H. N. "Gilgamesh, Enkidu, and the Heroic Life." *Journal of the American Oriental Society* 89:2 (1969): 392–398.

Wolkstein, Diane, and Samuel Noah Kramer. *Inanna: Queen of Heaven and Earth.* New York: Harper & Row, 1983.

Xiaomingxiong. "Chinese Mythology." *GLBTQ Archives,* 2002. http://www.glbtqarchive.com/literature/chinese_myth_L.pdf (accessed Nov. 23, 2016).

Zevallos, Dr. Zuleyka. "Rethinking Gender and Sexuality: Case Study of the Native American 'Two Spirit' People." *The Other Sociologist.* September 9, 2013. https://othersociologist.com/2013/09/09/two-spirit-people/ (accessed Dec. 31, 2016).

ONLINE WEBPAGE SOURCES

Association of Independent Readers & Rootworkers:
www.readersandrootworkers.org

Ago Laroye: www.agolaroye.com

Bible Hub: http://biblehub.com

Botánica Viejo Lázaro: https://www.viejolazaro.com/en/

Center for Muslim-Jewish Engagement:
http://www.cmje.org/religious-texts/

Encyclopedia of the Hellenic World: http://www.ehw.gr

Internet Classics Archive: http://classics.mit.edu

Internet Sacred Text Archive: http://sacred-texts.com

Kreol Magaine: http://www.kreolmagazine.com/

Mambo Ezili Danto: http://ezilidantor.tripod.com/

The Marconis: https://historicromance.wordpress.com

New World Encyclopedia: www.newworldencyclopedia.org

Online Etymology Dictionary: http://www.etymonline.com

Owlcation: https://owlcation.com

Queer Saints and Martyrs (and Others):
http://queering-the-church.blogspot.com

St. Sebastian Catholic Church: http://saintsebastiancatholic.com/

Theoi Greek Mythology: http://www.theoi.com

Viking Answer Lady: http://www.vikinganswerlady.com

GET MORE AT LLEWELLYN.COM

Visit us online to browse hundreds of our books and decks, plus sign up to receive our e-newsletters and exclusive online offers.

- Free tarot readings • Spell-a-Day • Moon phases
- Recipes, spells, and tips • Blogs • Encyclopedia
- Author interviews, articles, and upcoming events

GET SOCIAL WITH LLEWELLYN

Find us on [f]   [twitter] @LlewellynBooks
www.Facebook.com/LlewellynBooks

GET BOOKS AT LLEWELLYN

LLEWELLYN ORDERING INFORMATION

Order online: Visit our website at www.llewellyn.com to select your books and place an order on our secure server.

Order by phone:
- Call toll free within the US at 1-877-NEW-WRLD (1-877-639-9753)
- We accept VISA, MasterCard, American Express, and Discover.

Order by mail:
Send the full price of your order (MN residents add 6.875% sales tax) in US funds plus postage and handling to: Llewellyn Worldwide, 2143 Wooddale Drive, Woodbury, MN 55125-2989

POSTAGE AND HANDLING

STANDARD (US):(Please allow 12 business days)
$30.00 and under, add $6.00.
$30.01 and over, FREE SHIPPING.

CANADA:
We cannot ship to Canada. Please shop your local bookstore or Amazon Canada.

INTERNATIONAL:
Customers pay the actual shipping cost to the final destination, which includes tracking information.

Visit us online for more shipping options. Prices subject to change.

FREE CATALOG!

To order, call
1-877-
NEW-WRLD
ext. 8236
or visit our
website

TO WRITE TO THE AUTHOR

If you wish to contact the author or would like more information about this book, please write to the author in care of Llewellyn Worldwide and we will forward your request. Both the author and the publisher appreciate hearing from you and learning of your enjoyment of this book and how it has helped you. Llewellyn Worldwide cannot guarantee that every letter written to the author can be answered, but all will be forwarded.

Please write to:

Tomás Prower

℅ Llewellyn Worldwide

2143 Wooddale Drive

Woodbury, MN 55125-2989

Please enclose a self-addressed stamped envelope for reply
or $1.00 to cover costs. If outside the USA, enclose
an international postal reply coupon.

Many of Llewellyn's authors have websites with additional information and resources. For more information, please visit our website:

LLEWELLYN.COM